MICHAEL FRAYN

Plays: 4

Copenhagen
Democracy
Afterlife

with an introduction by the author

B L O O M S B U R Y

LONDON • NEW DELHI • NEW YORK • SYDNEY

Bloomsbury Methuen Drama

An imprint of Bloomsbury Publishing Plc

50 Bedford Square   1385 Broadway
London   New York
WC1B 3DP   NY 10018
UK   USA

www.bloomsbury.com

Bloomsbury is a registered trade mark of Bloomsbury Publishing Plc

This collection first published in Great Britain in 2010 by Methuen Drama

Copenhagen first published by Methuen Drama 1998.
© Michael Frayn 1998, 2000, 2002, 2003, 2009
Democracy first published by Methuen Publishing Limited 2003.
© 2003 Michael Frayn
Afterlife first published by Methuen Drama 2008.
Revised in this volume. © Michael Frayn 2008, 2010
Introduction © Michael Frayn 2010

British Library Cataloguing-in-Publication Data
A catalogue record for this book is available from the British Library.

ISBN: PB: 978-1-4081-2862-6

Library of Congress Cataloging-in-Publication Data
A catalog record for this book is available from the Library of Congress.

Typeset by Country Setting, Kingsdown, Kent
Printed and bound in Great Britain

Contents

Michael Frayn
Chronology

Introduction

I have spent most of my professional life writing fiction: recounting events that never happened, and that never happened to people who never existed. No one seems to believe, though, that writers of fiction sometimes make things up, so I have also often had to insist that the fiction *was* in fact fiction; and just occasionally to admit that here and there, in some places, I *had* borrowed a few details from real people and places, and confused the fiction with a fact or two.

My last three plays, the ones in this volume, have all had a rather different relationship to reality. The characters bear the names of people who were once actually alive (and in one or two cases still are), and I have derived their personalities and actions as best I could from the personalities that these real people really had, and the things they really did, as it emerges from the historical record.

When I began writing *Copenhagen*, the first of these plays, I found the prospect of trying to find some kind of embodiment for the real originals profoundly intimidating. If you invent your own characters you can construct them on a manageable scale, as God did when He created man – in His own image, certainly, but with vastly reduced levels of power and wisdom. Novelists and playwrights, likewise, tend to favour creatures who are notably less complicated than themselves; stupider, more consistently moral or immoral, and less afflicted by states which it's difficult to give any convincing account of, such as contentment and happiness. Niels Bohr and Werner Heisenberg, though, were two of the greatest physicists of the twentieth century. They had thought in ways where I could never hope to follow, and achieved things that I couldn't even begin to understand or describe. I also found myself up against an even more fundamental problem.

I've sometimes in the past suggested that all writers of fiction ought to be required by law to go and do a bit of reporting from time to time, just to remind them of how much more complex the world is than they can ever realise when they imagine it, how much more awkward to grasp and make sense of. Maybe this is why I've turned to history in my old age, in anticipation of my own proposed legislation. Writing about past situations and events, though, is very different from writing about the present. It doesn't, as reporting does, bring you face to face with the vast confusion of the world itself, where nothing has been discriminated or classified or named. That raw confusion has vanished forever into the irrecoverable limbo of time. It has already been converted into the symbols and representations, the words and numbers and images that constitute the historical record. (And even the numbers and images have to have words added to them before they can be understood as representations of particular states of affairs.)

So it wasn't just the science and the mathematics that I couldn't get hold of – I couldn't really begin to understand or describe *anything* about those long-dead protagonists of mine. In the simplest, most everday sense they had been thus and so, and not otherwise. However much I researched into what they had said and written, and into what other people had said and written about them, I couldn't go back in time to see and hear for myself what they were *like*.

In the end, of course, my 'Bohr' and 'Heisenberg' took matters into their own hands, just as all one's characters do. They stepped forward from the page as apparently autonomous beings with their own lives to lead. They began to speak their own words and initiate their own actions. Even historians and biographers, I imagine, must often have a similar sort of unexpected assistance from the characters they have so laboriously conjured up. Many historians, it's true, pride themselves on consciously excluding the personal, on limiting themselves to the bare facts and figures recorded in parish records and pipe-rolls, to trends and averages. All the same, there are ghostly presences telling them which facts and figures to select. There must be. The point of the figures and trends is in the end to suggest what individual lives were like, what the particular people who paid the tax and constituted the average felt and believed, what they were trying to achieve and what they were trying to avoid. A historian, just as much as a novelist or playwright, is trying to salvage a sense of present reality from the shadows of the past. In the end even the most austere historian is trading in personalities.

*

The playwright has an advantage here over the historian and the biographer – even over the novelist – because the words written on the page are eventually going to find incarnation in a living being, an actor, who will invest them with his own physical presence. For an hour or two each evening the actor will become the character he is embodying; the character will become the actor.

Modern theatre audiences are said to be too sophisticated to believe that the characters on stage are real people, to whom advice and encouragement can be shouted. I'm not sure, though, that the distinction is even now always so sharply set. I once saw a performance of *The Elephant Man* at the National Theatre where one of the cast collapsed on stage and rolled down the rake towards the front row of the stalls. Another member of the cast, Nicky Henson, put out a foot and saved him, then called to the stage manager to lower the curtain, which brought the fiction to an abrupt end.

Or did it? Nicky told me afterwards that a doctor who happened to be in the audience – a distinguished American heart physician, as it turned out – had at once gone backstage to help. After examining the patient he diagnosed not a heart attack but simple hyperventilation – then turned to Nicky and asked him with courteous professional deference if he agreed. Nicky looked round to see if there was a second doctor standing behind him. There was not. The second opinion was himself, or rather the character he had been playing on stage, who happened to be a doctor, and whom he evidently embodied offstage still, even in they eyes of a real doctor. 'If he had a few minutes' rest,' said the real doctor to his new-found colleague, 'he could probably quite safely carry on, wouldn't you think?' Dr Henson gravely concurred.

Various members of the audiences for *Copenhagen* in London who had actually met Heisenberg and the Bohrs complimented the actors on their extraordinary resemblance to the originals. Remarkable as all the performances were, resemblance in any literal sense seemed to me improbable (and see in the Postscript to the play what Heisenberg's son thought). It was a tribute, certainly, to the skill of the actors – but also to the power of the human mind to see what it chooses to see. Two of the backstage visitors during the run of *Democracy* were the historical originals themselves – Reinhard Wilke and Horst Ehmke. Neither of them, when I met them both later, seemed to me very much like my representations of them – though I realise with alarmed hindsight, looking at recent cases in the American film industry, they might have sued me for breaching their intellectual property rights by stealing their lives. They turned out to be very forgiving and genial. Whether they had recognised themselves or not, the generous supplies of red wine and indiscreet stories with which they kept the cast entertained into the small hours bore a remarkable resemblance to the red wine and intrigues that figured so largely both in the history of Brandt's government and in my play. And when they finally left, Ehmke's wife threw her arms around Roger Allam, who was playing Brandt, and cried, 'You even *smell* like Willy!'

Which was not something I'd got out of my researches, or Roger out of my stage directions.

*

Storytellers have of course been taking subjects from real history ever since stories were first told. Most of them have played much faster and looser with the record than I have. Everyone knows how boldly Shakespeare adapted Plutarch and Holinshed to his own ends. Schiller, perhaps next to Shakespeare the greatest practitioner of the historical drama, didn't hesitate (in *Don Carlos*) to make Philip II's disturbed and drunken son into a tragic hero, and to turn the boy's brief dynastic betrothal to his future stepmother at the age of fourteen into a lifelong love affair; or to make *Maria Stuart* pivot upon an entirely fictitious meeting between the Scottish queen and her cousin, the English queen who had imprisoned her. If history had been properly organised in the first place, Carlos *would* surely have been a potential hero; Mary Queen of Scots and Elizabeth I *would* have met; and all three of them would have expressed their inmost thoughts in trenchant German pentameters. But history never is so organised, and we expect writers of fiction to be bold in suggesting its hidden causality and ironies, and in imagining the thoughts and feelings that its protagonists so notoriously failed to express.

So I don't think my humble additions to the record need too much apology. It does seem to me reasonable, though, for readers and audiences to want to know where I've followed the record and where I've consciously embroidered upon it. It's often obvious from the context. I plainly can't have taken the conversation between the three characters in *Copenhagen* from the record, for instance, since they've all come back from beyond the grave to embark upon it. It's obvious that none of the words these characters say was ever uttered by their living originals, except perhaps for the crucial question that Heisenberg recalls putting to Bohr in 1941, and that so immediately upset and alienated him. (If, of course, Heisenberg ever *did* say what he says he said, which is one of the questions at issue between the two men.) You might wonder sometimes, though, whether the physics they discuss, and their account of atomic research, are themselves real or invented.

Elsewhere in these plays the relationship with actual history is rather more ambiguous. In Willy Brandt's speeches in *Democracy* about his hopes for rapprochement with Germany's former enemies in Eastern Europe, for example, I have used many of the things that he actually said, but I've brought them together to make a plainly stated whole, in a way that Brandt himself, in his efforts not to alarm the electorate, tended to avoid. In Reinhardt's speech to the Prince Archbishop at the beginning of *Afterlife* I have paraphrased various of Reinhardt's own writings, but used them in a way that Reinhardt never actually did, to make his case for being allowed to perform *Everyman* in front of the cathedral.

A play should surely be comprehensible to its audience in the theatre without a preface, but after each of the plays in this volume I have provided a postscript, for anyone interested in following up the record on which I have drawn, or seeing where I have departed from it.

*

The historical record itself, even if it's a simplification of the events it represents, is not as simple as all that. In fact it is often remarkably ambiguous and difficult to make sense of, and the line between the record and the inventions of fiction is not always a very distinct one.

Am I trying to weasel away at the notion of truth? To suggest, perhaps out of self-interest as a writer of stories, that there's no real difference between truth and falsehood, between fact and fiction? Not at all. It is a fact that Heisenberg went to Copenhagen in 1941; it is true that he did. But that fact, that truth, is still not the event itself. The actual event is now beyond our grasp. It is a *statement* about an event. This is what the historical record consists in, when you come right down to it – the statements of observers and participants, and the statements derived from them – and to say that a statement is true is in practice to say that it coheres reasonably well with other statements about the same event. Heisenberg says he went to Copenhagen, and so do plenty of other people who saw him there. No one says he didn't go.

Often, though, witnesses to the same event don't agree at all. In the first place, what they have seen is in the most literal sense never exactly the same event, because they have necessarily seen it from different standpoints in space. More significantly and elusively, they have almost certainly also seen it from different mental standpoints, determined by their varying preconceptions, expectations and interests.

In *Copenhagen* this is not just a difficulty in researching the background of the play but part of its subject. It's a particularly acute one because the two men were the only witnesses to their conversation, because the subject of that conversation was so complex and delicate, and because they were approaching the matter from opposite sides in the bitter conflict that had engulfed them. Another well-known example of the same thing can be found in *Wittgenstein's Poker*, the delightful book by David Edmonds and John Eidinow about something that happened in Cambridge on 25 October 1946, and it's perhaps even more striking because the event in this case was so simple, so accessible and uncontroversial, and because it was observed by so many intelligent and relatively disinterested witnesses – who nevertheless all saw quite different things.

Another problem is that memory introduces a further level of indeterminacy. Our recollections of what we have seen often change over time as we, quite unconsciously, rewrite them in the light of changing circumstances. This is no doubt one of the things that have made the accounts of the incident at the Cambridge Moral Science Club in 1946 so various. The people who were present have told the story many times in the sixty-odd years that have elapsed since, if only to themselves, and it has drifted in the telling. Then again, attitudes have changed. The reputations of the two protagonists – Wittengenstein, who made whatever gesture it was with the poker, and Popper, to whom (or *at* whom) he made it – have suffered various vicissitudes. Over the years people have become emboldened to adopt a somewhat more satirical view of Wittgenstein than many of them (apart from Bertrand Russell, in his memoirs, and Popper, in the story) would have dared to express during his lifetime, or for many years after his death.

Even the written record changes. Modern German history, for instance, from which *Democracy* takes its rise, is being continuously modified – particularly as German historians and writers at last start to investigate the sufferings not only of the Nazis' victims in Europe but of the Allies' in Germany, and also as the files of the KGB and the Stasi are opened. More revelations about Wehner's role in Brandt's downfall were emerging even as I wrote the play, and it has since become clear that the burden on his conscience lingering from his Communist past and his wartime exile in Moscow was even heavier than was realised at the time. It turns out that he had denounced many more of his comrades in the German Communist Party to the NKVD than he admitted – and not under duress, to save himself, as it was supposed, but quite voluntarily, out of an apparently sincere enthusiasm for the great Stalinist witch-hunt.

In the case of *Copenhagen* the historical record has been modified even by the acknowledged fiction that I derived from it. This was because the play aroused considerable dispute in America, mostly as to whether I had been over-generous to Heisenberg in suggesting that there was some uncertainty about his motivation or his readiness to serve the Nazis. I have recorded in the Post-Postscript to the play how the dispute led to the publication of documents that have changed our understanding of the events as they had hitherto been reconstructed by historians – even as they had been reconstructed by Heisenberg and Bohr themselves.

I've also described another possible modification of the historical record, occasioned this time not by the play but by the publication of Rainer Karlsch's book *Hitlers Bombe*, which suggests an even more intimate entanglement of history and fiction. If Karlsch is right, at least two of the physicists working on the German nuclear project managed to keep quiet, both during the war and after it, about a most extraordinary, and up to now completely unsuspected, development in their research. The story of this is in the Post-Postscript. By their silence, in Karlsch's version, they deceived not only British intelligence but also their colleagues, and all subsequent historians of the subject. One of the two men involved was Kurt Diebner, who was running a rival programme to Heisenberg's, and who seems from the known record to have been an unforthcoming and unimpressive man. In Karlsch's account, however, he emerges as profoundly devious, and much better-informed than he allowed himself to appear. The other conspirator was Walther Gerlach, the co-ordinator of the two programmes, who has always seemed to have been a somewhat ineffectual and ill-informed dilettante, but who in Karlsch's version of events becomes an administrator of remarkable energy and intellectual range. These two men, in other words (if Karlsch's version is itself fact!), were between them constructing a fictitious past, if only through what they so carefully failed to say, and in the process creating fictitious characters for themselves. And these fictions they managed to write into the historical record.

*

If justification is still in the end needed for piling acknowledged fiction on top of the already ambiguous structure of fact it's surely this: that all those internal states and events that so affect our perceptions and recollections – all our fears and hopes, our preconceptions and self-deceptions – cannot themselves be directly observed. The historical record depends upon them – but they are themselves beyond the reach of the record. The only way we can come at what other people think and feel is in the end through the imagination. Even our own thoughts and feelings often elude us. We have the experiences, certainly – we think the thoughts, we feel the feelings. But from inside those experiences we can't always stand back to identify and classify them. We know we're angry (though not always) – but often not exactly why. We may or may not realise that we share the common assumptions of the day, or have particular prejudices of our own, but we're unlikely to be able to see how they've affected our reading of the world around us.

Our intentions are often even more elusive. And yet, without some understanding of the intentions behind it, *no* human action can be judged, or even made sense of. You can pass judgment on Heisenberg, for example, only if you have some conception of what he was up to. Never mind judgment – to make *any* sense of his actions you have to make some estimate of what the aim of them was. Human intention is one of the forces that makes things happen (even when it's counter-effective, as it so often is), and we can no more understand the world of human activity without it than we can understand the natural world without the concept (almost equally elusive, according to some physicists) of energy. The question of intention arises not only in historical contexts, as in the case of Heisenberg in 1941, but over and over again in everyday life. Our only recourse, after we have taken note of everything that can be observed, remembered, and expressed in language, is to create for ourselves a kind of narrative of the unobservable internal events that seems consistent with the observable externals.

To write a fiction, in other words, based on the historical record.

Michael Frayn
April 2010

Copenhagen

Copenhagen was first previewed in the Cottesloe auditorium of the National Theatre, London, on 21 May 1998, and opened on 28 May 1998, with the following cast:

Margrethe   Sara Kestelman
Bohr   David Burke
Heisenberg   Matthew Marsh

Directed by Michael Blakemore
Designed by Peter J. Davison
Lighting by Mark Henderson
Sound by Simon Baker

This production transferred to the Duchess Theatre, London, where it was presented by Michael Godron and Lee Dean, and opened on 5 February 1999.

The play previewed at the Royale Theatre, New York, on 23 March 2000, and opened on 11 April 2000, with the following cast:

Margrethe   Blair Brown
Bohr   Philip Bosco
Heisenberg   Michael Cumpsty

Directed by Michael Blakemore
Designed by Peter J. Davison
Lighting by Mark Henderson and Michael Lincoln
Sound by Tony Meola

Characters

Margrethe
Bohr
Heisenberg

Act One

Margrethe   But why?

Bohr   You're still thinking about it?

Margrethe   Why did he come to Copenhagen?

Bohr   Does it matter, my love, now we're all three of us dead and gone?

Margrethe   Some questions remain long after their owners have died. Lingering like ghosts. Looking for the answers they never found in life.

Bohr   Some questions have no answers to find.

Margrethe   Why did he come? What was he trying to tell you?

Bohr   He did explain later.

Margrethe   He explained over and over again. Each time he explained it became more obscure.

Bohr   It was probably very simple, when you come right down to it: he wanted to have a talk.

Margrethe   A talk? To the enemy? In the middle of a war?

Bohr   Margrethe, my love, we were scarcely the enemy.

Margrethe   It was 1941!

Bohr   Heisenberg was one of our oldest friends.

Margrethe   Heisenberg was German. We were Danes. We were under German occupation.

Bohr   It put us in a difficult position, certainly.

Margrethe   I've never seen you as angry with anyone as you were with Heisenberg that night.

Bohr   Not to disagree, but I believe I remained remarkably calm.

Margrethe   I know when you're angry.

Bohr   It was as difficult for him as it was for us.

Margrethe   So why did he do it? Now no one can be hurt, now no one can be betrayed.

Bohr   I doubt if he ever really knew himself.

Margrethe   And he wasn't a friend. Not after that visit. That was the end of the famous friendship between Niels Bohr and Werner Heisenberg.

Heisenberg   Now we're all dead and gone, yes, and there are only two things the world remembers about me. One is the uncertainty principle, and the other is my mysterious visit to Niels Bohr in Copenhagen in 1941. Everyone understands uncertainty. Or thinks he does. No one understands my trip to Copenhagen. Time and time again I've explained it. To Bohr himself, and Margrethe. To interrogators and intelligence officers, to journalists and historians. The more I've explained, the deeper the uncertainty has become. Well, I shall be happy to make one more attempt. Now we're all dead and gone. Now no one can be hurt, now no one can be betrayed.

Margrethe   I never entirely liked him, you know. Perhaps I can say that to you now.

Bohr   Yes, you did. When he was first here in the twenties? Of course you did. On the beach at Tisvilde with us and the boys? He was one of the family.

Margrethe   Something alien about him, even then.

Bohr   So quick and eager.

Margrethe   Too quick. Too eager.

Bohr   Those bright watchful eyes.

Margrethe   Too bright. Too watchful.

Bohr   Well, he was a very great physicist. I never changed my mind about that.

Margrethe   They were all good, all the people who came to Copenhagen to work with you. You had most of the great pioneers in atomic theory here at one time or another.

Bohr   And the more I look back on it, the more I think Heisenberg was the greatest of them all.

Heisenberg   So what was Bohr? He was the first of us all, the father of us all. Modern atomic physics began when Bohr realised that quantum theory applied to matter as well as to energy. 1913. Everything we did was based on that great insight of his.

Bohr   When you think that he first came here to work with me in 1924 . . .

Heisenberg   I'd only just finished my doctorate, and Bohr was the most famous atomic physicist in the world.

Bohr   . . . and in just over a year he'd invented quantum mechanics.

Margrethe   It came out of his work with you.

Bohr   Mostly out of what he'd been doing with Max Born and Pascual Jordan at Göttingen. Another year or so and he'd got uncertainty.

Margrethe   And you'd done complementarity.

Bohr   We argued them both out together.

Heisenberg   We did most of our best work together.

Bohr   Heisenberg usually led the way.

Heisenberg   Bohr made sense of it all.

Bohr   We operated like a business.

Heisenberg   Chairman and managing director.

Margrethe   Father and son.

Heisenberg   A family business.

Margrethe   Even though we had sons of our own.

Bohr   And we went on working together long after he ceased to be my assistant.

Heisenberg   Long after I'd left Copenhagen in 1927 and gone back to Germany. Long after I had a chair and a family of my own.

Margrethe   Then the Nazis came to power . . .

Bohr   And it got more and more difficult. When the war broke out – impossible. Until that day in 1941.

Margrethe   When it finished forever.

Bohr   Yes, why did he do it?

Heisenberg   September, 1941. For years I had it down in my memory as October.

Margrethe   September. The end of September.

Bohr   A curious sort of diary memory is.

Heisenberg   You open the pages, and all the neat headings and tidy jottings dissolve around you.

Bohr   You step through the pages into the months and days themselves.

Margrethe   The past becomes the present inside your head.

Heisenberg   September, 1941, Copenhagen . . . And at once – here I am, getting off the night train from Berlin with my colleague Carl von Weizsäcker. Two plain civilian suits and raincoats among all the field-grey Wehrmacht uniforms arriving with us, all the naval gold braid, all the well-tailored black of the SS. In my bag I have the text of the lecture I'm giving. In my head is another communication that has to be delivered. The lecture is on astrophysics. The text inside my head is a more difficult one.

Bohr   We obviously can't go to the lecture.

Margrethe   Not if he's giving it at the German Cultural Institute – it's a Nazi propaganda organisation.

Bohr   He must know what we feel about that.

Heisenberg   Weizsacker has been my John the Baptist, and written to warn Bohr of my arrival.

Margrethe   He wants to see you?

Bohr   I assume that's why he's come.

Heisenberg   But how can the actual meeting with Bohr be arranged?

Margrethe   He must have something remarkably important to say.

Heisenberg   It has to seem natural. It has to be private.

Margrethe   You're not really thinking of inviting him to the house?

Bohr   That's obviously what he's hoping.

Margrethe   Niels! They've occupied our country!

Bohr   He is not they.

Margrethe   He's one of them.

Heisenberg   First of all there's an official visit to Bohr's workplace, the Institute for Theoretical Physics, with an awkward lunch in the old familiar canteen. No chance to talk to Bohr, of course. Is he even present? There's Rozental . . . Petersen, I think . . . Christian Møller, almost certainly . . . It's like being in a dream. You can never quite focus the precise details of the scene around you. At the head of the table – is that Bohr? I turn to look, and it's Bohr, it's Rozental, it's Møller, it's whoever I appoint to be there . . . A difficult occasion, though – I remember that clearly enough.

Bohr   It was a disaster. He made a very bad impression. Occupation of Denmark unfortunate. Occupation of Poland, however, perfectly acceptable. Germany now certain to win the war.

Heisenberg   Our tanks are almost at Moscow. What can stop us? Well, one thing, perhaps. One thing.

Bohr   He knows he's being watched, of course. One must remember that. He has to be careful about what he says.

Margrethe   Or he won't be allowed to travel abroad again.

Bohr   My love, the Gestapo planted microphones in his house. He told Goudsmit when he was in America. The SS brought him in for interrogation in the basement at the Prinz-Albrecht-Strasse.

Margrethe   And then they let him go again.

Heisenberg   I wonder if they suspect for one moment how painful it was to get permission for this trip. The humiliating appeals to the Party, the demeaning efforts to have strings pulled by our friends in the Foreign Office.

Margrethe   How did he seem? Is he greatly changed?

Bohr   A little older.

Margrethe   I still think of him as a boy.

Bohr   He's nearly forty. A middle-aged professor, fast catching up with the rest of us.

Margrethe   You still want to invite him here?

Bohr   Let's add up the arguments on either side in a reasonably scientific way. Firstly, Heisenberg is a friend . . .

Margrethe   Firstly, Heisenberg is a German.

Bohr   A White Jew. That's what the Nazis called him. He taught relativity, and they said it was Jewish physics. He couldn't mention Einstein by name, but he stuck with relativity, in spite of the most terrible attacks.

Margrethe   All the real Jews have lost their jobs. He's still teaching.

Bohr   He's still teaching relativity.

Margrethe   Still a professor at Leipzig.

Bohr   At Leipzig, yes. Not at Munich. They kept him out of the chair at Munich.

Margrethe   He could have been at Columbia.

Bohr   Or Chicago. He had offers from both.

Margrethe   He wouldn't leave Germany.

Bohr   He wants to be there to rebuild German science when Hitler goes. He told Goudsmit.

Margrethe   And if he's being watched it will all be reported upon. Who he sees. What he says to them. What they say to him.

Heisenberg   I carry my surveillance around like an infectious disease. But then I happen to know that Bohr is also under surveillance.

Margrethe   And you know you're being watched yourself.

Bohr   By the Gestapo?

Heisenberg   Does he realise?

Bohr   I've nothing to hide.

Margrethe   By our fellow-Danes. It would be a terrible betrayal of all their trust in you if they thought you were collaborating.

Bohr   Inviting an old friend to dinner is hardly collaborating.

Margrethe   It might appear to be collaborating.

Bohr   Yes. He's put us in a difficult position.

Margrethe   I shall never forgive him.

Bohr   He must have good reason. He must have very good reason.

Heisenberg   This is going to be a deeply awkward occasion.

Margrethe   You won't talk about politics?

Bohr   We'll stick to physics. I assume it's physics he wants to talk to me about.

Margrethe   I think you must also assume that you and I aren't the only people who hear what's said in this house. If you want to speak privately you'd better go out in the open air.

Bohr   I shan't want to speak privately.

Margrethe   You could go for another of your walks together.

Heisenberg   Shall I be able to suggest a walk?

Bohr   I don't think we shall be going for any walks. Whatever he has to say he can say where everyone can hear it.

Margrethe   Some new idea he wants to try out on you, perhaps.

Bohr   What can it be, though? Where are we off to next?

Margrethe   So now of course your curiosity's aroused, in spite of everything.

Heisenberg   So now here I am, walking out through the autumn twilight to the Bohrs' house at Ny-Carlsberg. Followed, presumably, by my invisible shadow. What am I feeling? Fear, certainly – the touch of fear that one always feels for a teacher, for an employer, for a parent. Much worse fear about what I have to say. About how to express it. How to broach it in the first place. Worse fear still about what happens if I fail.

Margrethe   It's not something to do with the war?

Bohr   Heisenberg is a theoretical physicist. I don't think anyone has yet discovered a way you can use theoretical physics to kill people.

Margrethe   It couldn't be something about fission?

Bohr   Fission? Why would he want to talk to me about fission?

Margrethe   Because you're working on it.

Bohr   Heisenberg isn't.

Margrethe   Isn't he? Everybody else in the world seems to be. And you're the acknowledged authority.

Bohr   He hasn't published on fission.

Margrethe   It was Heisenberg who did all the original work on the physics of the nucleus. And he consulted you then, he consulted you at every step.

Bohr   That was back in 1932. Fission's only been around for the last three years.

Margrethe   But if the Germans were developing some kind of weapon based on nuclear fission . . .

Bohr   My love, no one is going to develop a weapon based on nuclear fission.

Margrethe   But if the Germans were trying to, Heisenberg would be involved.

Bohr   There's no shortage of good German physicists.

Margrethe   There's no shortage of good German physicists in America or Britain.

Bohr   The Jews have gone, obviously.

Heisenberg   Einstein, Wolfgang Pauli, Max Born . . . Otto Frisch, Lise Meitner . . . We led the world in theoretical physics! Once.

Margrethe   So who is there still working in Germany?

Bohr   Sommerfeld, of course. Von Laue.

Margrethe   Old men.

Bohr   Wirtz. Harteck.

Margrethe   Heisenberg is head and shoulders above all of them.

Bohr   Otto Hahn – he's still there. He discovered fission, after all.

Margrethe   Hahn's a chemist. I thought that what Hahn discovered . . .

Bohr   . . . was that Enrico Fermi had discovered it in Rome four years earlier. Yes – he just didn't realise it was fission. It didn't occur to anyone that the uranium atom might have split, and turned into an atom of barium and an atom of krypton. Not until Hahn and Strassmann did the analysis, and detected the barium.

Margrethe   Fermi's in Chicago.

Bohr   His wife's Jewish.

Margrethe   So Heisenberg would be in charge of the work?

Bohr   Margrethe, there is no work! John Wheeler and I did it all in 1939. One of the implications of our paper is that there's no way in the foreseeable future in which fission can be used to produce any kind of weapon.

Margrethe   Then why is everyone still working on it?

Bohr   Because there's an element of magic in it. You fire a neutron at the nucleus of a uranium atom and it splits into two other elements. It's what the alchemists were trying to do – to turn one element into another.

Margrethe   So why is he coming?

Bohr   Now your curiosity's aroused.

Margrethe   My forebodings.

Heisenberg   I crunch over the familiar gravel to the Bohrs' front door, and tug at the familiar bell-pull. Fear, yes. And another sensation, that's become painfully familiar over the past year. A mixture of self-importance and sheer helpless absurdity – that of all the 2,000 million people in this world, I'm the one who's been charged with this impossible responsibility . . . The heavy door swings open.

Bohr   My dear Heisenberg!

Heisenberg   My dear Bohr!

Bohr   Come in, come in . . .

Margrethe   And of course as soon as they catch sight of each other all their caution disappears. The old flames leap up from the ashes. If we can just negotiate all the treacherous little opening civilities . . .

Heisenberg   I'm so touched you felt able to ask me.

Bohr   We must try to go on behaving like human beings.

Heisenberg   I realise how awkward it is.

Bohr   We scarcely had a chance to do more than shake hands at lunch the other day.

Heisenberg   And Margrethe I haven't seen . . .

Bohr   Since you were here four years ago.

Margrethe   Niels is right. You look older.

Heisenberg   I had been hoping to see you both in 1938, at the congress in Warsaw . . .

Bohr   I believe you had some personal trouble.

Heisenberg   A little business in Berlin.

Margrethe   In the Prinz-Albrecht-Strasse?

Heisenberg   A slight misunderstanding.

Bohr   We heard, yes. I'm so sorry.

Heisenberg   These things happen. The question is now resolved. Happily resolved. We should all have met in Zürich . . .

Bohr   In September 1939.

Heisenberg   Only of course . . .

Margrethe   There was an unfortunate clash with the outbreak of war.

Heisenberg   Sadly.

Bohr   Sadly for us, certainly.

Margrethe   A lot more sadly still for many people.

Heisenberg   Yes. Indeed.

Bohr   Well, there it is.

Heisenberg   What can I say?

Margrethe   What can any of us say, in the present circumstances?

Heisenberg   No. And your sons?

Margrethe   Are well, thank you. Elisabeth? The children?

Heisenberg   Very well. They send their love, of course.

Margrethe   They so much wanted to see each other, in spite of everything! But now the moment has come they're so busy avoiding each other's eye that they can scarcely see each other at all.

Heisenberg   I wonder if you realise how much it means to me to be back here in Copenhagen. In this house. I have become rather isolated in these last few years.

Bohr   I can imagine.

Margrethe   Me he scarcely notices. I watch him discreetly from behind my expression of polite interest as he struggles on.

Heisenberg   Have things here been difficult?

Bohr   Difficult?

Margrethe   Of course. He has to ask. He has to get it out of the way.

Bohr   Difficult . . . What can I say? We've not so far been treated to the gross abuses that have occurred elsewhere. The race laws have not been enforced.

Margrethe   Yet.

Bohr   A few months ago they started deporting Communists and other anti-German elements.

Heisenberg   But you personally . . . ?

Bohr   Have been left strictly alone.

Heisenberg   I've been anxious about you.

Bohr   Kind of you. No call for sleepless nights in Leipzig so far, though.

Margrethe   Another silence. He's done his duty. Now he can begin to steer the conversation round to pleasanter subjects.

Heisenberg   Are you still sailing?

Bohr   Sailing?

Margrethe   Not a good start.

Bohr   No, no sailing.

Heisenberg   The Sound is . . . ?

Bohr   Mined.

Heisenberg   Of course.

Margrethe   I assume he won't ask if Niels has been skiing.

Heisenberg   You've managed to get some skiing?

Bohr   Skiing? In Denmark?

Heisenberg   In Norway. You used to go to Norway.

Bohr   I did, yes.

Heisenberg   But since Norway is also . . . well. . .

Bohr   Also occupied? Yes, that might make it easier. In fact I suppose we could now holiday almost anywhere in Europe.

Heisenberg   I'm sorry. I hadn't thought of it quite in those terms.

Bohr   Perhaps I'm being a little oversensitive.

Heisenberg   Of course not. I should have thought.

Margrethe   He must almost be starting to wish he was back in the Prinz-Albrecht-Strasse.

Heisenberg   I don't suppose you feel you could ever come to Germany . . .

Margrethe   The boy's an idiot.

Bohr   My dear Heisenberg, it would be an easy mistake to make, to think that the citizens of a small nation, of a small nation overrun, wantonly and cruelly overrun, by its more powerful neighbour, don't have exactly the same feelings of national pride as their conquerors, exactly the same love of their country.

Margrethe   Niels, we agreed.

Bohr   To talk about physics, yes.

Margrethe   Not about politics.

Bohr   I'm sorry.

Heisenberg   No, no – I was simply going to say that I still have my old ski-hut at Bayrischzell. So if by any chance . . . at any time . . . for any reason . . .

Bohr   Perhaps Margrethe would be kind enough to sew a yellow star on my ski-jacket.

Heisenberg   Yes. Yes. Stupid of me.

Margrethe   Silence again. Those first brief sparks have disappeared, and the ashes have become very cold indeed. So now of course I'm starting to feel almost sorry for him. Sitting here all on his own in the midst of people who hate him, all on his own against the two of us. He looks younger again, like the boy who first came here in 1924. Younger than Christian would have been now. Shy and arrogant and anxious to be loved. Homesick and pleased to be away from home at last. And, yes, it's sad, because Niels loved him, he was a father to him.

Heisenberg   So . . . what are you working on?

Margrethe   And all he can do is press forward.

Bohr   Fission, mostly.

Heisenberg   I saw a couple of papers in the *Physical Review*. The velocity-range relations of fission fragments . . . ?

Bohr   And something about the interactions of nuclei with deuterons. And you?

Heisenberg   Various things.

Margrethe   Fission?

Heisenberg   I sometimes feel very envious of your cyclotron.

Margrethe   Why? Are you working on fission yourself?

Heisenberg   There are over thirty in the United States. Whereas in the whole of Germany. . . Well . . . You still get to your country place, at any rate?

Bohr   We still go to Tisvilde, yes.

Margrethe   In the whole of Germany, you were going to say . . .

Bohr   . . . there is not one single cyclotron.

Heisenberg   So beautiful at this time of year. Tisvilde.

Bohr   You haven't come to borrow the cyclotron, have you? That's not why you've come to Copenhagen?

Heisenberg   That's not why I've come to Copenhagen.

Bohr   I'm sorry. We mustn't jump to conclusions.

Heisenberg   No, we must none of us jump to conclusions of any sort.

Margrethe   We must wait patiently to be told.

Heisenberg   It's not always easy to explain things to the world at large.

Bohr   I realise that we must always be conscious of the wider audience our words may have. But the lack of cyclotrons in Germany is surely not a military secret.

Heisenberg   I've no idea what's a secret and what isn't.

Bohr   No secret, either, about why there aren't any. You can't say it but I can. It's because the Nazis have systematically undermined theoretical physics. Why? Because so many people working in the field were Jews. And why were so many of them Jews? Because theoretical physics, the sort of physics done by Einstein, by Schrödinger and Pauli, by Born and Sommerfeld, by you and me, was always regarded in Germany as inferior to experimental physics, and the theoretical chairs and lectureships were the only ones that Jews could get.

Margrethe   Physics, yes? Physics.

Bohr   This is physics.

Margrethe   It's also politics.

Heisenberg   The two are sometimes painfully difficult to keep apart.

Bohr   So, you saw those two papers. I haven't seen anything by you recently.

Heisenberg   No.

Bohr   Not like you. Too much teaching?

Heisenberg   I'm not teaching. Not at the moment.

Bohr   My dear Heisenberg – they haven't pushed you out of your chair at Leipzig? That's not what you've come to tell us?

Heisenberg   No, I'm still at Leipzig. For part of each week.

Bohr   And for the rest of the week?

Heisenberg   Elsewhere. The problem is more work, not less.

Bohr   I see. Do I?

Heisenberg   Are you in touch with any of our friends in England? Born? Chadwick?

Bohr   Heisenberg, we're under German occupation. Germany's at war with Britain.

Heisenberg   I thought you might still have contacts of some sort. Or people in America? We're not at war with America.

Margrethe   Yet.

Heisenberg   You've heard nothing from Pauli, in Princeton? Goudsmit? Fermi?

Bohr   What do you want to know?

Heisenberg   I was simply curious . . . I was thinking about Robert Oppenheimer the other day. I had a great set-to with him in Chicago in 1939.

Bohr   About mesons.

Heisenberg   Is he still working on mesons?

Bohr   I'm quite out of touch.

Margrethe   The only foreign visitor we've had was from Germany. Your friend Weizsäcker was here in March.

Heisenberg   *My* friend? *Your* friend, too. I hope. You know he's come back to Copenhagen with me? He's very much hoping to see you again.

Margrethe   When he came here in March he brought the head of the German Cultural Institute with him.

Heisenberg   I'm sorry about that. He did it with the best of intentions. He may not have explained to you that the Institute is run by the Cultural Division of the Foreign Office. We have good friends in the foreign service. Particularly at the Embassy here.

Bohr   Of course. I knew his father when he was Ambassador in Copenhagen in the twenties.

Heisenberg   It hasn't changed so much since then, you know, the German foreign service.

Bohr   It's a department of the Nazi government.

Heisenberg   Germany is more complex than it may perhaps appear from the outside. The different organs of state have quite different traditions, in spite of all attempts at reform. Particularly the foreign service. Our people in the Embassy here are quite old-fashioned in the way they use their influence. They would certainly be trying to see that distinguished local citizens were able to work undisturbed.

Bohr   Are you telling me that I'm being protected by your friends in the Embassy?

Heisenberg   What I'm saying, in case Weizsäcker failed to make it clear, is that you would find congenial company there. I know people would be very honoured if you felt able to accept an occasional invitation.

Bohr   To cocktail parties at the Germany Embassy? To coffee and cakes with the Nazi plenipotentiary?

Heisenberg   To lectures, perhaps. To discussion groups. Social contacts of any sort could be helpful.

Bohr   I'm sure they could.

Heisenberg   Essential, perhaps, in certain circumstances.

Bohr   In what circumstances?

Heisenberg   I think we both know.

Bohr   Because I'm half-Jewish?

Heisenberg   We all at one time or another may need the help of our friends.

Bohr   Is this why you've come to Copenhagen? To invite me to watch the deportation of my fellow-Danes from a grandstand seat in the windows of the German Embassy?

Heisenberg   Bohr, please! Please! What else can I do? How else can I help? It's an impossibly difficult situation for you, I understand that. It's also an impossibly difficult one for me.

Bohr   Yes. I'm sorry. I'm sure you also have the best of intentions.

Heisenberg   Forget what I said. Unless . . .

Bohr   Unless I need to remember it.

Heisenberg   In any case it's not why I've come.

Margrethe   Perhaps you should simply say what it is you want to say.

Heisenberg   What you and I often used to do in the old days was to take an evening stroll.

Bohr   Often. Yes. In the old days.

Heisenberg   You don't feel like a stroll this evening, for old times' sake?

Bohr   A little chilly tonight, perhaps, for strolling.

Heisenberg   This is so difficult. You remember where we first met?

Bohr   Of course. At Göttingen in 1922.

Heisenberg   At a lecture festival held in your honour.

Bohr   It was a high honour. I was very conscious of it.

Heisenberg   You were being honoured for two reasons. Firstly because you were a great physicist. . .

Bohr   Yes, yes.

Heisenberg   . . . and secondly because you were one of the very few people in Europe who were prepared to have dealings with Germany. The war had been over for four years, and we were still lepers. You held out your hand to us. You've always inspired love, you know that. Wherever you've been, wherever you've worked. Here in Denmark. In England, in America. But in Germany we worshipped you. Because you held out your hand to us.

Bohr   Germany's changed.

Heisenberg   Yes. Then we were down. And you could be generous.

Margrethe   And now you're up.

Heisenberg   And generosity's harder. But you held out your hand to us then, and we took it.

Bohr   Yes . . . No! Not you. As a matter of fact. You bit it.

Heisenberg   Bit it?

Bohr   Bit my hand! You did! I held it out, in my most statesmanlike and reconciliatory way, and you gave it a very nasty nip.

Heisenberg   *I* did?

Bohr   The first time I ever set eyes on you. At one of those lectures I was giving in Göttingen.

Heisenberg   What are you talking about?

Bohr   You stood up and laid into me.

Heisenberg   Oh . . . I offered a few comments.

Bohr   Beautiful summer's day. The scent of roses drifting in from the gardens. Rows of eminent physicists and mathematicians, all nodding approval of my benevolence and wisdom. Suddenly, up jumps a cheeky young pup and tells me that my mathematics are wrong.

Heisenberg   They were wrong.

Bohr   How old were you?

Heisenberg   Twenty.

Bohr   Two years younger than the century.

Heisenberg   Not quite.

Bohr   December 5th, yes?

Heisenberg   1.93 years younger than the century.

Bohr   To be precise.

Heisenberg   No – to two places of decimals. To be *precise*, 1.928 . . . 7 . . . 6 . . . 7 . . . 1 . . .

Bohr   I can always keep track of you, all the same. And the century.

Margrethe   And Niels has suddenly decided to love him again, in spite of everything. Why? What happened? Was it the recollection of that summer's day in Göttingen? Or everything? Or nothing at all? Whatever it was, by the time we've sat down to dinner the cold ashes have started into flame once again.

Bohr   You were always so combative! It was the same when we played table tennis at Tisvilde. You looked as if you were trying to kill me.

Heisenberg   I wanted to win. Of course I wanted to win. *You* wanted to win.

Bohr   I wanted an agreeable game of table tennis.

Heisenberg   You couldn't see the expression on your face.

Bohr   I could see the expression on yours.

Heisenberg   What about those games of poker in the ski-hut at Bayrischzell, then? You once cleaned us all out! You remember that? With a non-existent straight! We're all mathematicians – we're all counting the cards – we're 90 per cent certain he hasn't got anything. But on he goes, raising us, raising us. This insane confidence. Until our faith in mathematical probability begins to waver, and one by one we all throw in.

Bohr   I thought I *had* a straight! I misread the cards! I bluffed myself!

Margrethe   Poor Niels.

Heisenberg   Poor Niels? He won! He bankrupted us! You were insanely competitive! He got us all playing poker once with imaginary cards!

Bohr   You played chess with Weizsäcker on an imaginary board!

Margrethe   Who won?

Bohr   Need you ask? At Bayrischzell we'd ski down from the hut to get provisions, and he'd make even that into some kind of race! You remember? When we were there with Weizsäcker and someone? You got out a stopwatch.

Heisenberg   It took poor Weizsäcker eighteen minutes.

Bohr   You were down there in ten, of course.

Heisenberg   Eight.

Bohr   I don't recall how long I took.

Heisenberg   Forty-five minutes.

Bohr   Thank you.

Margrethe   Some rather swift skiing going on here, I think.

Heisenberg   Your skiing was like your science. What were you waiting for? Me and Weizsäcker to come back and suggest some slight change of emphasis?

Bohr   Probably.

Heisenberg   You were doing seventeen drafts of each slalom?

Margrethe   And without me there to type them out.

Bohr   At least I knew where I was. At the speed you were going you were up against the uncertainty relationship. If you knew where you were when you were down you didn't know how fast you'd got there. If you knew how fast you'd been going you didn't know you were down.

Heisenberg   I certainly didn't stop to think about it.

Bohr   Not to criticise, but that's what might be criticised with some of your science.

Heisenberg   I usually got there, all the same.

Bohr   You never cared what got destroyed on the way, though. As long as the mathematics worked out you were satisfied.

Heisenberg   If something works it works.

Bohr   But the question is always, what does the mathematics mean, in plain language? What are the philosophical implications?

Heisenberg   I always knew you'd be picking your way step by step down the slope behind me, digging all the capsized meanings and implications out of the snow.

Margrethe   The faster you ski the sooner you're across the cracks and crevasses.

Heisenberg   The faster you ski the better you think.

Bohr   Not to disagree, but that is most . . . most interesting.

Heisenberg   By which you mean it's nonsense. But it's not nonsense. Decisions make themselves when you're coming downhill at seventy kilometres an hour. Suddenly there's the edge of nothingness in front of you. Swerve left? Swerve right? Or think about it and die? In your head you swerve both ways . . .

Margrethe   Like that particle.

Heisenberg   What particle?

Margrethe   The one that you said goes through two different slits at the same time.

Heisenberg   Oh, in our old thought-experiment. Yes. Yes!

Margrethe   Or Schrödinger's wretched cat.

Heisenberg   That's alive and dead at the same time.

Margrethe   Poor beast.

Bohr   My love, it was an imaginary cat.

Margrethe   I know.

Bohr   Locked away with an imaginary phial of cyanide.

Margrethe   I know, I know.

Heisenberg   So the particle's here, the particle's there . . .

Bohr   The cat's alive, the cat's dead . . .

Margrethe   You've swerved left, you've swerved right. . .

Heisenberg   Until the experiment is over, this is the point, until the sealed chamber is opened, the abyss detoured; and it turns out that the particle has met itself again, the cat's dead . . .

Margrethe   And you're alive.

Bohr   Not so fast, Heisenberg. . .

Heisenberg   The swerve itself was the decision.

Bohr   Not so fast, not so fast!

Heisenberg   Isn't that how you shot Hendrik Casimir
dead?

Bohr   Hendrik Casimir?

Heisenberg   When he was working here at the Institute.

Bohr   I never shot Hendrik Casimir.

Heisenberg   You told me you did.

Bohr   It was George Gamow. I shot George Gamow. *You*
don't know – it was long after your time.

Heisenberg   Bohr, you shot Hendrik Casimir.

Bohr   Gamow, Gamow. Because he insisted that it was
always quicker to act than to react. To make a decision to do
something rather than respond to someone else's doing it.

Heisenberg   And for that you shot him?

Bohr   It was him! He went out and bought a pair of pistols!
He puts one in his pocket, I put one in mine, and we get
on with the day's work. Hours go by, and we're arguing
ferociously about – I can't remember – our problems with the
nitrogen nucleus, I expect – when suddenly Gamow reaches
into his pocket. . .

Heisenberg   Cap-pistols.

Bohr   Cap-pistols, yes. Of course.

Heisenberg   Margrethe was looking a little worried.

Margrethe   No – a little surprised. At the turn of events.

Bohr   Now you remember how quick he was.

Heisenberg   Casimir?

Bohr   Gamow.

Heisenberg   Not as quick as me.

Bohr   Of course not. But compared with me.

Heisenberg   A fast neutron. However, or so you're going to tell me . . .

Bohr   However, yes, before his gun is even out of his pocket . . .

Heisenberg   You've drafted your reply.

Margrethe   I've typed it out.

Heisenberg   You've checked it with Klein.

Margrethe   I've retyped it.

Heisenberg   You've submitted it to Pauli in Hamburg.

Margrethe   I've retyped it again.

Bohr   Before his gun is even out of his pocket, mine is in my hand.

Heisenberg   And poor Casimir has been blasted out of existence.

Bohr   Except that it was Gamow.

Heisenberg   It was Casimir! He told me!

Bohr   Yes, well, one of the two.

Heisenberg   Both of them simultaneously alive and dead in our memories.

Bohr   Like a pair of Schrödinger cats. Where were we?

Heisenberg   Skiing. Or music. That's another thing that decides everything for you. I play the piano and the way seems to open in front of me – all I have to do is follow. That's how I had my one success with women. At a musical evening at the Bückings in Leipzig – we've assembled a piano trio. 1937, just when all my troubles with the . . . when my troubles are coming to a head. We're playing the Beethoven G major. We finish the scherzo, and I look up from the piano to see if the others are ready to start the final presto. And in that instant I catch a glimpse of a young woman sitting at the side of the room. Just the briefest glimpse, but of course at once I've carried her off to Bayrischzell, we're engaged, we're married, etc. – the usual hopeless romantic fantasies. Then off we go into the presto, and it's terrifyingly fast – so fast there's no time to be afraid. And suddenly everything in the world seems easy. We reach the end and I just carry on skiing. Get myself introduced to the young woman – see her home – and, yes, a week later I've carried her off to Bayrischzell – another week and we're engaged – three months and we're married. All on the sheer momentum of that presto!

Bohr   You were saying you felt isolated. But you do have a companion, after all.

Heisenberg   Music?

Bohr   Elisabeth!

Heisenberg   Oh. Yes. Though, what with the children, and so on . . . I've always envied the way you and Margrethe manage to talk about everything. Your work. Your problems. Me, no doubt.

Bohr   I was formed by nature to be a mathematically curious entity: not one but half of two.

Heisenberg   Mathematics becomes very odd when you apply it to people. One plus one can add up to so many different sums . . .

Margrethe   Silence. What's he thinking about now? His life? Or ours?

Bohr   So many things we think about at the same time. Our lives and our physics.

Margrethe   All the things that come into our heads out of nowhere.

Bohr   Our private consolations. Our private agonies.

Heisenberg   Silence. And of course they're thinking about their children again.

Margrethe   The same bright things. The same dark things. Back and back they come.

Heisenberg   Their four children living, and their two children dead.

Margrethe   Harald. Lying alone in that ward.

Bohr   She's thinking about Christian and Harald.

Heisenberg   The two lost boys. Harald . . .

Bohr   All those years alone in that terrible ward.

Heisenberg   And Christian. The firstborn. The eldest son.

Bohr   And once again I see those same few moments that I see every day.

Heisenberg   Those short moments on the boat, when the tiller slams over in the heavy sea, and Christian is falling.

Bohr   If I hadn't let him take the helm . . .

Heisenberg   Those long moments in the water.

Bohr   Those endless moments in the water.

Heisenberg   When he's struggling towards the lifebuoy.

Bohr   So near to touching it.

Margrethe   I'm at Tisvilde. I look up from my work. There's Niels in the doorway, silently watching me. He turns his head away, and I know at once what's happened.

Bohr   So near, so near! So slight a thing!

Heisenberg   Again and again the tiller slams over. Again and again . . .

Margrethe   Niels turns his head away . . .

Bohr   Christian reaches for the lifebuoy . . .

Heisenberg   But about some things even they never speak.

Bohr   About some things even we only think.

Margrethe   Because there's nothing to be said.

Bohr   Well . . . perhaps we *should* be warm enough. You suggested a stroll.

Heisenberg   In fact the weather is remarkably warm.

Bohr   We shan't be long.

Heisenberg   A week at most.

Bohr   What – our great hike through Zealand?

Heisenberg   We went to Elsinore. I often think about what you said there.

Bohr   You don't mind, my love? Half an hour?

Heisenberg   An hour, perhaps. No, the whole appearance of Elsinore, you said, was changed by our knowing that Hamlet had lived there. Every dark corner there reminds us of the darkness inside the human soul. . .

Margrethe   So, they're walking again. He's done it. And if they're walking they're talking. Talking in a rather different way, no doubt – I've typed out so much in my time about how differently particles behave when they're unobserved . . . I knew Niels would never hold out if they could just get through the first few minutes. If only out of curiosity . . . Now they're started an hour will mean two, of course, perhaps three . . . The first thing they ever did was to go for a walk together. At Göttingen, after that lecture. Niels immediately went to look for the presumptuous young man who'd queried his mathematics, and swept him off for a tramp in the country. Walk – talk – make his acquaintance. And when Heisenberg arrived here to work for him, off they go again, on their great tour of Zealand. A lot of this century's physics they did in the open air. Strolling around the forest paths at Tisvilde. Going down to the beach with the children. Heisenberg holding Christian's hand. Yes, and every evening in Copenhagen, after dinner, they'd walk round Faelled Park behind the Institute, or out along Langelinie into the harbour. Walk, and talk. Long, long before walls had ears . . . But this time, in 1941, their walk takes a different course. Ten minutes after they set out . . . they're back! I've scarcely had the table cleared when there's Niels in the doorway. I see at once how upset he is – he can't look me in the eye.

Bohr   Heisenberg wants to say goodbye. He's leaving.

Margrethe   *He* won't look at me, either.

Heisenberg   Thank you. A delightful evening. Almost like old times. So kind of you.

Margrethe   You'll have some coffee? A glass of something?

Heisenberg   I have to get back and prepare for my lecture.

Margrethe   But you'll come and see us again before you leave?

Bohr   He has a great deal to do.

Margrethe   It's like the worst moments of 1927 all over again, when Niels came back from Norway and first read Heisenberg's uncertainty paper. Something they both seemed to have forgotten about earlier in the evening, though I hadn't. Perhaps they've both suddenly remembered that time. Only from the look on their faces something even worse has happened.

Heisenberg   Forgive me if I've done or said anything that . . .

Bohr   Yes, yes.

Heisenberg   It meant a great deal to me, being here with you both again. More perhaps than you realise.

Margrethe   It was a pleasure for us. Our love to Elisabeth.

Bohr   Of course.

Margrethe   And the children.

Heisenberg   Perhaps, when this war is over . . . If we're all spared . . . Goodbye.

Margrethe   Politics?

Bohr   Physics. He's not right, though. How can he be right?
John Wheeler and I . . .

Margrethe   A breath of air as we talk, why not?

Bohr   A breath of air?

Margrethe   A turn around the garden. Healthier than
staying indoors, perhaps.

Bohr   Oh. Yes.

Margrethe   For everyone concerned.

Bohr   Yes. Thank you . . . How can he possibly be right?
Wheeler and I went through the whole thing in 1939.

Margrethe   What did he say?

Bohr   Nothing. I don't know. I was too angry to take it in.

Margrethe   Something about fission?

Bohr   What happens in fission? You fire a neutron at a
uranium nucleus, it splits, and it releases energy.

Margrethe   A huge amount of energy. Yes?

Bohr   About enough to move a speck of dust. But it also
releases two or three more neutrons. Each of which has the
chance of splitting another nucleus.

Margrethe   So then those two or three split nuclei each
release energy in their turn?

Bohr   And two or three more neutrons.

Heisenberg   You start a trickle of snow sliding as you ski.
The trickle becomes a snowball . . .

Bohr   An ever-widening chain of split nuclei forks through
the uranium, doubling and quadrupling in millionths of a
second from one generation to the next. First two splits, let's
say for simplicity. Then two squared, two cubed, two to the
fourth, two to the fifth, two to the sixth . . .

Heisenberg   The thunder of the gathering avalanche echoes from all the surrounding mountains . . .

Bohr   Until eventually, after, let's say, eighty generations, 2^{80} specks of dust have been moved. 2^{80} is a number with 24 noughts. Enough specks of dust to constitute a city, and all who live in it.

Heisenberg   But there is a catch.

Bohr   There is a catch, thank God. Natural uranium consists of two different isotopes. Most of it's U-238, which you can only fission with fast neutrons. Most neutrons, though, will only fission the other isotope, U-235 – and less than one per cent of natural uranium is U-235.

Heisenberg   This was Bohr's great insight. Another of his amazing intuitions. It came to him when he was at Princeton in 1939, walking across the campus with Wheeler. A characteristic Bohr moment – I wish I'd been there to enjoy it. Five minutes deep silence as they walked, then: 'Now hear this – I have understood everything.'

Bohr   In fact it's a double catch, because the 238 also slows neutrons down and absorbs them. So an explosive chain reaction will never occur in natural uranium. To make an explosion you will have to separate out pure 235. And to make the chain long enough for a large explosion . . .

Heisenberg   Eighty generations, let's say . . .

Bohr   . . . you would need many tons of it. And it's extremely difficult to separate.

Heisenberg   Tantalisingly difficult.

Bohr   Mercifully difficult. The best estimates, when I was in America in 1939, were that to produce even one gram of U-235 would take 26,000 years. By which time, surely, this war will be over. So he's wrong, you see, he's wrong! Or could *I* be wrong? Could I have miscalculated? Let me see . . . What are the absorption rates for fast neutrons in 238? What's the mean free path of slow neutrons in 235 . . . ?

Margrethe   But what exactly had Heisenberg said? That's what everyone wanted to know, then and for ever after.

Bohr   It's what the British wanted to know, as soon as Chadwick managed to get in touch with me. What exactly did Heisenberg say?

Heisenberg   And what exactly did Bohr reply? That was of course the first thing my colleagues asked me when I got back to Germany.

Margrethe   What did Heisenberg tell Niels – what did Niels reply? The person who wanted to know most of all was Heisenberg himself.

Bohr   You mean when he came back to Copenhagen after the war, in 1947?

Margrethe   Escorted this time not by unseen agents of the Gestapo, but by a very conspicuous minder from British intelligence.

Bohr   I think he wanted various things.

Margrethe   Two things. Food parcels . . .

Bohr   For his family in Germany. They were on the verge of starvation.

Margrethe   And for you to agree what you'd said to each other in 1941.

Bohr   The conversation went wrong almost as fast as it did before.

Margrethe   You couldn't even agree where you'd walked that night.

Heisenberg   Where we walked? Faelled Park, of course. Where we went so often in the old days.

Margrethe   But Faelled Park is behind the Institute, four kilometres away from where we live!

Heisenberg   I can see the drift of autumn leaves under the street lamps next to the bandstand.

Bohr   Yes, because you remember it as October!

Margrethe   And it was September.

Bohr   No fallen leaves!

Margrethe   And it was 1941. No street lamps!

Bohr   I thought we hadn't got any further than my study. What I can see is the drift of papers under the reading lamp on my desk.

Heisenberg   We must have been outside! What I was going to say was treasonable. If I'd been overheard I'd have been executed.

Margrethe   So what was this mysterious thing you said?

Heisenberg   There's no mystery about it. There never was any mystery. I remember it absolutely clearly, because my life was at stake, and I chose my words very carefully. I simply asked you if as a physicist one had the moral right to work on the practical exploitation of atomic energy. Yes?

Bohr   I don't recall.

Heisenberg   You don't recall, no, because you immediately became alarmed. You stopped dead in your tracks.

Bohr   I was horrified.

Heisenberg   Horrified. Good, you remember that. You stood there gazing at me, horrified.

Bohr   Because the implication was obvious. That you *were* working on it.

Heisenberg   And you jumped to the conclusion that I was trying to provide Hitler with nuclear weapons.

Bohr   And you were!

Heisenberg   No! A reactor! That's what we were trying to build! A machine to produce power! To generate electricity, to drive ships!

Bohr   You didn't say anything about a reactor.

Heisenberg   I didn't say anything about anything! Not in so many words. I couldn't! I'd no idea how much could be overheard. How much you'd repeat to others.

Bohr   But then I asked you if you actually thought that uranium fission could be used for the construction of weapons.

Heisenberg   Ah! It's coming back!

Bohr   And I clearly remember what you replied.

Heisenberg   I said I now knew that it could be.

Bohr   This is what really horrified me.

Heisenberg   Because you'd always been confident that weapons would need 235, and that we could never separate enough of it.

Bohr   A reactor – yes, maybe, because you can keep a slow chain reaction going in natural uranium.

Heisenberg   What we'd realised, though, was that if we could once get the reactor going . . .

Bohr   The 238 in the natural uranium would absorb the fast neutrons . . .

Heisenberg   Exactly as you predicted in 1939 – everything we were doing was based on that fundamental insight of yours. The 238 would absorb the fast neutrons. And would be transformed by them into a new element altogether.

Bohr   Neptunium. Which would decay in its turn into another new element. . .

Heisenberg   At least as fissile as the 235 that we couldn't separate . . .

Margrethe   Plutonium.

Heisenberg   Plutonium.

Bohr   I should have worked it out for myself.

Heisenberg   If we could build a reactor we could build bombs. That's what had brought me to Copenhagen. But none of this could I say. And at this point you stopped listening. The bomb had already gone off inside your head. I realised we were heading back towards the house. Our walk was over. Our one chance to talk had gone forever.

Bohr   Because I'd grasped the central point already. That one way or another you saw the possibility of supplying Hitler with nuclear weapons.

Heisenberg   You grasped at least four different central points, all of them wrong. You told Rozental that I'd tried to pick your brains about fission. You told Weisskopf that I'd asked you what you knew about the Allied nuclear programme. Chadwick thought I was hoping to persuade you that there was no German programme. But then you seem to have told some people that I'd tried to recruit you to work on it!

Bohr   Very well. Let's start all over again from the beginning. No Gestapo in the shadows this time. No British intelligence officer. No one watching us at all.

Margrethe   Only me.

Bohr   Only Margrethe. We're going to make the whole thing clear to Margrethe. You know how strongly I believe that we don't do science for ourselves, that we do it so we can explain to others . . .

Heisenberg   In plain language.

Bohr   In plain language. Not your view, I know – you'd be happy to describe what you were up to purely in differential equations if you could – but for Margrethe's sake . . .

Heisenberg   Plain language.

Bohr   Plain language. All right, so here we are, walking along the street once more. And this time I'm absolutely calm, I'm listening intently. What is it you want to say?

Heisenberg   It's not just what *I* want to say! The whole German nuclear team in Berlin! Not Diebner, of course, not the Nazis – but Weizsäcker, Hahn, Wirtz, Jensen, Houtermanns – they all wanted me to come and discuss it with you. We all see you as a kind of spiritual father.

Margrethe   The Pope. That's what you used to call Niels behind his back. And now you want him to give you absolution.

Heisenberg   Absolution? No!

Margrethe   According to your colleague Jensen.

Heisenberg   Absolution is the last thing I want!

Margrethe   You told one historian that Jensen had expressed it perfectly.

Heisenberg   Did I? Absolution . . . Is that what I've come for? It's like trying to remember who was at that lunch you gave me at the Institute. Around the table sit all the different explanations for everything I did. I turn to look . . . Petersen, Rozental, and . . . yes . . . now the word absolution is taking its place among them all . . .

Margrethe   Though I thought absolution was granted for sins past and repented, not for sins intended and yet to be committed.

Heisenberg   Exactly! That's why I was so shocked!

Bohr   *You* were shocked?

Heisenberg   Because you *did* give me absolution! That's exactly what you did! As we were hurrying back to the house. You muttered something about everyone in wartime being obliged to do his best for his own country. Yes?

Bohr   Heaven knows what I said. But now here I am, profoundly calm and conscious, weighing my words. You don't want absolution. I understand. You want me to tell you *not* to do it? All right. I put my hand on your arm. I look you in the eye in my most papal way. Go back to Germany,

Heisenberg. Gather your colleagues together in the laboratory. Get up on a table and tell them: 'Niels Bohr says that in his considered judgment supplying a homicidal maniac with an improved instrument of mass murder is . . . ' What shall I say? ' . . . an interesting idea.' No, not even an interesting idea. ' . . . a really rather seriously uninteresting idea.' What happens? You all fling down your Geiger counters?

Heisenberg   Obviously not.

Bohr   Because they'll arrest you.

Heisenberg   Whether they arrest us or not it won't make any difference. In fact it will make things worse. I'm running my programme for the Kaiser Wilhelm Institute. But there's a rival one at Army Ordnance, run by Kurt Diebner, and he's a party member. If I go they'll simply get Diebner to take over my programme as well. He should be running it anyway. Wirtz and the rest of them only smuggled me in to keep Diebner and the Nazis out of it. My one hope is to remain in control.

Bohr   So you don't want me to say yes and you don't want me to say no.

Heisenberg   What I want is for you to listen carefully to what I'm going on to say next, instead of running off down the street like a madman.

Bohr   Very well. Here I am, walking very slowly and popishly. And I listen most carefully as you tell me . . .

Heisenberg   That nuclear weapons will require an enormous technical effort.

Bohr   True.

Heisenberg   That they will suck up huge resources.

Bohr   Huge resources. Certainly.

Heisenberg   That sooner or later governments will have to turn to scientists and ask whether it's worth committing those resources – whether there's any hope of producing the weapons in time for them to be used.

Bohr   Of course, but. . .

Heisenberg   Wait. So they will have to come to you and me. We are the ones who will have to advise them whether to go ahead or not. In the end the decision will be in our hands, whether we like it or not.

Bohr   And that's what you want to tell me?

Heisenberg   That's what I want to tell you.

Bohr   That's why you have come all this way, with so much difficulty? That's why you have thrown away nearly twenty years of friendship? Simply to tell me that?

Heisenberg   Simply to tell you that.

Bohr   But, Heisenberg, this is more mysterious than ever! What are you telling it me *for*? What am I supposed to do about it? The government of occupied Denmark isn't going to come to me and ask me whether we should produce nuclear weapons!

Heisenberg   No, but sooner or later, if I manage to remain in control of our programme, the German government is going to come to *me*! They will ask *me* whether to continue or not! *I* will have to decide what to tell them!

Bohr   Then you have an easy way out of your difficulties. You tell them the simple truth that you've just told me. You tell them how difficult it will be. And perhaps they'll be discouraged. Perhaps they'll lose interest.

Heisenberg   But, Bohr, where will that lead? What will be the consequences if we manage to fail?

Bohr   What can I possibly tell you that you can't tell yourself?

Heisenberg   There was a report in a Stockholm paper that the Americans are working on an atomic bomb.

Bohr   Ah. Now it comes, now it comes. Now I understand everything. You think I have contacts with the Americans?

Heisenberg   You may. It's just conceivable. If anyone in Occupied Europe does it will be you.

Bohr   So you *do* want to know about the Allied nuclear programme.

Heisenberg   I simply want to know if there is one. Some hint. Some clue. I've just betrayed my country and risked my life to warn you of the German programme . . .

Bohr   And now I'm to return the compliment?

Heisenberg   Bohr, I have to know! I'm the one who has to decide! If the Allies are building a bomb, what am I choosing for my country? You said it would be easy to imagine that one might have less love for one's country if it's small and defenceless. Yes, and it would be another easy mistake to make, to think that one loved one's country less because it happened to be in the wrong. Germany is where I was born. Germany is where I became what I am. Germany is all the faces of my childhood, all the hands that picked me up when I fell, all the voices that encouraged me and set me on my way, all the hearts that speak to my heart. Germany is my widowed mother and my impossible brother. Germany is my wife. Germany is our children. I have to know what I'm deciding for them! Is it another defeat? Another nightmare like the nightmare I grew up with? Bohr, my childhood in Munich came to an end in anarchy and civil war. Are more children going to starve, as we did? Are they going to have to spend winter nights as I did when I was a schoolboy, crawling on my hands and knees through the enemy lines, creeping out into the country under cover of darkness in the snow to find food for my family? Are they going to sit up all night, as I did at the age of seventeen, guarding some terrified prisoner, talking to him and talking to him through the small hours, because he's going to be executed in the morning?

Bohr But, my dear Heisenberg, there's nothing I can tell you. I've no idea whether there's an Allied nuclear programme.

Heisenberg It's just getting under way even as you and I are talking. And maybe I'm choosing something worse even than defeat. Because the bomb they're building is to be used on us. On the evening of Hiroshima Oppenheimer said it was his one regret. That they hadn't produced the bomb in time to use on Germany.

Bohr He tormented himself afterwards.

Heisenberg Afterwards, yes. At least we tormented ourselves a little beforehand. Did a single one of them stop to think, even for one brief moment, about what they were doing? Did Oppenheimer? Did Fermi, or Teller, or Szilard? Did Einstein, when he wrote to Roosevelt in 1939 and urged him to finance research on the bomb? Did you, when you escaped from Copenhagen two years later, and went to Los Alamos?

Bohr My dear, good Heisenberg, we weren't supplying the bomb to Hitler!

Heisenberg You weren't dropping it on Hitler, either. You were dropping it on anyone who was in reach. On old men and women in the street, on mothers and their children. And if you'd produced it in time they would have been my fellow countrymen. My wife. My children. That was the intention. Yes?

Bohr That was the intention.

Heisenberg You never had the slightest conception of what happens when bombs are dropped on cities. Even conventional bombs. None of you ever experienced it. Not a single one of you. I walked back from the centre of Berlin to the suburbs one night, after one of the big raids. No transport moving, of course. The whole city on fire. Even the puddles in the streets are burning. They're puddles of molten phosphorus. It gets on your shoes like some kind of incandescent dog-muck – I have to keep scraping it off – as if the streets have been fouled by the hounds of hell. It would have made you laugh – my shoes keep bursting into flame. All around me, I suppose, there are people trapped, people in various stages of burning to death. And all I can think is, how will I ever get hold of another pair of shoes in times like these?

Bohr   You know why Allied scientists worked on the bomb.

Heisenberg   Of course. Fear.

Bohr   The same fear that was consuming you. Because they were afraid that *you* were working on it.

Heisenberg   But, Bohr, you could have told them!

Bohr   Told them what?

Heisenberg   What I told you in 1941! That the choice is in our hands! In mine – in Oppenheimer's! That if I can tell them the simple truth when they ask me, the simple discouraging truth, so can he!

Bohr   This is what you want from me? Not to tell you what the Americans are doing but to stop them?

Heisenberg   To tell them that we can stop it together.

Bohr   I had no contact with the Americans!

Heisenberg   You did with the British.

Bohr   Only later.

Heisenberg   The Gestapo intercepted the message you sent them about our meeting.

Margrethe   And passed it to you?

Heisenberg   Why not? They'd begun to trust me. This is what gave me the possibility of remaining in control of events.

Bohr   Not to criticise, Heisenberg, but if this is your plan in coming to Copenhagen, it's . . . what can I say? It's most interesting.

Heisenberg   It's not a plan. It's a hope. Not even a hope. A microscopically fine thread of possibility. A wild improbability. Worth trying, though, Bohr! Worth trying, surely! But already you're too angry to understand what I'm saying.

Margrethe   No – why he's angry is because he *is* beginning to understand! The Germans drive out most of their best physicists because they're Jews. America and Britain give them sanctuary. Now it turns out that this might offer the Allies a hope of salvation. And at once you come howling to Niels begging him to persuade them to give it up.

Bohr   Margrethe, my love, perhaps we should try to express ourselves a little more temperately.

Margrethe   But the gall of it! The sheer, breathtaking gall of it!

Bohr   Bold skiing, I have to say.

Heisenberg   But, Bohr, we're not skiing now! We're not playing table tennis! We're not juggling with cap-pistols and non-existent cards! I refused to believe it, when I first heard the news of Hiroshima. I thought that it was just one of the strange dreams we were living in at the time. They'd got stranger and stranger, God knows, as Germany fell into ruins in those last months of the war. But by then we were living in the strangest of them all. The ruins had suddenly vanished – just the way things do in dreams – and all at once we're in a stately home in the middle of the English countryside. We've been rounded up by the British – the whole team, everyone who worked on atomic research – and we've been spirited away. To Farm Hall, in Huntingdonshire, in the water meadows of the River Ouse. Our families in Germany are starving, and there are we sitting down each evening to an excellent formal dinner with our charming host, the British officer in charge of us. It's like a pre-war house party – one of those house parties in a play, that's cut off from any contact with the outside world, where you know the guests have all been invited for some secret sinister purpose. No one knows we're there – no one in England, no one in Germany, not even our families. But the war's over. What's happening? Perhaps, as in a play, we're going to be quietly murdered, one by one. In the meanwhile it's all delightfully civilised. I entertain the party with Beethoven piano sonatas. Major Rittner, our hospitable gaoler, reads Dickens to us, to improve our English . . . Did these things really happen to me . . . ? We wait for the point of it all to be revealed to us. Then one evening it is. And it's even more grotesque than the one we were fearing. It's on the radio: you have actually done the deed that we were tormenting ourselves about. That's why we're there, dining with our gracious host, listening to our Dickens. We've been kept locked up to stop us discussing the subject with anyone until it's too late. When Major Rittner tells us I simply refuse to believe it until I hear it with my own ears on the nine o'clock news. We'd no idea how far ahead you'd got. I can't describe the effect it has on us. You play happily with your toy cap-pistol. Then someone else picks it up and pulls the trigger . . . and all at once there's blood everywhere and people screaming, because it wasn't a toy at all . . . We sit up half the night, talking about it, trying to take it in. We're all literally in shock.

Margrethe   Because it had been done? Or because it wasn't you who'd done it?

Heisenberg   Both. Both. Otto Hahn wants to kill himself, because it was he who discovered fission, and he can see the blood on his hands. Gerlach, our old Government administrator, also wants to die, because his hands are so shamefully clean. You've done it, though. You've built the bomb.

Bohr   Yes.

Heisenberg   And you've used it on a living target.

Bohr   On a living target.

Margrethe   You're not suggesting that Niels did anything wrong in working at Los Alamos?

Heisenberg   Of course not. Bohr has never done anything wrong.

Margrethe   The decision had been taken long before Niels arrived. The bomb would have been built whether Niels had gone or not.

Bohr   In any case, my part was very small.

Heisenberg   Oppenheimer described you as the team's father-confessor.

Bohr   It seems to be my role in life.

Heisenberg   He said you made a great contribution.

Bohr   Spiritual, possibly. Not practical.

Heisenberg   Fermi says it was you who worked out how to trigger the Nagasaki bomb.

Bohr   I put forward an idea.

Margrethe   You're not implying that there's anything that *Niels* needs to explain or defend?

Heisenberg   No one has ever expected him to explain or defend anything. He's a profoundly good man.

Bohr   It's not a question of goodness. I was spared the decision.

Heisenberg   Yes, and I was not. So explaining and defending myself was how I spent the last thirty years of my life. When I went to America in 1949 a lot of physicists wouldn't even shake my hand. Hands that had actually built the bomb wouldn't touch mine.

Margrethe   And let me tell you, if you think you're making it any clearer to me now, you're not.

Bohr   Margrethe, I understand his feelings . . .

Margrethe   I don't. I'm as angry as you were before! It's so easy to make you feel conscience-stricken. Why should he transfer his burden to you? Because what does he do after his great consultation with you? He goes back to Berlin and tells the Nazis that he can produce atomic bombs!

Heisenberg   But what I stress is the difficulty of separating 235.

Margrethe   You tell them about plutonium.

Heisenberg   I tell some of the minor officials. I have to keep people's hopes alive!

Margrethe   Otherwise they'll send for the other one.

Heisenberg   Diebner. Very possibly.

Margrethe   There's always a Diebner at hand ready to take over our crimes.

Heisenberg   Diebner might manage to get a little further than me.

Bohr   Diebner?

Heisenberg   Might. Just possibly might.

Bohr   He hasn't a quarter of your ability!

Heisenberg   Not a tenth of it. But he has ten times the eagerness to do it. It might be a very different story if it's Diebner who puts the case at our meeting with Albert Speer, instead of me.

Margrethe   The famous meeting with Speer.

Heisenberg   But this is when it counts. This is the real moment of decision. It's June 1942. Nine months after my trip to Copenhagen. All research cancelled by Hitler unless it produces immediate results – and Speer is the sole arbiter of what will qualify. Now, we've just got the first sign that our reactor's going to work. Our first increase in neutrons. Not much – thirteen per cent – but it's a start.

Bohr   June 1942? You're slightly ahead of Fermi in Chicago.

Heisenberg   Only we don't know that. But the RAF have begun terror-bombing. They've obliterated half of Lubeck, and the whole centre of Rostock and Cologne. We're desperate for new weapons to strike back with. If ever there's a moment to make our case, this is it.

Margrethe   You don't ask him for the funding to continue?

Heisenberg   To continue with the reactor? Of course I do. But I ask for so little that he doesn't take the programme seriously.

Margrethe   Do you tell him the reactor will produce plutonium?

Heisenberg   I don't tell him the reactor will produce plutonium. Not Speer, no. I don't tell him the reactor will produce plutonium.

Bohr   A striking omission, I have to admit.

Heisenberg   And what happens? It works! He gives us barely enough money to keep the reactor programme ticking over. And that is the end of the German atomic bomb. That is the end of it.

Margrethe   You go on with the reactor, though.

Heisenberg   We go on with the reactor. Of course. Because now there's no risk of getting it running in time to produce enough plutonium for a bomb. No, we go on with the reactor all right. We work like madmen on the reactor. We have to drag it all the way across Germany, from east to west, from Berlin to Swabia, to get it away from the bombing, to keep it out of the hands of the Russians. Diebner tries to hijack it on the way. We get it away from him, and we set it up in a little village in the Swabian Jura.

Bohr   This is Haigerloch?

Heisenberg   There's a natural shelter there – the village inn has a wine cellar cut into the base of a cliff. We dig a hole in the floor for the reactor, and I keep that programme going, I keep it under my control, until the bitter end.

Bohr   But, Heisenberg, with respect now, with the greatest respect, you couldn't even keep the reactor under your control. That reactor was going to kill you.

Heisenberg   It wasn't put to the test. It never went critical.

Bohr   Thank God. Hambro and Perrin examined it after the Allied troops took over. They said it had no cadmium control rods. There was nothing to absorb any excess of neutrons, to slow the reaction down when it overheated.

Heisenberg   No rods, no.

Bohr   You believed the reaction would be self-limiting.

Heisenberg   That's what I originally believed.

Bohr   Heisenberg, the reaction would not have been self-limiting.

Heisenberg   By 1945 I understood that.

Bohr   So if you ever had got it to go critical, it would have melted down, and vanished into the centre of the earth!

Heisenberg   Not at all. We had a lump of cadmium to hand.

Bohr   A *lump* of cadmium? What were you proposing to do with a *lump* of cadmium?

Heisenberg   Throw it into the water.

Bohr   What water?

Heisenberg   The heavy water. The moderator that the uranium was immersed in.

Bohr   My dear good Heisenberg, not to criticise, but you'd all gone mad!

Heisenberg   We were almost there! We had this fantastic neutron growth! We had 670 per cent growth!

Bohr   You'd lost all contact with reality down in that hole!

Heisenberg   Another week. Another fortnight. That's all we needed!

Bohr   It was only the arrival of the Allies that saved you!

Heisenberg   We'd almost reached the critical mass! A tiny bit bigger and the chain would sustain itself indefinitely. All we need is a little more uranium. I set off with Weizsäcker to try and get our hands on Diebner's. Another hair-raising journey all the way back across Germany. Constant air raids – no trains – we try bicycles – we never make it! We end up stuck in a little inn somewhere in the middle of nowhere, listening to the thump of bombs falling all round us. And on the radio someone playing the Beethoven G minor cello sonata . . .

Bohr   And everything was still under your control?

Heisenberg   Under my control – yes! That's the point! Under my control!

Bohr   Nothing was under anyone's control by that time!

Heisenberg   Yes, because at last we were free of all constraints! The nearer the end came the faster we could work!

Bohr   You were no longer running that programme, Heisenberg. The programme was running you.

Heisenberg   Two more weeks, two more blocks of uranium, and it would have been German physics that achieved the world's first self-sustaining chain reaction.

Bohr   Except that Fermi had already done it in Chicago, two years earlier.

Heisenberg   We didn't know that.

Bohr   You didn't know anything down in that cave. You were as blind as moles in a hole. Perrin said that there wasn't even anything to protect you all from the radiation.

Heisenberg   We didn't have time to think about it.

Bohr   So if it *had* gone critical . . .

Margrethe You'd all have died of radiation sickness.

Bohr My dear Heisenberg! My dear boy!

Heisenberg Yes, but by then the reactor would have been running.

Bohr I should have been there to look after you.

Heisenberg That's all we could think of at the time. To get the reactor running, to get the reactor running.

Bohr You always needed me there to slow you down a little. Your own walking lump of cadmium.

Heisenberg If I had died then, what should I have missed? Thirty years of attempting to explain. Thirty years of reproach and hostility. Even you turned your back on

Margrethe You came to Copenhagen again. You came to Tisvilde.

Heisenberg It was never the same.

Bohr No. It was never the same.

Heisenberg I sometimes think that those final few weeks at Haigerloch were the last happy time in my life. In a strange way it was very peaceful. Suddenly we were out of all the politics of Berlin. Out of the bombing. The war was coming to an end. There was nothing to think about except the reactor. And we didn't go mad, in fact. We didn't work all the time. There was a monastery on top of the rock above our cave. I used to retire to the organ loft in the church, and play Bach fugues.

Margrethe Look at him. He's lost. He's like a lost child. He's been out in the woods all day, running here, running there. He's shown off, he's been brave, he's been cowardly. He's done wrong, he's done right. And now the evening's come, and all he wants is to go home, and he's lost.

Heisenberg Silence.

Bohr Silence.

Margrethe   Silence.

Heisenberg   And once again the tiller slams over, and Christian is falling.

Bohr   Once again he's struggling towards the lifebuoy.

Margrethe   Once again I look up from my work, and there's Niels in the doorway, silently watching me . . .

Bohr   So, Heisenberg, why did you come to Copenhagen in 1941? It was right that you told us about all the fears you had. But you didn't really think I'd tell you whether the Americans were working on a bomb.

Heisenberg   No.

Bohr   You didn't seriously hope that I'd stop them.

Heisenberg   No.

Bohr   You were going back to work on that reactor whatever I said.

Heisenberg   Yes.

Bohr   So, Heisenberg, why did you come?

Heisenberg   Why did I come?

Bohr   Tell us once again. Another draft of the paper. And this time we shall get it right. This time we shall understand.

Margrethe   Maybe you'll even understand yourself.

Bohr   After all, the workings of the atom were difficult to explain. We made many attempts. Each time we tried they became more obscure. We got there in the end, however. So – another draft, another draft.

Heisenberg   Why did I come? And once again I go through that evening in 1941. I crunch over the familiar gravel, and tug at the familiar bell-pull. What's in my head? Fear, certainly, and the absurd and horrible importance of someone bearing bad news. But . . . yes . . . something else as

well. Here it comes again. I can almost see its face.
Something good. Something bright and eager and hopeful.

Bohr I open the door . . .

Heisenberg And there he is. I see his eyes light up at the
sight of me.

Bohr He's smiling his wary schoolboy smile.

Heisenberg And I feel a moment of such consolation.

Bohr A flash of such pure gladness.

Heisenberg As if I'd come home after a long journey.

Bohr As if a long-lost child had appeared on the doorstep.

Heisenberg Suddenly I'm free of all the dark tangled
currents in the water.

Bohr Christian is alive, Harald still unborn.

Heisenberg The world is at peace again.

Margrethe Look at them. Father and son still. Just for a
moment. Even now we're all dead.

Bohr For a moment, yes, it's the twenties again.

Heisenberg And we shall speak to each other and
understand each other in the way we did before.

Margrethe And from those two heads the future will
emerge. Which cities will be destroyed, and which survive.
Who will die, and who will live. Which world will go down
to obliteration, and which will triumph.

Bohr My dear Heisenberg!

Heisenberg My dear Bohr!

Bohr Come in, come in . . .

Act Two

Heisenberg It was the very beginning of spring. The first time I came to Copenhagen, in 1924. March: raw, blustery northern weather. But every now and then the sun would come out and leave that first marvellous warmth of the year on your skin. That first breath of returning life.

Bohr You were twenty-two. So I must have been . . .

Heisenberg Thirty-eight.

Bohr Almost the same age as you were when you came in 1941.

Heisenberg So what do we do?

Bohr Put on our boots and rucksacks . . .

Heisenberg Take the tram to the end of the line . . .

Bohr And start walking!

Heisenberg Northwards to Elsinore.

Bohr If you walk you talk.

Heisenberg Then westwards to Tisvilde.

Bohr And back by way of Hillerød.

Heisenberg Walking, talking, for a hundred miles.

Bohr After which we talked more or less non-stop for the next three years.

Heisenberg We'd split a bottle of wine over dinner in your flat at the Institute.

Bohr Then I'd come up to your room . . .

Heisenberg That terrible little room in the servants' quarters in the attic.

Bohr And we'd talk on into the small hours.

Heisenberg   How, though?

Bohr   How?

Heisenberg   How did we talk? In Danish?

Bohr   In German, surely.

Heisenberg   I lectured in Danish. I had to give my first colloquium when I'd only been here for ten weeks.

Bohr   I remember it. Your Danish was already excellent.

Heisenberg   No. You did a terrible thing to me. Half an hour before it started you said casually, 'Oh, I think we'll speak English today.'

Bohr   But when you explained . . . ?

Heisenberg   Explain to the Pope? I didn't dare. That excellent Danish you heard was my first attempt at English.

Bohr   My dear Heisenberg! On our own together, though? My love, do you recall?

Margrethe   What language you spoke when I wasn't there? You think I had microphones hidden?

Bohr   No, no – but patience, my love, patience!

Margrethe   Patience?

Bohr   You sounded a little sharp.

Margrethe   Not at all.

Bohr   We have to follow the threads right back to the beginning of the maze.

Margrethe   I'm watching every step.

Bohr   You didn't mind? I hope.

Margrethe   Mind?

Bohr   Being left at home?

Margrethe   While you went off on your hike? Of course not. Why should I have minded? You had to get out of the house. Two new sons arriving on top of each other would be rather a lot for any man to put up with.

Bohr   Two new sons?

Margrethe   Heisenberg.

Bohr   Yes, yes.

Margrethe   And our own son.

Bohr   Aage?

Margrethe   Ernest!

Bohr   1924 – of course – Ernest.

Margrethe   Number five. Yes?

Bohr   Yes, yes, yes. And if it was March, you're right – he couldn't have been much more than . . .

Margrethe   One week.

Bohr   One week? One week, yes. And you really didn't mind?

Margrethe   Not at all. I was pleased you had an excuse to get away. And you always went off hiking with your new assistants. You went off with Kramers, when he arrived in 1916.

Bohr   Yes, when I suppose Christian was still only . . .

Margrethe   One week.

Bohr   Yes . . . Yes . . . I almost killed Kramers, you know.

Heisenberg   Not with a cap-pistol?

Bohr   With a mine. On our walk.

Heisenberg   Oh, the mine. Yes, you told me, on ours. Never mind Kramers – you almost killed yourself!

Bohr   A mine washed up in the shallows . . .

Heisenberg   And of course at once they compete to throw stones at it. What were you thinking of?

Bohr   I've no idea.

Heisenberg   A touch of Elsinore there, perhaps.

Bohr   Elsinore?

Heisenberg   The darkness inside the human soul.

Bohr   You did something just as idiotic.

Heisenberg   *I* did?

Bohr   With Dirac in Japan. You climbed a pagoda.

Heisenberg   Oh, the pagoda.

Bohr   Then balanced on the pinnacle. According to Dirac. On one foot. In a high wind. I'm glad I wasn't there.

Heisenberg   Elsinore, I confess.

Bohr   Elsinore, certainly.

Heisenberg   I was jealous of Kramers, you know.

Bohr   His Eminence. Isn't that what you called him?

Heisenberg   Because that's what he was. Your leading cardinal. Your favourite son. Till I arrived on the scene.

Margrethe   He was a wonderful cellist.

Bohr   He was a wonderful everything.

Heisenberg   Far too wonderful.

Margrethe   I liked him.

Heisenberg   I was terrified of him. When I first started at the Institute. I was terrified of all of them. All the boy wonders you had here – they were all so brilliant and accomplished. But Kramers was the heir apparent. All the rest of us had to work in the general study hall. Kramers had the private office next to yours, like the electron on the inmost orbit around the nucleus. And he didn't think much of my physics. He insisted you could explain everything about the atom by classical mechanics.

Bohr   Well, he was wrong.

Margrethe   And very soon the private office was vacant.

Bohr   And there was another electron on the inmost orbit.

Heisenberg   Yes, and for three years we lived inside the atom.

Bohr   With other electrons on the outer orbits around us all over Europe.

Heisenberg   Max Born and Pascual Jordan in Göttingen.

Bohr   Yes, but Schrödinger in Zürich, Fermi in Rome.

Heisenberg   Chadwick and Dirac in England.

Bohr   Joliot and de Broglie in Paris.

Heisenberg   Gamow and Landau in Russia.

Bohr   Everyone in and out of each other's departments.

Heisenberg   Papers and drafts of papers on every international mail train.

Bohr   You remember when Goudsmit and Uhlenbeck did spin?

Heisenberg   There's this one last variable in the quantum state of the atom that no one can make sense of. The last hurdle . . .

Bohr   And these two crazy Dutchmen go back to a ridiculous idea that electrons can spin in different ways.

Heisenberg   And of course the first thing that everyone wants to know is, what line is Copenhagen going to take?

Bohr   I'm on my way to Leiden, as it happens.

Heisenberg   And it turns into a papal progress! The train stops on the way at Hamburg . . .

Bohr   Pauli and Stern are waiting on the platform to ask me what I think about spin.

Heisenberg   You tell them it's wrong.

Bohr   No, I tell them it's very. . .

Heisenberg   Interesting.

Bohr   I think that is precisely the word I choose.

Heisenberg   Then the train pulls into Leiden.

Bohr   And I'm met at the barrier by Einstein and Ehrenfest. And I change my mind because Einstein – Einstein, you see? – I'm the Pope – he's God – because Einstein has made a relativistic analysis, and it resolves all my doubts.

Heisenberg   Meanwhile I'm standing in for Max Born at Göttingen, so you make a detour there on your way home.

Bohr   And you and Jordan meet me at the station.

Heisenberg   Same question: what do you think of spin?

Bohr   And when the train stops at Berlin there's Pauli on the platform.

Heisenberg   Wolfgang Pauli, who never gets out of bed if he can possibly avoid it . . .

Bohr   And who's already met me once at Hamburg on the journey out . . .

Heisenberg   He's travelled all the way from Hamburg to Berlin purely in order to see you for the second time round . . .

Bohr   And find out how my ideas on spin have developed en route.

Heisenberg   Oh, those years! Those amazing years! Those three short years!

Bohr   From 1924 to 1927.

Heisenberg   From when I arrived in Copenhagen to work with you . . .

Bohr   To when you departed, to take up your chair at Leipzig.

Heisenberg   Three years of raw, bracing northern springtime.

Bohr   At the end of which we had quantum mechanics, we had uncertainty. . .

Heisenberg   We had complementarity . . .

Bohr   We had the whole Copenhagen Interpretation.

Heisenberg   Europe in all its glory again. A new Enlightenment, with Germany back in her rightful place at the heart of it. And who led the way for everyone else?

Margrethe   You and Niels.

Heisenberg   Well, we did.

Bohr   We did.

Margrethe   And that's what you were trying to get back to in 1941?

Heisenberg   To something we did in those three years . . . Something we said, something we thought . . . I keep almost seeing it out of the corner of my eye as we talk! Something about the way we worked. Something about the way we did all those things . . .

Bohr   Together.

Heisenberg   Together. Yes, together.

Margrethe   No.

Bohr   No? What do you mean, no?

Margrethe   Not together. You didn't do any of those things together.

Bohr   Yes, we did. Of course we did.

Margrethe   No, you didn't. Every single one of them you did when you were apart. *You* first worked out quantum mechanics on Heligoland.

Heisenberg   Well, it was summer by then. I had my hay fever.

Margrethe   And on Heligoland, on your own, on a rocky bare island in the middle of the North Sea, you said there was nothing to distract you . . .

Heisenberg   My head began to clear, and I had this very sharp picture of what atomic physics ought to be like. I suddenly realised that we had to limit it to the measurements we could actually make, to what we could actually observe. We can't see the electrons inside the atom . . .

Margrethe   Any more than Niels can see the thoughts in your head, or you the thoughts in Niels's.

Heisenberg   All we can see are the effects that the electrons produce, on the light that they reflect. . .

Bohr   But the difficulties you were trying to resolve were the ones we'd explored together, over dinner in the flat, on the beach at Tisvilde.

Heisenberg   Of course. But I remember the evening when the mathematics first began to chime with the principle.

Margrethe   On Heligoland.

Heisenberg   On Heligoland.

Margrethe   On your own.

Heisenberg   It was terribly laborious – I didn't understand matrix calculus then . . . I get so excited I keep making mistakes. But by three in the morning I've got it. I seem to be looking through the surface of atomic phenomena into a strangely beautiful interior world. A world of pure mathematical structures. I'm too excited to sleep. I go down to the southern end of the island. There's a rock jutting out into the sea that

I've been longing to climb. I get up it in the half-light before the dawn, and lie on top, gazing out to sea.

Margrethe   On your own.

Heisenberg   On my own. And yes – I was happy.

Margrethe   Happier than you were back here with us all in Copenhagen the following winter.

Heisenberg   What, with all the Schrödinger nonsense?

Bohr   Nonsense? Come, come. Schrödinger's wave formulation?

Margrethe   Yes, suddenly everyone's turned their backs on your wonderful new matrix mechanics.

Heisenberg   No one can understand it.

Margrethe   And they *can* understand Schrödinger's wave mechanics.

Heisenberg   Because they'd learnt it in school! We're going backwards to classical physics! And when I'm a little cautious about accepting it . . .

Bohr   A little cautious? Not to criticise, but. . .

Margrethe   . . . You described it as repulsive!

Heisenberg   I said the physical implications were repulsive. Schrödinger said my mathematics were repulsive.

Bohr   I seem to recall you used the word . . . well, I won't repeat it in mixed company.

Heisenberg   In private. But by that time people had gone crazy.

Margrethe   They thought you were simply jealous.

Heisenberg   Someone even suggested some bizarre kind of intellectual snobbery. You got extremely excited.

Bohr   On your behalf.

Heisenberg   You invited Schrödinger here . . .

Bohr   To have a calm debate about our differences.

Heisenberg   And you fell on him like a madman. You meet him at the station – of course – and you pitch into him before he's even got his bags off the train. Then you go on at him from first thing in the morning until last thing at night.

Bohr   *I* go on? *He* goes on!

Heisenberg   Because you won't make the least concession!

Bohr   Nor will he!

Heisenberg   You made him ill! He had to retire to bed to get away from you!

Bohr   He had a slight feverish cold.

Heisenberg   Margrethe had to nurse him!

Margrethe   I dosed him with tea and cake to keep his strength up.

Heisenberg   Yes, while you pursued him even into the sickroom! Sat on his bed and hammered away at him!

Bohr   Perfectly politely.

Heisenberg   You were the Pope and the Holy Office and the Inquisition all rolled into one! And then, and then, after Schrödinger had fled back to Zürich – and this I will never forget, Bohr, this I will never let you forget – you started to take his side! You turned on me!

Bohr   Because *you'd* gone mad by this time! You'd become fanatical! You were refusing to allow wave theory any place in quantum mechanics at all!

Heisenberg   You'd completely turned your coat!

Bohr   I said wave mechanics and matrix mechanics were simply alternative tools.

Heisenberg   Something you're always accusing me of. 'If it works it works.' Never mind what it means.

Bohr   Of course I mind what it means.

Heisenberg   What it means in language.

Bohr   In plain language, yes.

Heisenberg   What something means is what it means in mathematics.

Bohr   You think that so long as the mathematics works out, the sense doesn't matter.

Heisenberg   Mathematics *is* sense! That's what sense is!

Bohr   But in the end, in the end, remember, we have to be able to explain it all to Margrethe!

Margrethe   Explain it to me? You couldn't even explain it to each other! You went on arguing into the small hours every night! You both got so angry!

Bohr   We also both got completely exhausted.

Margrethe   It was the cloud chamber that finished you.

Bohr   Yes, because if you detach an electron from an atom, and send it through a cloud chamber, you can see the track it leaves.

Heisenberg   And it's a scandal. There shouldn't be a track!

Margrethe   According to your quantum mechanics.

Heisenberg   There *isn't* a track! No orbits! No tracks or trajectories! Only external effects!

Margrethe   Only there the track is. I've seen it myself, as clear as the wake left by a passing ship.

Bohr   It was a fascinating paradox.

Heisenberg   You actually loved the paradoxes, that's your problem. You revelled in the contradictions.

Bohr   Yes, and you've never been able to understand the suggestiveness of paradox and contradiction. That's *your* problem. You live and breathe paradox and contradiction, but you can no more see the beauty of them than the fish can see the beauty of the water.

Heisenberg   I sometimes felt as if I was trapped in a kind of windowless hell. You don't realise how aggressive you are. Prowling up and down the room as if you're going to eat someone – and I can guess who it's going to be.

Bohr   That's the way we did the physics, though.

Margrethe   No. No! In the end you did it on your own again! Even you! You went off skiing in Norway.

Bohr   I had to get away from it all!

Margrethe   And you worked out complementarity in Norway, on your own.

Heisenberg   The speed he skis at, he had to do *something* to keep the blood going round. It was either physics or frostbite.

Bohr   Yes, and you stayed behind in Copenhagen . . .

Heisenberg   And started to think at last.

Margrethe   You're a lot better off apart, you two.

Heisenberg   Having him out of town was as liberating as getting away from my hay fever on Heligoland.

Margrethe   I shouldn't let you sit anywhere near each other, if I were the teacher.

Heisenberg   And that's when I did uncertainty. Walking round Faelled Park on my own one horrible raw February night. It's very late, and as soon as I've turned off into the park I'm completely alone in the darkness. I start to think about what you'd see, if you could train a telescope on me from the mountains of Norway. You'd see me by the street lamps on the Blegdamsvej, then nothing as I vanished into the darkness, then another glimpse of me as I passed the lamp post in front of the bandstand. And that's what we see in the cloud chamber. Not a continuous track but a series of glimpses – a series of collisions between the passing electron and various molecules of water vapour . . . Or think of you, on your great papal progress to Leiden in 1925. What did Margrethe see of that, at home here in Copenhagen? A picture postcard from Hamburg, perhaps. Then one from Leiden. One from Göttingen. One from Berlin. Because what we see in the cloud chamber are not even the collisions themselves, but the water droplets that condense around them, as big as cities around a traveller – no, vastly bigger still, relatively – complete countries – Germany . . . Holland . . . Germany again. There is no track, there are no precise addresses; only a vague list of countries visited. I don't know why we hadn't thought of it before, except that we were too busy arguing to think at all.

Bohr   You seem to have given up on all forms of discussion. By the time I get back from Norway I find you've done a draft of your uncertainty paper and you've already sent it for publication!

Margrethe   And an even worse battle begins.

Bohr   My dear good Heisenberg, it's not open behaviour to rush a first draft into print before we've discussed it together! It's not the way we work!

Heisenberg   No, the way we work is that you hound me from first thing in the morning till last thing at night! The way we work is that you drive me mad!

Bohr   Yes, because the paper contains a fundamental error.

Margrethe   And here we go again.

Heisenberg   No, but I show him the strangest truth about the universe that any of us has stumbled on since relativity – that you can never know everything about the whereabouts of a particle, or anything else, even Bohr now, as he prowls up and down the room in that maddening way of his, because we can't observe it without introducing some new element into the situation, a molecule of water vapour for it to hit, or a piece of light – things which have an energy of their own, and which therefore have an effect on what they hit. A small one, admittedly, in the case of Bohr . . .

Bohr   Yes, if you know where I am with the kind of accuracy we're talking about when we're dealing with particles, you can still measure my velocity to within – what . . . ?

Heisenberg   Something like a billionth of a billionth of a kilometre per second. The theoretical point remains, though, that you have no absolutely determinate situation in the world, which among other things lays waste to the idea of causality, the whole foundation of science – because if you don't know how things are today you certainly can't know how they're going to be tomorrow. I shatter the objective universe around you – and all you can say is that there's an error in the formulation!

Bohr   There is!

Margrethe   Tea, anyone? Cake?

Heisenberg   Listen, in my paper what we're trying to locate is not a free electron off on its travels through a cloud chamber, but an electron when it's at home, moving around inside an atom . . .

Bohr   And the uncertainty arises not, as you claim, through its indeterminate recoil when it's hit by an incoming photon . . .

Heisenberg   Plain language, plain language!

Bohr   This *is* plain language.

Heisenberg   Listen . . .

Bohr   The language of classical mechanics.

Heisenberg   Listen! Copenhagen is an atom. Margrethe is its nucleus. About right, the scale? Ten thousand to one?

Bohr   Yes, yes.

Heisenberg   Now, Bohr's an electron. He's wandering about the city somewhere in the darkness, no one knows where. He's here, he's there, he's everywhere and nowhere. Up in Faelled Park, down at Carlsberg. Passing City Hall, out by the harbour. I'm a photon. A quantum of light. I'm despatched into the darkness to find Bohr. And I succeed, because I manage to collide with him . . . But what's happened? Look – he's been slowed down, he's been deflected! He's no longer doing exactly what he was so maddeningly doing when I walked into him!

Bohr   But, Heisenberg, Heisenberg! You also have been deflected! If people can see what's happened to you, to their piece of light, then they can work out what must have happened to me! The trouble is knowing what's happened to you! Because to understand how people see you we have to treat you not just as a particle, but as a wave. I have to use not only your particle mechanics, I have to use the Schrödinger wave function.

Heisenberg   I know – I put it in a postscript to my paper.

Bohr   Everyone remembers the paper – no one remembers the postscript. But the question is fundamental. Particles are things, complete in themselves. Waves are disturbances in something else.

Heisenberg   I know. Complementarity. It's in the postscript.

Bohr   They're either one thing or the other. They can't be both. We have to choose one way of seeing them or the other. But as soon as we do we can't know everything about them.

Heisenberg   And off he goes into orbit again. Incidentally exemplifying another application of complementarity. Exactly where you go as you ramble around is of course completely determined by your genes and the various physical forces acting on you. But it's also completely determined by your own entirely inscrutable whims from one moment to the next. So we can't completely understand your behaviour without seeing it both ways at once, and that's impossible. Which means that your extraordinary peregrinations are not fully objective aspects of the universe. They exist only partially, through the efforts of me or Margrethe, as our minds shift endlessly back and forth between the two approaches.

Bohr   You've never absolutely and totally accepted complementarity, have you?

Heisenberg   Yes! Absolutely and totally! I defended it at the Como Conference in 1927! I have adhered to it ever afterwards with religious fervour! You convinced me. I humbly accepted your criticisms.

Bohr   Not before you'd said some deeply wounding things.

Heisenberg   Good God, at one point you literally reduced me to tears!

Bohr   Forgive me, but I diagnosed them as tears of frustration and rage.

Heisenberg   I was having a tantrum?

Bohr   I have brought up children of my own.

Heisenberg   And what about Margrethe? Was *she* having a tantrum? Klein told me you reduced *her* to tears after I'd gone, making her type out your endless redraftings of the complementarity paper.

Bohr   I don't recall that.

Margrethe   I do.

Heisenberg   We had to drag Pauli out of bed in Hamburg once again to come to Copenhagen and negotiate peace.

Bohr   He succeeded. We ended up with a treaty. Uncertainty and complementarity became the two central tenets of the Copenhagen Interpretation of Quantum Mechanics.

Heisenberg   A political compromise, of course, like most treaties.

Bohr   You see? Somewhere inside you there are still secret reservations.

Heisenberg   Not at all – it works. That's what matters. It works, it works, it works!

Bohr   It works, yes. But it's more important than that. Because you see what we did in those three years, Heisenberg? Not to exaggerate, but we turned the world inside out! Yes, listen, now it comes, now it comes . . . We put man back at the centre of the universe. Throughout history we keep finding ourselves displaced. We keep exiling ourselves to the periphery of things. First we turn ourselves into a mere adjunct of God's unknowable purposes, tiny figures kneeling in the great cathedral of creation. And no sooner have we recovered ourselves in the Renaissance, no sooner has man become, as Protagoras proclaimed him, the measure of all things, than we're pushed aside again by the products of our own reasoning! We're dwarfed again as physicists build the great new cathedrals for us to wonder at – the laws of classical mechanics that pre-date us from the beginning of eternity, that will survive us to eternity's end, that exist whether we exist or not. Until we come to the beginning of the twentieth century, and we're suddenly forced to rise from our knees again.

Heisenberg   It starts with Einstein.

Bohr   It starts with Einstein. He shows that measurement – measurement, on which the whole possibility of science depends – measurement is not an impersonal event that occurs with impartial universality. It's a human act, carried out from a specific point of view in time and space, from the one particular viewpoint of a possible observer. Then, here in Copenhagen in those three years in the mid-twenties we discover that there is no precisely determinable objective universe. That the universe exists only as a series of approximations. Only within the limits determined by our relationship with it. Only through the understanding lodged inside the human head.

Margrethe   So this man you've put at the centre of the universe – is it you, or is it Heisenberg?

Bohr   Now, now, my love.

Margrethe   Yes, but it makes a difference.

Bohr   Either of us. Both of us. Yourself. All of us.

Margrethe   If it's Heisenberg at the centre of the universe, then the one bit of the universe that he can't see is Heisenberg.

Heisenberg   So . . .

Margrethe   So it's no good asking him why he came to Copenhagen in 1941. He doesn't know!

Heisenberg   I thought for a moment just then I caught a glimpse of it.

Margrethe   Then you turned to look.

Heisenberg   And away it went.

Margrethe   Complementarity again. Yes?

Bohr   Yes, yes.

Margrethe   I've typed it out often enough. If you're doing something you have to concentrate on you can't also be thinking about doing it, and if you're thinking about doing it then you can't actually be doing it. Yes?

Heisenberg   Swerve left, swerve right, or think about it and die.

Bohr   But *after* you've done it. . .

Margrethe   You look back and make a guess, just like the rest of us. Only a worse guess, because you didn't see yourself doing it, and we did. Forgive me, but you don't even know why you did uncertainty in the first place.

Bohr   Whereas if *you're* the one at the centre of the universe . . .

Margrethe   Then I can tell you that it was because you wanted to drop a bomb on Schrödinger.

Heisenberg   I wanted to show he was wrong, certainly.

Margrethe   And Schrödinger was winning the war. When the Leipzig chair first became vacant that autumn he was short-listed for it and you weren't. You needed a wonderful new weapon.

Bohr   Not to criticise, Margrethe, but you have a tendency to make everything personal.

Margrethe   Because everything *is* personal! You've just read us all a lecture about it! You know how much Heisenberg wanted a chair. You know the pressure he was under from his family. I'm sorry, but you want to make everything seem heroically abstract and logical. And when you tell the story, yes, it all falls into place, it all has a beginning and a middle and an end. But I was there, and when I remember what it was like I'm there still, and I look around me and what I see isn't a story! It's confusion and rage and jealousy and tears and no one knowing what things mean or which way they're going to go.

Heisenberg   All the same, it works, it works.

Margrethe   Yes, it works wonderfully. Within three months of publishing your uncertainty paper you're offered Leipzig.

Heisenberg   I didn't mean that.

Margrethe   Not to mention somewhere else and somewhere else.

Heisenberg   Halle and Munich and Zürich.

Bohr   And various American universities.

Heisenberg   But I didn't mean that.

Margrethe   And when you take up your chair at Leipzig you're how old?

Heisenberg   Twenty-six.

Bohr   The youngest full professor in Germany.

Heisenberg   I mean the Copenhagen Interpretation. The Copenhagen Interpretation works. However we got there, by whatever combination of high principles and low calculation, of most painfully hard thought and most painfully childish tears, it works. It goes on working.

Margrethe   Yes, and why did you both accept the Interpretation in the end? Was it really because you wanted to re-establish humanism?

Bohr   Of course not. It was because it was the only way to explain what the experimenters had observed.

Margrethe   Or was it because now you were becoming a professor you wanted a solidly established doctrine to teach? Because you wanted to have your new ideas publicly endorsed by the head of the church in Copenhagen? And perhaps Niels agreed to endorse them in return for your accepting *his* doctrines. For recognising him as head of the church. And if you want to know why you came to Copenhagen in 1941 I'll tell you that as well. You're right – there's no great mystery about it. You came to show yourself off to us.

Bohr   Margrethe!

Margrethe   No! When he first came in 1924 he was a humble assistant lecturer from a humiliated nation, grateful to have a job. Now here you are, back in triumph – the leading scientist in a nation that's conquered most of Europe. You've come to show us how well you've done in life.

Bohr   This is so unlike you!

Margrethe   I'm sorry, but isn't that really why he's here? Because he's burning to let us know that he's in charge of some vital piece of secret research. And that even so he's preserved a lofty moral independence. Preserved it so famously that he's being watched by the Gestapo. Preserved it so successfully that he's now also got a wonderfully important moral dilemma to face.

Bohr Yes, well, now you're simply working yourself up.

Margrethe A chain reaction. You tell one painful truth and it leads to two more. And as you frankly admit, you're going to go back and continue doing precisely what you were doing before, whatever Niels tells you.

Heisenberg Yes.

Margrethe Because you wouldn't dream of giving up such a wonderful opportunity for research.

Heisenberg Not if I can possibly help it.

Margrethe Also you want to demonstrate to the Nazis how useful theoretical physics can be. You want to save the honour of German science. You want to be there to re-establish it in all its glory as soon as the war's over.

Heisenberg All the same, I don't tell Speer that the reactor . . .

Margrethe . . . will produce plutonium, no, because you're afraid of what will happen if the Nazis commit huge resources, and you fail to deliver the bombs. Please don't try to tell us that you're a hero of the resistance.

Heisenberg I've never claimed to be a hero.

Margrethe Your talent is for skiing too fast for anyone to see where you are. For always being in more than one position at a time, like one of your particles.

Heisenberg I can only say that it worked. Unlike most of the gestures made by heroes of the resistance. It worked! I know what you think. You think I should have joined the plot against Hitler, and got myself hanged like the others.

Bohr Of course not.

Heisenberg You don't say it, because there are some things that can't be said. But you think it.

Bohr No.

Heisenberg What would it have achieved? What would it have achieved if you'd dived in after Christian, and drowned as well? But that's another thing that can't be said.

Bohr Only thought.

Heisenberg Yes. I'm sorry.

Bohr And rethought. Every day.

Heisenberg You had to be held back, I know.

Margrethe Whereas you held yourself back.

Heisenberg Better to stay on the boat, though, and fetch it about. Better to remain alive, and throw the lifebuoy. Surely!

Bohr Perhaps. Perhaps not.

Heisenberg Better. Better.

Margrethe Really it is ridiculous. You reasoned your way, both of you, with such astonishing delicacy and precision into the tiny world of the atom. Now it turns out that everything depends upon these really rather large objects on our shoulders. And what's going on in there is . . .

Heisenberg Elsinore.

Margrethe Elsinore, yes.

Heisenberg And you may be right. I *was* afraid of what would happen. I *was* conscious of being on the winning side . . . So many explanations for everything I did! So many of them sitting round the lunch table! Somewhere at the head of the table, I think, is the real reason I came to Copenhagen. Again I turn to look . . . And for a moment I almost see its face. Then next time I look the chair at the head of the table is completely empty. There's no reason at all. I didn't tell Speer simply because I didn't think of it. I came to Copenhagen simply because I did think of it. A million things we might do or might not do every day. A million decisions that make themselves. Why didn't you kill me?

Bohr   Why didn't I . . . ?

Heisenberg   Kill me. Murder me. That evening in 1941.
Here we are, walking back towards the house, and you've just
leapt to the conclusion that I'm going to arm Hitler with
nuclear weapons. You'll surely take any reasonable steps to
prevent it happening.

Bohr   By murdering you?

Heisenberg   We're in the middle of a war. I'm an enemy.
There's nothing odd or immoral about killing enemies.

Bohr   I should fetch out my cap-pistol?

Heisenberg   You won't need your cap-pistol. You won't
even need a mine. You can do it without any loud bangs,
without any blood, without any spectacle of suffering. As
cleanly as a bomb-aimer pressing his release three thousand
metres above the earth. You simply wait till I've gone. Then
you sit quietly down in your favourite armchair here and
repeat aloud to Margrethe, in front of our unseen audience,
what I've just told you. I shall be dead almost as soon as poor
Casimir. A lot sooner than Gamow.

Bohr   My dear Heisenberg, the suggestion is of course . . .

Heisenberg   Most interesting. So interesting that it never
even occurred to you. Complementarity, once again. I'm
your enemy; I'm also your friend. I'm a danger to mankind;
I'm also your guest. I'm a particle; I'm also a wave. We have
one set of obligations to the world in general, and we have
other sets, never to be reconciled, to our fellow countrymen,
to our neighbours, to our friends, to our family, to our
children. We have to go through not two slits at the same
time but twenty-two. All we can do is to look afterwards, and
see what happened.

Margrethe   I'll tell you another reason why you did
uncertainty: you have a natural affinity for it.

Heisenberg   Well, I must cut a gratifyingly chastened figure when I return in 1947. Crawling on my hands and knees again. My nation back in ruins.

Margrethe   Not really. You're demonstrating that once more you personally have come out on top.

Heisenberg   Begging for food parcels?

Margrethe   Established in Göttingen under British protection, in charge of post-war German science.

Heisenberg   That first year in Göttingen I slept on straw.

Margrethe   Elisabeth said you had a most charming house thereafter.

Heisenberg   I was given it by the British.

Margrethe   Your new foster-parents. Who'd confiscated it from someone else.

Bohr   Enough, my love, enough.

Margrethe   No, I've kept my thoughts to myself for all these years. But it's maddening to have this clever son forever dancing about in front of our eyes, forever demanding our approval, forever struggling to shock us, forever begging to be told what the limits to his freedom are, if only so that he can go out and transgress them! I'm sorry, but really . . . On your hands and knees? It's my dear, good, kind husband who's on his hands and knees! Literally. Crawling down to the beach in the darkness in 1943, fleeing like a thief in the night from his own homeland to escape being murdered. The protection of the German Embassy that you boasted about didn't last for long. We were incorporated into the Reich.

Heisenberg   I warned you in 1941. You wouldn't listen. At least Bohr got across to Sweden.

Margrethe   And even as the fishing boat was taking him across the Sound two freighters were arriving in the harbour to ship the entire Jewish population of Denmark eastwards.

That great darkness inside the human soul was flooding out to engulf us all.

Heisenberg   I did try to warn you.

Margrethe   Yes, and where are you? Shut away in a cave like a savage, trying to conjure an evil spirit out of a hole in the ground. That's what it came down to in the end, all that shining springtime in the 1920s, that's what it produced – a more efficient machine for killing people.

Bohr   It breaks my heart every time I think of it.

Heisenberg   It broke all our hearts.

Margrethe   And this wonderful machine may yet kill every man, woman, and child in the world. And if we really are the centre of the universe, if we really are all that's keeping it in being, what will be left?

Bohr   Darkness. Total and final darkness.

Margrethe   Even the questions that haunt us will at last be extinguished. Even the ghosts will die.

Heisenberg   I can only say that I didn't do it. I didn't build the bomb.

Margrethe   No, and why didn't you? I'll tell you that, too. It's the simplest reason of all. Because you couldn't. You didn't understand the physics.

Heisenberg   That's what Goudsmit said.

Margrethe   And Goudsmit knew. He was one of your magic circle. He and Uhlenbeck were the ones who did spin.

Heisenberg   All the same, he had no idea of what I did or didn't understand about a bomb.

Margrethe   He tracked you down across Europe for Allied intelligence. He interrogated you after you were captured.

Heisenberg   He blamed me, of course. His parents died in Auschwitz. He thought I should have done something to save them. I don't know what. So many hands stretching up from the darkness for a lifeline, and no lifeline that could ever reach them . . .

Margrethe   He said you didn't understand the crucial difference between a reactor and a bomb.

Heisenberg   I understood very clearly. I simply didn't tell the others.

Margrethe   Ah.

Heisenberg   I understood, though.

Margrethe   But secretly.

Heisenberg   You can check if you don't believe me.

Margrethe   There's evidence, for once?

Heisenberg   It was all most carefully recorded.

Margrethe   Witnesses, even?

Heisenberg   Unimpeachable witnesses.

Margrethe   Who wrote it down?

Heisenberg   Who recorded it and transcribed it.

Margrethe   Even though you didn't tell anyone?

Heisenberg   I told one person. I told Otto Hahn. That terrible night at Farm Hall, after we'd heard the news. Somewhere in the small hours, after everyone had finally gone to bed, and we were alone together. I gave him a reasonably good account of how the bomb had worked.

Margrethe   After the event.

Heisenberg   After the event. Yes. When it didn't matter any more. All the things Goudsmit said I didn't understand. Fast neutrons in 235. The plutonium option. A reflective shell to reduce neutron escape. Even the method of triggering it.

Bohr   The critical mass. That was the most important thing. The amount of material you needed to establish the chain reaction. Did you tell him the critical mass?

Heisenberg   I gave him a figure, yes. You can look it up! Because that was the other secret of the house party. Diebner asked me when we first arrived if I thought there were hidden microphones. I laughed. I told him the British were far too old-fashioned to know about Gestapo methods. I underestimated them. They had microphones everywhere – they were recording everything. Look it up! Everything we said. Everything we went through that terrible night. Everything I told Hahn alone in the small hours.

Bohr   But the critical mass. You gave him a figure. What was the figure you gave him?

Heisenberg   I forget.

Bohr   Heisenberg . . .

Heisenberg   It's all on the record. You can see for yourself.

Bohr   The figure for the Hiroshima bomb . . .

Heisenberg   Was fifty kilograms.

Bohr   So that was the figure you gave Hahn? Fifty kilograms?

Heisenberg   I said about a ton.

Bohr   About a ton? A thousand kilograms? Heisenberg, I believe I am at last beginning to understand something.

Heisenberg   The one thing I was wrong about.

Bohr   You were twenty times over.

Heisenberg   The one thing.

Bohr   But, Heisenberg, your mathematics, your mathematics! How could they have been so far out?

Heisenberg   They weren't. As soon as I calculated the diffusion I got it just about right.

Bohr   As soon as you calculated it?

Heisenberg   I gave everyone a seminar on it a week later. It's in the record! Look it up!

Bohr   You mean . . . you hadn't calculated it before? You hadn't done the diffusion equation?

Heisenberg   There was no need to.

Bohr   No need to?

Heisenberg   The calculation had already been done.

Bohr   Done by whom?

Heisenberg   By Perrin and Flügge in 1939.

Bohr   By Perrin and Flügge? But, my dear Heisenberg, that was for natural uranium. Wheeler and I showed that it was only the 235 that fissioned.

Heisenberg   Your great paper. The basis of everything we did.

Bohr   So you needed to calculate the figure for pure 235.

Heisenberg   Obviously.

Bohr   And you didn't?

Heisenberg   I didn't.

Bohr   And that's why you were so confident you couldn't do it until you had the plutonium. Because you spent the entire war believing that it would take not a few kilograms of 235, but a ton or more. And to make a ton of 235 in any plausible time . . .

Heisenberg   Would have needed something like two hundred million separator units. It was plainly unimaginable.

Bohr   If you'd realised you had to produce only a few kilograms . . .

Heisenberg   Even to make a single kilogram would need something like two hundred thousand units.

Bohr   But two hundred million is one thing; two hundred thousand is another. You might just possibly have imagined setting up two hundred thousand.

Heisenberg   Just possibly.

Bohr   The Americans did imagine it.

Heisenberg   Because Otto Frisch and Rudolf Peierls actually did the calculation. They solved the diffusion equation.

Bohr   Frisch was my old assistant.

Heisenberg   Peierls was my old pupil.

Bohr   An Austrian and a German.

Heisenberg   So they should have been making their calculation for us, at the Kaiser Wilhelm Institute in Berlin. But instead they made it at the University of Birmingham, in England.

Margrethe   Because they were Jews.

Heisenberg   There's something almost mathematically elegant about that.

Bohr   They also started with Perrin and Flügge.

Heisenberg   They also thought it would take tons. They also thought it was unimaginable.

Bohr   Until one day . . .

Heisenberg   They did the calculation.

Bohr   They discovered just how fast the chain reaction would go.

Heisenberg   And therefore how little material you'd need.

Bohr   They said slightly over half a kilogram.

Heisenberg   About the size of a tennis ball.

Bohr   They were wrong, of course.

Heisenberg   They were a hundred times under.

Bohr   Which made it seem a hundred times more imaginable than it actually was.

Heisenberg   Whereas I left it seeming twenty times less imaginable.

Bohr   So all your agonising in Copenhagen about plutonium was beside the point. You could have done it without ever building the reactor. You could have done it with 235 all the time.

Heisenberg   Almost certainly not.

Bohr   Just possibly, though.

Heisenberg   Just possibly.

Bohr   And *that* question you'd settled long before you arrived in Copenhagen. Simply by failing to try the diffusion equation.

Heisenberg   Such a tiny failure.

Bohr   But the consequences went branching out over the years, doubling and redoubling.

Heisenberg   Until they were large enough to save a city. Which city? Any of the cities that we never dropped our bomb on.

Bohr   London, presumably, if you'd had it in time. If the Americans had already entered the war, and the Allies had begun to liberate Europe, then . . .

Heisenberg   Who knows? Paris as well. Amsterdam. Perhaps Copenhagen.

Bohr   So, Heisenberg, tell us this one simple thing: why didn't you do the calculation?

Heisenberg   The question is why Frisch and Peierls *did* do it. It was a stupid waste of time. However much 235 it turned out to be, it was obviously going to be more than anyone could imagine producing.

Bohr   Except that it wasn't!

Heisenberg   Except that it wasn't.

Bohr   So why . . . ?

Heisenberg   I don't know! I don't know why I didn't do it! Because I never thought of it! Because it didn't occur to me! Because I assumed it wasn't worth doing!

Bohr   Assumed? Assumed? You never assumed things! That's how you got uncertainty, because you rejected our assumptions! You calculated, Heisenberg! You calculated everything! The first thing you did with a problem was the mathematics!

Heisenberg   You should have been there to slow me down.

Bohr   Yes, you wouldn't have got away with it if I'd been standing over you.

Heisenberg   Though in fact you made exactly the same assumption! You thought there was no danger for exactly the same reason as I did! Why didn't *you* calculate it?

Bohr   Why didn't *I* calculate it?

Heisenberg   Tell us why *you* didn't calculate it and we'll know why *I* didn't!

Bohr   It's obvious why *I* didn't!

Heisenberg   Go on.

Margrethe   Because he wasn't trying to build a bomb!

Heisenberg   Yes. Thank you. Because he wasn't trying to build a bomb. I imagine it was the same with me. Because *I* wasn't trying to build a bomb. Thank you.

Bohr   So, you bluffed yourself, the way I did at poker with the straight I never had. But in that case . . .

Heisenberg   Why did I come to Copenhagen? Yes, why did I come . . . ?

Bohr   One more draft, yes? One final draft!

Heisenberg   And once again I crunch over the familiar gravel to the Bohrs' front door, and tug at the familiar bell-pull. Why have I come? I know perfectly well. Know so well that I've no need to ask myself. Until once again the heavy front door opens.

Bohr   He stands on the doorstep blinking in the sudden flood of light from the house. Until this instant his thoughts have been everywhere and nowhere, like unobserved particles, through all the slits in the diffraction grating simultaneously. Now they have to be observed and specified.

Heisenberg   And at once the clear purposes inside my head lose all definite shape. The light falls on them and they scatter.

Bohr   My dear Heisenberg!

Heisenberg   My dear Bohr!

Bohr   Come in, come in . . .

Heisenberg   How difficult it is to see even what's in front of one's eyes. All we possess is the present, and the present endlessly dissolves into the past. Bohr has gone even as I turn to see Margrethe.

Margrethe   Niels is right. You look older.

Bohr   I believe you had some personal trouble.

Heisenberg   Margrethe slips into history even as I turn back to Bohr. And yet how much more difficult still it is to catch the slightest glimpse of what's behind one's eyes. Here I am at the centre of the universe, and yet all I can see are two smiles that don't belong to me.

Margrethe   How is Elisabeth? How are the children?

Heisenberg   Very well. They send their love, of course . . . I can feel a third smile in the room, very close to me. Could it be the one I suddenly see for a moment in the mirror there?

And is the awkward stranger wearing it in any way connected with this presence that I can feel in the room? This all-enveloping, unobserved presence?

Margrethe   I watch the two smiles in the room, one awkward and ingratiating, the other rapidly fading from incautious warmth to bare politeness. There's also a third smile in the room, I know, unchangingly courteous, I hope, and unchangingly guarded.

Heisenberg   You've managed to get some skiing?

Bohr   I glance at Margrethe, and for a moment I see what she can see and I can't – myself, and the smile vanishing from my face as poor Heisenberg blunders on.

Heisenberg   I look at the two of them looking at me, and for a moment I see the third person in the room as clearly as I see them. Their importunate guest, stumbling from one crass and unwelcome thoughtfulness to the next.

Bohr   I look at him looking at me, anxiously, pleadingly, urging me back to the old days, and I see what he sees. And yes – now it comes, now it comes – there's someone missing from the room. He sees me. He sees Margrethe. He doesn't see himself.

Heisenberg   Two thousand million people in the world, and the one who has to decide their fate is the only one who's always hidden from me.

Bohr   You suggested a stroll.

Heisenberg   You remember Elsinore? The darkness inside the human soul . . . ?

Bohr   And out we go. Out under the autumn trees. Through the blacked-out streets.

Heisenberg   Now there's no one in the world except Bohr and the invisible other. Who is he, this all-enveloping presence in the darkness?

Margrethe   The flying particle wanders the darkness, no one knows where. It's here, it's there, it's everywhere and nowhere.

Bohr   With careful casualness he begins to ask the question he's prepared.

Heisenberg   Does one as a physicist have the moral right to work on the practical exploitation of atomic energy?

Margrethe   The great collision.

Bohr   I stop. He stops . . .

Margrethe   This is how they work.

Heisenberg   He gazes at me, horrified.

Margrethe   Now at last he knows where he is and what he's doing.

Heisenberg   He turns away.

Margrethe   And even as the moment of collision begins it's over.

Bohr   Already we're hurrying back towards the house.

Margrethe   Already they're both flying away from each other into the darkness again.

Heisenberg   Our conversation's over.

Bohr   Our great partnership.

Heisenberg   All our friendship.

Margrethe   And everything about him becomes as uncertain as it was before.

Bohr   Unless . . . yes . . . a thought-experiment . . . Let's suppose for a moment that I don't go flying off into the night. Let's see what happens if instead I remember the paternal role I'm supposed to play. If I stop, and control my anger, and turn to him. And ask him why.

Heisenberg   Why?

Bohr   Why are you confident that it's going to be so reassuringly difficult to build a bomb with 235? Is it because you've done the calculation?

Heisenberg   The calculation?

Bohr   Of the diffusion in 235. No. It's because you haven't calculated it. You haven't considered calculating it. You hadn't consciously realised there was a calculation to be made.

Heisenberg   And of course now I *have* realised. In fact it wouldn't be all that difficult. Let's see . . . The scattering cross-section's about 6×10^{-24}, so the mean free path would be . . . Hold on . . .

Bohr   And suddenly a very different and very terrible new world begins to take shape . . .

Margrethe   That was the last and greatest demand that Heisenberg made on his friendship with you. To be understood when he couldn't understand himself. And that was the last and greatest act of friendship for Heisenberg that you performed in return. To leave him misunderstood.

Heisenberg   Yes. Perhaps I should thank you.

Bohr   Perhaps you should.

Margrethe   Anyway, it was the end of the story.

Bohr   Though perhaps there was also something I should thank *you* for. That summer night in 1943, when I escaped across the Sound in the fishing boat, and the freighters arrived from Germany. . .

Margrethe   What's that to do with Heisenberg?

Bohr   When the ships arrived on the Wednesday there were eight thousand Jews in Denmark to be arrested and crammed into their holds. On the Friday evening, at the start of the Sabbath, when the SS began their round-up, there was scarcely a Jew to be found.

Margrethe   They'd all been hidden in churches and hospitals, in people's homes and country cottages.

Bohr   But how was that possible? – Because we'd been tipped off by someone in the German Embassy.

Heisenberg   Georg Duckwitz, their shipping specialist.

Bohr   Your man?

Heisenberg   One of them.

Bohr   He was a remarkable informant. He told us the day before the freighters arrived – the very day that Hitler issued the order. He gave us the exact time that the SS would move.

Margrethe   It was the Resistance who got them out of their hiding places and smuggled them across the Sound.

Bohr   For a handful of us in one fishing smack to get past the German patrol boats was remarkable enough. For a whole armada to get past, with the best part of eight thousand people on board, was like the Red Sea parting.

Margrethe   I thought there *were* no German patrol boats that night?

Bohr   No – the whole squadron had suddenly been reported unseaworthy.

Heisenberg   How they got away with it I can't imagine.

Bohr   Duckwitz again?

Heisenberg   He also went to Stockholm and asked the Swedish Government to accept everyone.

Bohr   So perhaps I should thank you.

Heisenberg   For what?

Bohr   My life. All our lives.

Heisenberg   Nothing to do with me by that time. I regret to say.

Bohr   But after I'd gone you came back to Copenhagen.

Heisenberg   To make sure that our people didn't take over the Institute in your absence.

Bohr   I've never thanked you for that, either.

Heisenberg   You know they offered me your cyclotron?

Bohr   You could have separated a little 235 with it.

Heisenberg   Meanwhile you were going on from Sweden to Los Alamos.

Bohr   To play my small but helpful part in the deaths of a hundred thousand people.

Margrethe   Niels, you did nothing wrong!

Bohr   Didn't I?

Heisenberg   Of course not. You were a good man, from first to last, and no one could ever say otherwise. Whereas I . . .

Bohr   Whereas you, my dear Heisenberg, never managed to contribute to the death of one single solitary person in all your life.

Margrethe   Well, yes.

Heisenberg   Did I?

Margrethe   One. Or so you told us. The poor fellow you guarded overnight, when you were a boy in Munich, while he was waiting to be shot in the morning.

Bohr   All right then, one. One single soul on his conscience, to set against all the others.

Margrethe   But that one single soul was emperor of the universe, no less than each of us. Until the morning came.

Heisenberg   No, when the morning came I persuaded them to let him go.

Bohr   Heisenberg, I have to say – if people are to be measured strictly in terms of observable quantities . . .

Heisenberg   Then we should need a strange new quantum ethics. There'd be a place in heaven for me. And another one for the SS man I met on my way home from Haigerloch. That was the end of my war. The Allied troops were closing in; there was nothing more we could do. Elisabeth and the children had taken refuge in a village in Bavaria, so I went to see them before I was captured. I had to go by bicycle – there were no trains or road transport by that time – and I had to travel by night and sleep under a hedge by day, because all through the daylight hours the skies were full of Allied planes, scouring the roads for anything that moved. A man on a bicycle would have been the biggest target left in Germany. Three days and three nights I travelled. Out of Württemberg, down through the Swabian Jura and the first foothills of the Alps. Across my ruined homeland. Was this what I'd chosen for it? This endless rubble? This perpetual smoke in the sky? These hungry faces? Was this my doing? And all the desperate people on the roads. The most desperate of all were the SS. Bands of fanatics with nothing left to lose, roaming around shooting deserters out of hand, hanging them from roadside trees. The second night, and suddenly there it is – the terrible familiar black tunic emerging from the twilight in front of me. On his lips as I stop – the one terrible familiar word. 'Deserter,' he says. He sounds as exhausted as I am. I give him the travel order I've written for myself. But there's hardly enough light in the sky to read by, and he's too weary to bother. He begins to open his holster instead. He's going to shoot me because it's simply less labour. And suddenly I'm thinking very quickly and clearly – it's like skiing, or that night on Heligoland, or the one in Faelled Park. What comes into my mind this time is the pack of American cigarettes I've got in my pocket. And already it's in my hand – I'm holding it out to him. The most desperate solution to a problem yet. I wait while he stands there looking at it, trying to make it out, trying to think, his left hand holding my useless piece of paper, his right on the fastening of the holster. There are two simple words in large print on the pack: Lucky Strike. He closes the holster, and takes the cigarettes instead . . . It had worked, it had worked! Like all the other solutions to all the other problems. For twenty cigarettes he let me live. And on I went. Three days and three nights. Past the weeping children, the lost and hungry children, drafted to fight, then abandoned by their commanders. Past the starving slave-labourers walking home to France, to Poland, to Estonia. Through Gammertingen and Biberach and Memmingen. Mindelheim, Kaufbeuren, and Schöngau. Across my beloved homeland. My ruined and dishonoured and beloved homeland.

Bohr   My dear Heisenberg! My dear friend!

Margrethe   Silence. The silence we always in the end return to.

Heisenberg   And of course I know what they're thinking about.

Margrethe   All those lost children on the road.

Bohr   Heisenberg wandering the world like a lost child himself.

Margrethe   Our own lost children.

Heisenberg   And over goes the tiller once again.

Bohr   So near, so near! So slight a thing!

Margrethe   He stands in the doorway, watching me, then he turns his head away . . .

Heisenberg   And once again away he goes, into the dark waters.

Bohr   Before we can lay our hands on anything, our life's over.

Heisenberg   Before we can glimpse who or what we are, we're gone and laid to dust.

Bohr   Settled among all the dust we raised.

Margrethe   And sooner or later there will come a time when all our children are laid to dust, and all our children's children.

Bohr   When no more decisions, great or small, are ever made again. When there's no more uncertainty, because there's no more knowledge.

Margrethe   And when all our eyes are closed, when even the ghosts have gone, what will be left of our beloved world? Our ruined and dishonoured and beloved world?

Heisenberg   But in the meanwhile, in this most precious meanwhile, there it is. The trees in Faelled Park. Gammertingen and Biberach and Mindelheim. Our children and our children's children. Preserved, just possibly, by that one short moment in Copenhagen. By some event that will never quite be located or defined. By that final core of uncertainty at the heart of things.

Postscript

Where a work of fiction features historical characters and historical events it's reasonable to want to know how much of it is fiction and how much of it is history. So let me make it as clear as I can in regard to this play.

The central event in it is a real one. Heisenberg *did* go to Copenhagen in 1941, and there *was* a meeting with Bohr, in the teeth of all the difficulties encountered by my characters. He probably went to dinner at the Bohrs' house, and the two men probably went for a walk to escape from any possible microphones, though there is some dispute about even these simple matters. The question of what they actually said to each other has been even more disputed, and where there's ambiguity in the play about what happened, it's because there is in the recollection of the participants. Much more sustained speculation still has been devoted to the question of what Heisenberg was hoping to achieve by the meeting. All the alternative and co-existing explications offered in the play, except perhaps the final one, have been aired at various times, in one form or another.

Most anxious of all to establish some agreed version of the meeting was Heisenberg himself. He did indeed go back in 1947 with his British minder, Ronald Fraser, and attempted to find some common ground in the matter with Bohr. But it proved to be too delicate a task, and (according to Heisenberg, at any rate, in his memoirs) 'We both came to feel that it would be better to stop disturbing the spirits of the past.' This is where my play departs from the historical record, by supposing that at some later time, when everyone involved had become spirits of the past themselves, they argued the question out further, until they had achieved a little more understanding of what was going on, just as they had so many times when they were alive with the intractable difficulties presented by the internal workings of the atom.

The account of these earlier discussions in the twenties reflects at any rate one or two of the key topics, and the passion with which the argument was conducted, as it emerges from the biographical and autobiographical record.

I am acutely aware of how over-simplified my version is. Max Born described the real story as not so much 'a straight staircase upwards, but a tangle of interconnected alleys', and I have found it impossible to follow these in any detail (even where I can begin to understand them). In particular I have grossly understated the crucial role played by Born himself and by his pupil Pascual Jordan at Göttingen in formulating quantum mechanics (it was Born who supplied the understanding of matrices that Heisenberg lacked, and the statistical interpretation of Schrödinger's wave function), and of Wolfgang Pauli in Hamburg, whose exclusion principle filled in one of the key pieces in the puzzle.

But the account of the German and American bomb programmes, and of the two physicists' participation in them, is taken from the historical record; so is the fate of Danish Jewry; Heisenberg's experiences in Germany before and during the war, his subsequent internment, and the depression that clouded his later years. I have filled out some of the details, but in general what he says happened to him – at the end of the First World War, on Heligoland, during his nocturnal walk in Faelled Park, during the Berlin air raid and his internment, and on his ride across Germany, with its near-fatal encounter along the way – is based very closely upon the accounts he gave in life.

The actual words spoken by my characters are of course entirely their own. If this needs any justification then I can only appeal to Heisenberg himself. In his memoirs dialogue plays an important part, he says, because he hopes 'to demonstrate that science is rooted in conversations'. But, as he explains, conversations, even real conversations, cannot be reconstructed literally several decades later. So he freely reinvents them, and appeals in his turn to Thucydides. (Heisenberg's father was a professor of classics, and he was an accomplished classicist himself, on top of all his other distinctions.) Thucydides explains in his preface to the *History of the Peloponnesian War* that, although he had avoided all 'storytelling', when it came to the speeches, 'I have found it impossible to remember their exact wording. Hence I have made each orator speak as, in my opinion, he would have done in the circumstances, but keeping as close as I could to the train of thought that guided his actual speech.'

Thucydides was trying to give an account of speeches that had actually been made, many of which he had himself heard. Some of the dialogue in my play represents speeches that must have been made in one form or another; some of it speeches that were certainly never made at all. I hope, though, that in some sense it respects the Thucydidean principle, and that speeches (and indeed actions) follow in so far as possible the original protagonists' train of thought. But how far is it possible to know what their train of thought was? This is where I have departed from the established historical record – from any possible historical record. The great challenge facing the storyteller and the historian alike is to get inside people's heads, to stand where they stood and see the world as they saw it, to make some informed estimate of their motives and intentions – and this is precisely where recorded and recordable history cannot reach. Even when all the external evidence has been mastered, the only way into the protagonists' heads is through the imagination. This indeed is the substance of the play.

*

I can't claim to be the first person to notice the parallels between Heisenberg's science and his life. They provide David Cassidy with the title (*Uncertainty*) for his excellent biography (the standard work in English). 'Especially difficult and controversial,' says Cassidy in his introduction, 'is a retrospective evaluation of Heisenberg's activities during the Third Reich and particularly during World War II. Since the end of the war, an enormous range of views about this man and his behaviour have been expressed, views that have been fervently, even passionately, held by a variety of individuals. It is as if, for some, the intense emotions unleashed by the unspeakable horrors of that war and regime have combined with the many ambiguities, dualities, and compromises of Heisenberg's life and actions to make Heisenberg himself subject to a type of uncertainty principle . . . ' Thomas Powers makes a similar point in his extraordinary and encyclopaedic book *Heisenberg's War*, which first aroused my interest in the trip to Copenhagen; he says that Heisenberg's later reticence on his role in the failure of the German bomb programme 'introduces an element of irreducible uncertainty'.

Cassidy does not explore the parallel further. Powers even appends a footnote to his comment: 'Forgive me.' The apology seems to me unnecessary. It's true that the concept of uncertainty is one of those scientific notions that has become common coinage, and generalised to the point of losing much of its original meaning. The idea as introduced by Heisenberg into quantum mechanics was precise and technical. It didn't suggest that everything about the behaviour of particles was unknowable, or hazy. What it limited was the simultaneous measurement of 'canonically conjugate variables', such as position and momentum, or energy and time. The more precisely you measure one variable, it said, the less precise your measurement of the related variable can be; and this ratio, the uncertainty relationship, is itself precisely formulable.

None of this, plainly, applies directly to our observations of thought and intention. Thoughts are not locatable by pairs of conjugate variables, so there can be no question of a ratio of precision. Powers seems to imply that in Heisenberg's case the uncertainty arises purely because 'questions of motive and intention cannot be established more clearly than he was willing to state them'. It's true that Heisenberg was under contradictory pressures after the war which made it particularly difficult for him to explain what he had been trying to do. He wanted to distance himself from the Nazis, but he didn't want to suggest that he had been a traitor. He was reluctant to claim to his fellow-Germans that he had deliberately lost them the war, but he was no less reluctant to suggest that he had failed them simply out of incompetence.

But the uncertainty surely begins long before the point where Heisenberg might have offered an explanation. He was under at least as many contradictory pressures at the time to shape the actions he later failed to explain, and the uncertainty would still have existed, for us and for him, even if he had been as open, honest, and helpful as it is humanly possible to be.

What people say about their own motives and intentions, even when they are not caught in the traps that entangled Heisenberg, is always subject to question – as subject to question as what anybody else says about them. Thoughts and intentions, even one's own – perhaps one's own most of all – remain shifting and elusive. There is not one single thought or intention of any sort that can ever be precisely established.

What the uncertainty of thoughts does have in common with the uncertainty of particles is that the difficulty is not just a practical one, but a systematic limitation which cannot even in theory be circumvented. It is patently not resolved by the efforts of psychologists and psychoanalysts, and it will not be resolved by neurologists, either, even when everything is known about the structure and workings of the brain, any more than semantic questions can be resolved by looking at the machine code of a computer. And since, according to the so-called 'Copenhagen Interpretation' of quantum mechanics – the interconnected set of theories that was developed by Heisenberg, Bohr and others in the twenties – the whole possibility of saying or thinking anything about the world, even the most apparently objective, abstract aspects of it studied by the natural sciences, depends upon human observation, and is subject to the limitations which the human mind imposes, this uncertainty in our thinking is also fundamental to the nature of the world.

'Uncertainty' is not a very satisfactory word to come at this. It sits awkwardly even in its original context. You can be uncertain about things which are themselves entirely definite, and about which you could be entirely certain if you were simply better informed. Indeed, the very idea of uncertainty seems to imply the possibility of certainty. Heisenberg and Bohr used several different German words in different contexts. Bohr (who spoke more or less perfect German) sometimes referred to *Unsicherheit,* which means quite simply unsureness. In Heisenberg's original paper he talks about *Ungenauigkeit* – inexactness – and the most usual term now in German seems to be *Unschärfe* – blurredness or fuzziness. But the word he adopts in his general conclusion, and which he uses when he refers back to the period later in his memoirs, is *Unbestimmtheit*, for which it's harder to find a satisfactory English equivalent. Although it means uncertainty in the sense of vagueness, it's plainly derived from *bestimmen*, to determine or to ascertain. This is reflected better in the other English translation which is sometimes used, but which seems to be less familiar: indeterminacy. 'Undeterminedness' would be closer still, though clumsy. Less close to the German, but even closer to the reality of the situation, would be 'indeterminability'.

Questions of translation apart, Heisenberg's choice of word suggests that, at the time he wrote his paper, he had not fully grasped the metaphysical implications of what he was saying. Indeed, he concludes that the experiments concerned are affected by *Unbestimmtheit* 'purely empirically'. He was not, as Bohr complained, at that time greatly interested in the philosophical fallout from physics and mathematics (though he became much more so later on in life), and he was publishing in a hurry, as Bohr also complained, before he had had a chance to discuss the work with either Bohr or anyone else. His paper seems to imply that electrons have definite orbits, even if these are unknowable; he talks about a quantum of light completely throwing the electron out of its 'orbit', even though he puts the word into inverted commas, and says that it has no rational sense here. The title of the paper itself reinforces this impression: *Über den anschaulichen Inhalt der quantentheoretischen Kinematik und Mechanik.* Again there are translation problems. '*Anschaulich*' means graphic, concrete, 'look-at-able'; the title is usually translated as referring to the 'perceptual' content of the disciplines concerned, which again seems to suggest a contrast with their unperceived aspects – as if Heisenberg were concerned merely about our difficulties in visualising abstractions, not about the physical implications of this.

*

The Copenhagen Interpretation of quantum mechanics was scientific orthodoxy for most of the twentieth century, and is the theoretical basis (for better or worse) on which the century's dramatic physical demonstrations of nuclear forces were constructed. But it has not gone unchallenged. Einstein never accepted it, though he could never find a way round it. The mathematician Roger Penrose regards the present state of quantum theory as 'provisional', and quotes Schrödinger, de Broglie, and Dirac as forerunners in this view.

An alternative to the Copenhagen Interpretation, explaining the apparent superimposition of different states that appears at the quantum level in terms of a multiplicity of parallel worlds, was developed after the Second World War by Hugh Everett III, who had been a graduate student of John Wheeler, Bohr's associate in the famous paper which opened the way to an understanding of uranium fission. David Deutsch, who proposes an extreme version of Everett's ideas in his book *The Fabric of Reality*, claims that 'hardly anyone' still believes in the Copenhagen Interpretation. I have put this view to a number of physicists. They all seemed greatly surprised by it; but maybe I have hit upon precisely the supposed handful who remain in the faith.

Another follower of Everett (though he seems to differ quite sharply from Deutsch) is Murray Gell-Mann, who with Yuval Ne'eman revolutionised elementary particle theory in the sixties with the introduction of the quark, in its three different 'colours' and six different 'flavours', as the fundamental unit of the material world. Gell-Mann believes that quantum mechanics is the fundamental tool for understanding the universe, but he sees the Copenhagen Interpretation, with its dependence upon an observer and the human act of measurement, as anthropocentric, and as characterising merely a special case that he calls 'the approximate quantum mechanics of measured systems'. I hesitate to express any reservations about something I understand so little, particularly when it comes from such an authority, but it seems to me that the view which Gell-Mann favours, and which involves what he calls alternative 'histories' or 'narratives', is precisely as anthropocentric as Bohr's, since histories and narratives are not freestanding elements of the universe, but human constructs as subjective and as restricted in their viewpoint as the act of observation.

The relevance of indeterminacy to quantum mechanics has also been challenged. A version of the famous thought experiment involving two slits has now actually been carried out in the laboratory (at the University of Konstanz). It confirms, as Bohr hypothesised, that while an unobserved particle seems to pass through both slits, so that it forms a characteristic interference pattern on a screen beyond them, any act of observation that attempts to determine which of the two paths the particle actually follows necessarily destroys the phenomenon, so that the interference pattern vanishes. But the experiment appears to suggest that, although the uncertainty principle is true, it accounts for discrepancies far too small to explain the loss of interference. The observation in the laboratory experiment, moreover, was carried out not, as in the old thought experiment, by hitting the particle involved with a photon, which transfers part of its energy to the particle and so alters its path, but by a way of marking with microwaves which has almost no effect on the particle's momentum.

Some physicists now accept that the loss of interference is caused by a much stranger and less quasi-classical aspect of the quantum world – entanglement. The notion was introduced by Schrödinger in 1935, and suggests that where quantum-mechanical entities become involved with each other (as with the particle and the photon), they form states of affairs which continue to have a collective identity and behaviour, even though their components have physically separated again. The difficulties in this are obvious, but there is no interpretation of quantum-mechanical phenomena that does not involve breathtaking challenges to the logic of our everyday experience.

For the references to all these developments see the bibliography at the end of this Postscript.

*

What about my characters? Are they anything like their originals?

It's impossible to catch the exact tone of voice of people one never knew, with only the written record to go on,

especially when most of what their contemporaries recall
them as saying was originally said in other languages. There
are also more particular problems with all three of my
protagonists.

Bohr, for a start, was as notorious for his inarticulacy and
inaudibility as he was famous for his goodness and lovability.
He was fluent in various languages, but I have heard it said
that the problem was to know which language he was being
fluent in. Schrödinger, after his epic confrontation with Bohr
in 1926, described him as often talking 'for minutes almost in
a dreamlike, visionary and really quite unclear manner, partly
because he is so full of consideration and constantly hesitates –
fearing that the other might take a statement of his [Bohr's]
point of view as an insufficient appreciation of the other's . . . '
My Bohr is necessarily a little more coherent than this – and
I have been told by various correspondents who knew him
that in private, if not in public, he could be much more
cogent and incisive than Schrödinger evidently found him.

The problem with Margrethe is that there is relatively little
biographical material to go on. She and Niels were plainly
mutually devoted, and everything suggests that she was as
generally loved as he was. She had no scientific training, but
Bohr constantly discussed his work with her, presumably
avoiding technical language – though she must have become
fairly familiar with even that since she typed out each draft
of his papers. I suspect she was more gracious and reserved
than she appears here, but she plainly had great firmness of
character – in later life she was known as *Dronning* (Queen)
Margrethe. She was always cooler about Heisenberg than
Bohr was, and she was openly angry about his visit in 1941.
According to Bohr she objected strongly to his being invited
to the house, and relented only when Bohr promised to avoid
politics and restrict the conversation to physics. Bohr himself
always refused to be drawn about Heisenberg's trip in 1941,
but she insisted, even after the war, even after all Heisenberg's
attempts to explain, 'No matter what anyone says, that was a
hostile visit.'

The problem with Heisenberg is his elusiveness and
ambiguity, which is of course what the play is attempting to

elucidate. The one thing about him that everyone agreed upon was what Max Born, his mentor in Göttingen, called 'his unbelievable quickness and precision of understanding'. The contrast with Bohr is almost comic. 'Probably [Bohr's] most characteristic property,' according to George Gamow, 'was the slowness of his thinking and comprehension.'

As a young man Heisenberg seems to have had an appealing eagerness and directness. Born described him as looking like a simple farm boy, with clear bright eyes, and a radiant expression on his face. Somebody else thought he looked 'like a bright carpenter's apprentice just returned from technical school'. Victor Weisskopf says that he made friends easily, and that everyone liked him. Bohr, after their first meeting in 1922, was delighted by Heisenberg's 'nice shy nature, his good temper, his eagerness and his enthusiasm'. There was something about him of the prize-winning student, who is good at everything required of him, and Bohr was not the only father-figure to whom he appealed. He had a somewhat similar relationship to Sommerfeld, his first professor in Munich, and in his difficulties with the Nazis he turned to two elders of German physics for counsel, Max Planck and Max von Laue. His closest friend and colleague was probably Carl Friedrich von Weizsäcker, who was younger than him, but it is striking that during his internment the person he chose to confide his explanation of the Hiroshima bomb to was not Weizsäcker, who was interned with him (although he may well have discussed it with him already), but the 66-year-old Otto Hahn.

The American physicist Jeremy Bernstein says that 'he had the first truly quantum-mechanical mind – the ability to take the leap beyond the classical visualising pictures into the abstract, all-but-impossible-to-visualise world of the subatomic . . . ' Cassidy believes that a great part of his genius was his 'ability to adopt a serviceable solution regardless of accepted wisdom'. Rudolf Peierls stresses his intuition. He would 'almost always intuitively know the answer to a problem, then look for a mathematical solution to give it to him'. The obverse of this, according to Peierls, is that 'he was always very casual about numbers' – a weakness that seems to have contributed to his downfall – or his salvation – in the atomic bomb programme.

Margrethe always found him difficult, closed, and over-sensitive, and this propensity to be withdrawn and inturned was exacerbated as life went on – first by his political problems in the thirties, and then by his efforts to reconcile the moral irreconcilables of his wartime work. His autobiographical writing is rather stiff and formal, and his letters to Bohr, even during the twenties and thirties, are correct rather than intimate. Throughout the period of their closest friendship they addressed each other with the formal *Sie*, and switched to *Du* only when Heisenberg also had a chair.

The conversations that Heisenberg claimed such freedom to recreate in his memoirs are stately. Much more plausibly colloquial is the transcript of David Irving's long interview with him for *The Virus House*, Irving's history of the German bomb programme, though he is still (naturally) watchful. In the transcripts of the relatively unguarded conversations that the German atomic team had among themselves during their internment, where Heisenberg emerges as the dominant figure, both morally and practically, a certain hard-headed worldliness can be detected. He is much concerned with professional prospects, and with how they might make some money out of their wartime researches. When one of the others says that if they agree to work on atomic matters under Allied control they will be looked down upon as traitors 'in the eyes of the masses', Heisenberg replies: 'No. One must do that cleverly. As far as the masses are concerned it will look as though we unfortunately have to continue our scientific work under the wicked Anglo-Saxon control, and that we can do nothing about it. We will have to appear to accept this control with fury and gnashing of teeth.'

There was always something a little sharp and harsh about him, something that at its best inspired respect rather than love, and that after the war occasioned really quite astonishing hostility and contempt. Even Samuel Goudsmit turned against him. Goudsmit was an old friend and colleague; when the investigators of the Alsos mission, the Allied agency for gathering intelligence on German atomic research, for which he was working, finally broke into Heisenberg's office in 1945, one of the first things they saw was a picture of the two of them together that Heisenberg had kept there as a memento of happier days. But when Goudsmit subsequently interrogated Heisenberg he found him arrogant and self-involved. Goudsmit had understandably bitter feelings at the time – he had just discovered the record of his parents' death in Auschwitz. Heisenberg was also caught in a false position. Confident that his team had been far ahead of the Americans, he offered Goudsmit his services in initiating them into the secrets of uranium fission. (Goudsmit did nothing to correct his misapprehension, which gave Heisenberg, when the truth finally came out, grounds for returning Goudsmit's bitterness.) In his superficial and strangely unimpressive book on Alsos, Goudsmit wrote about Heisenberg and his team with contemptuous dismissal and, in the year-long correspondence in the American press that followed its publication, accused him of self-importance and dishonesty.

Weisskopf gave a reception for Heisenberg during his trip to America in 1949, but about half the guests – including many people from the Los Alamos team – failed to appear, explaining to Weisskopf that they didn't want to shake the hand of the man who had tried to build a bomb for Hitler. Even Cassidy, who gives full measure to Heisenberg as a physicist in his biography, is notably cool and cautious in his assessment of Heisenberg's role in the German bomb programme. Ronald Fraser, the British intelligence officer who escorted Heisenberg back to Copenhagen in 1947 (the British seem to have been frightened that he would defect to the Russians, or be kidnapped by them) replied to Irving's inquiry about the trip in tones of patronising contempt that seem slightly unhinged. 'The whole story of "a kind of confrontation",' he wrote to Irving, 'in the matter of his 1941 natter with Bohr in the Tivoli Gardens [sic] is a typical Heisenberg fabrication – maybe a bit brighter than a thousand others, but like them all a product of his *Blut und Boden* guilt complex, which he rationalises that quickly that the stories become *for him* the truth, the whole truth, and nothing but the truth. Pitiful, in a man of his mental stature.'

The historian Paul Lawrence Rose, who has focused upon Heisenberg as an emblem for what he regards as the general failings of German culture, also takes a remarkably high moral tone. In a paper he wrote in 1984, entitled *Heisenberg, German Morality and the Atomic Bomb,* he talked about Heisenberg's 'guff', his 'self-serving, self-deluding claims', and his 'elementary moral stupidity'. After a further fourteen years research Professor Rose returned to the subject in 1998 in a full-length book which was published after the play was produced, and which has attracted considerable attention, *Heisenberg and the Nazi Atomic Bomb Project: a Study in German Culture.* His contempt for Heisenberg remains unmoderated. He believes that Heisenberg failed, in spite of his perfect readiness to serve the Nazi regime, because of his arrogance and wrong-headedness, and because he embodied various vices of German culture in general, and of the Nazi regime in particular, whose values he had absorbed.

It is a difficult book to read – Rose can scarcely quote a word of Heisenberg's without adding his own disparaging qualification. Here is a selection of his interjections on two facing pages taken more or less at random: ' . . . self-incriminating . . . a somewhat inadequate explanation . . . this inconsistency . . . the falseness of these lame excuses . . . a characteristic Heisenberg lie . . . Heisenberg's usual facile rationalising ability . . . Heisenberg then went on glibly to recollect . . . the delusory nature of Heisenberg's memory . . . '

You wonder at times whether it wouldn't look better if it were handwritten in green ink, with no paragraph breaks. Rose seems to be aware himself of the effect he is producing. He realises, he says, that some readers may 'find distasteful the recurrent moral judgments passed on Heisenberg'. They may also, he thinks, be put off by what seems a 'lack of sympathy with German culture' – he cannot say, he confesses, that his 'British background' has made him entirely sympathetic to it. He is at pains to distance himself from any unfortunate echoes that this attitude may awaken: he hopes that readers will not accuse him of 'unthinkingly preaching a crude view of German "national character", whatever that term may mean'. What he is concerned with, he explains, is not that at all, but 'the enduring nature of what one might call the "deep culture" of Germany . . . In this book I have tried to penetrate into how Germans think – or rather, perhaps, used to think – and to show how radically different are German and what I have termed "Western" mentalities and sensibilities.' It is this that underlies what he calls, without apparent irony, 'the Heisenberg problem'.

Some of his evidence induces a certain dizziness. He quotes without comment, as the epigraph to a chapter, a remark by Albert Speer, the Nazi Minister of Armaments: 'I do hope Heisenberg is not now claiming that they tried, for reasons of principle, to sabotage the project by asking for such minimal support!' It's true that any claim to have sabotaged the project, particularly for reasons of principle, would represent an astonishing departure from Heisenberg's habitual caution on the subject. But the question is not what Speer hoped, but whether Heisenberg *did* make such a claim.

So did he or didn't he? Rose doesn't tell us, and the only reference he gives is Gitta Sereny's new book, *Albert Speer: His Battle with Truth*. The allusion is to the crucial meeting at Harnack House in 1942, mentioned in the play. Speer said in his memoirs that he was 'rather put out' by the very small amount of money that Heisenberg requested to run the nuclear research programme. In an earlier draft of the manuscript (the 'Spandau draft'), says Sereny, he had added in brackets the remark that Rose quotes – and Heisenberg, she says, 'did in fact try precisely that after the war'.

So he *did* make the claim! But when and where? Sereny doesn't tell us. The only references to the smallness of the sums of money he asked for that I can find in the record are the one quoted, by Speer himself, and another by Field Marshal Milch, Goering's deputy in the Luftwaffe, who was also present at the meeting. There's certainly nothing about it in Heisenberg's memoirs, or in Robert Jungk's book, *Brighter Than a Thousand Suns*, or in Heisenberg's long interview with Irving, or in the other two obvious places, his interview with *Der Spiegel* in 1967, when Irving's book was published, or his review of the book in the *Frankfurter Allgemeine Zeitung*. I hardly like to put myself forward to fill the gap, but so far as I know the only reference he made to the subject was posthumously and fictitiously in my play.

Sereny, like Rose, is markedly unenthusiastic about Heisenberg in general. She goes on to argue that Heisenberg's claims about his intentions in meeting Bohr in 1941 'are now shown by Speer's Spandau account to be false', though quite how this is so she doesn't explain. About what she calls 'the facts' of the Copenhagen meeting she is remarkably brisk. In the conversation '. . . which Bohr subsequently reported to his associates at the Niels Bohr Institute, Heisenberg had made his political stand crystal clear. His team, he told Bohr, had gone some way towards discovering a way to produce an atom bomb. Germany was going to win the war, probably quite soon, and Bohr should join them now in their efforts.'

The idea that Heisenberg was inviting Bohr to work on the German bomb is on the face of it the least plausible out of all the possible interpretations that have been offered. It is completely at odds with what Weisskopf recalls Bohr as saying in 1948, and with what Bohr is on record as telling Chadwick at the time. In any case, the suggestion that Heisenberg thought he might be able to import someone half-Jewish into the most secret research programme in Nazi Germany is frankly preposterous.

So what is Sereny's evidence for her account of the meeting? At this point the sense of vertigo returns, and one begins to have the feeling that one is in an Escher drawing, where the stairs up to the floor above somehow lead back to the floor one is already on, because the only reference she gives is . . . Powers, Heisenberg's great champion, in *Heisenberg's War.*

And it's true – Powers *does* quote an opinion to this effect (and it's the only possible source for it anywhere, so far as I know). He says he was told by Weizsäcker that some person or persons unnamed in Copenhagen, 44 years after the event, had told *him* that this is what Bohr had said he had believed Heisenberg's intention to be. One might think that this is rather faint evidence. In any case, even if it really is what Bohr believed, it is of course not what Weizsäcker believed, or Powers either. They are reporting Bohr's alleged belief as a possible misapprehension on his part which might have explained his anger. Indeed, Powers's own reading of the situation is precisely the one that Sereny claims to be discredited by Speer's remark.

Goudsmit gradually modified his opinion, and his final judgment on Heisenberg, when he died in 1976, was a generous one which goes some way to expunging the dismissive tone of his book: 'Heisenberg was a very great physicist, a deep thinker, a fine human being, and also a courageous person. He was one of the greatest physicists of our time, but he suffered severely under the unwarranted attacks by fanatical colleagues. In my opinion he must be considered to have been in some respects a victim of the Nazi regime.'

Robert Jungk, one of the few authors who have ever attempted to defend Heisenberg, modified his opinion in the opposite direction. In *Brighter Than a Thousand Suns*, originally published in 1956, he suggested that the German physicists had managed to avoid building nuclear weapons for conscientious reasons, and quoted Heisenberg as saying that, 'under a dictatorship active resistance can only be practised by those who pretend to collaborate with the regime. Anyone speaking out openly against the system thereby indubitably deprives himself of any chance of active resistance.' But Jungk later changed his mind, and described the notion of passive resistance on the part of the German physicists as a 'myth'. He had contributed to spreading it, he said, out of an 'esteem for those impressive personalities which I have since realised to be out of place'.

For a really spirited and sustained defence Heisenberg had to wait until Powers published his book in 1993. It is a remarkable piece of work, journalistic in tone, but generous in its understanding and huge in its scope. A little too huge, perhaps, because Powers is unable to resist being sidetracked from the main narrative by the amazing byways that he perpetually finds opening off it. I recommend it particularly to other dramatists and screenwriters; there is material here for several more plays and films yet.

His central argument is that the Allied bomb programme succeeded because of the uninhibited eagerness of the scientists to do it, particularly of those exiles who had known Nazism at first hand, and who were desperate to pre-empt Hitler; while the German programme failed because of the underlying reluctance of scientists in Germany to arm Hitler with the bomb, however strong their patriotism, and however much they wanted to profit from the possibilities for research. 'Zeal was needed,' he says. 'Its absence was lethal, like a poison that leaves no trace.'

But he goes further, and argues that Heisenberg 'did not simply withhold himself, stand aside, let the project die. He killed it.' He tries to show that at every point Heisenberg was careful to hold out enough hope to the authorities to ensure that he and his team were left in charge of the project, but never enough to attract the total commitment and huge investment that would have offered the only real hope of success. 'Heisenberg's caution saved him. He was free to do what he could to guide the German atomic research effort into a broom closet, where scientists tinkered until the war ended.'

Cassidy, reviewing the book in *Nature*, described it as a good story, but insisted that 'as history it is incredible'. Rose dismisses it as 'entirely bogus' and 'a scholarly disaster'. Powers acknowledged ruefully, in a recent letter to the *Times Literary Supplement*, that he had failed to convince any historian who had pronounced upon the matter.

The play is not an attempt to adjudicate between these differing views of Heisenberg's personality, or these differing accounts of his activities. But it would have been impossible to write it without taking *some* view of Powers' version of events, so here, for what it is worth, is a brief summary of the case, and of my own hesitant view of it. The evidence is confused and contradictory, and making any sense of it involves balancing probabilities and possibilities almost as indeterminable as Heisenberg found events inside the atom.

*

Some of the evidence undoubtedly appears to support Powers's thesis in its stronger form, that Heisenberg deliberately sabotaged the project.

In the first place there are two scraps of direct testimony. One is a message brought to America in 1941 by a departing

German Jewish academic called Fritz Reiche. It was from Fritz Houtermans, the German physicist who had just realised that if they could get a reactor going it would produce plutonium, and that plutonium would be a fissile alternative to the U-235 that they could not separate. Reiche testified later that he had passed it on to a group of scientists working at Princeton, including Wolfgang Pauli, John von Neumann, and Hans Bethe. As Rudolf Ladenburg, the physicist who arranged the meeting, recorded it afterwards, Houtermans wanted it to be known that 'a large number of German physicists are working intensively on the problem of the uranium bomb under the direction of Heisenberg', and that 'Heisenberg himself tries to delay the work as much as possible, fearing the catastrophic results of a success'.

Rose dismisses Houtermans as a proven liar, and records that Reiche later appeared to withdraw his belief in Heisenberg's opposition to the project. But neither of these objections seems immediately relevant to the consistency of Reiche's and Ladenburg's testimony.

The second scrap of evidence is even more direct, but much more dubious. Heisenberg's American editor, Ruth Nanda Anshen, records receiving a letter from him in 1970 in which he claimed that, 'Dr Hahn, Dr von Laue and I falsified the mathematics in order to avoid the development of the atom bomb by German scientists.'

The letter itself has apparently vanished from the record. Rose nonetheless accepts it as beyond doubt genuine, and sees it as a yet more blatant attempt at self-justification. It is not, however, called into evidence by Powers, even though it would appear to support his case, and he mentions it only in his notes, and with the greatest reserve. Jeremy Bernstein, who seems to me the best-informed and most fair-minded of all Heisenberg's critics, and whose book *Hitler's Uranium Club* will be relied upon in understanding the scientific considerations that follow, dismisses it as 'incredible' and 'a chimera'. It is entirely at odds with Heisenberg's careful moderation in all his other references to the matter, and the inclusion of Hahn and von Laue in the plot is nonsensical. Hahn was a chemist, not a physicist, and, as will be plain from what comes later, had no knowledge whatsoever of the relevant mathematics, while von Laue is famous as an outspoken opponent of Nazism who never worked on the German nuclear programme at all.

So much for the direct evidence, true or false. All the rest of the evidence is indirect, and relates to whether Heisenberg did actually have some understanding of the relevant physics and concealed it, or whether he failed out of ignorance. It centres on the question of critical mass, the amount of fissile material (U-235 or plutonium) large enough to support an explosive chain reaction. An estimate of this amount was crucial to the decision about proceeding with a serious nuclear weapons programme because of the enormous difficulty and expense of separating the U-235 from the U-238 that makes up the vast bulk of natural uranium, and the length of time it would take to develop a reactor capable of transmuting the uranium into plutonium. At the beginning of the war it was believed by scientists on both sides that the answer would be in tons, which put the possibility of producing it beyond practical consideration. The idea became imaginable only when two scientists working in Britain, Rudolf Peierls and Otto Frisch, did the calculation and realised quite how fast the reaction would go with fast neutrons in pure U-235, and consequently how little fissile material you would need: not tons but kilograms. (The various ironies associated with this are explored in the play, and I will not repeat them here.)

Powers argues that the idea never became imaginable in Germany because Heisenberg 'cooked up a plausible method of estimating critical mass which gave an answer in tons'. He believes that Heisenberg 'well knew how to make a bomb with far less, but kept the knowledge to himself'.

There is a certain amount of evidence that the German team did at one point arrive at a much lower figure for the critical mass – indeed, for one in kilograms, that bore some relation to the estimate made by Frisch and Peierls, and to the actual mass of the Hiroshima bomb (56 kg). Manfred von Ardenne, who was running an alternative nuclear programme for the German Post Office, later claimed in his memoirs that in the late autumn of 1941 he was informed independently by both Heisenberg and Hahn that they had worked out the critical mass for a U-235 bomb and found it to be about 10 kilograms. This information was subsequently withdrawn by von Weizsäcker, who told him that he and Heisenberg had decided that a U-235 bomb was impossible (because the heat of the reaction would expand the uranium too fast for it to continue). But Heisenberg, so far as I know, never commented on this, and von Weizsäcker, according to Bernstein, 'essentially denied' that any such conversation ever took place.

As Bernstein says, it is difficult to know what to make of all this – it is 'one of several brick walls anyone who studies this subject runs into'. I think it's difficult to take von Ardenne's recollection entirely literally. Hahn, as I noted before, plainly had no understanding of the mathematics, nor of any of the other issues involved, and, as we shall see, had to have them explained to him by Heisenberg later. On the other hand (and this story has more other hands than a Hindu god), in von Weizsäcker's report on the possibility of an American bomb programme, written in September 1941, he talked about the destructive effects of a bomb weighing 5 kg. Then again, in February 1942 a brief progress report for German Army Ordnance, authors unnamed, suggested without further explanation a critical mass of between 10 and 100 kg. And at the crucial meeting with Speer at Harnack House in June 1942, when Field Marshal Milch asked him how large an atomic bomb would have to be to destroy a city, Heisenberg replied, or so he said in his interview with Irving, that it, or at any rate its 'essentially active part', would have to be 'about the size of a pineapple'.

In the end, though, I believe that the crucial piece of evidence lies elsewhere, in a source that was denied to everyone who wrote about Heisenberg until recently – the transcripts of the Farm Hall recordings. Bernstein, Powers, and Rose were the first commentators to have access to them.

Though of course they still don't reach the same conclusions from them.

*

The story of Farm Hall is another complete play in itself. Sir Charles Frank, the British atomic physicist, in his admirably fair and clear introduction to the text of the transcripts that was published in Britain, regrets that they were not released in time for Dürrenmatt to make use of.

At the end of the war troops of the Alsos mission, to which Goudsmit was attached, made their way through what was left of the German front line and located the remains of the German reactor at Haigerloch, with the intention of finally reassuring themselves that Germany would not be able to spring some terrible nuclear surprise at the last moment. They also seized the team of scientists themselves, making a special armed sortie to Urfeld, in Bavaria, to collect Heisenberg from his home. Hechingen, the nearby town where the team was based, and Haigerloch itself were in the French sector. The scientists were abstracted secretly, from under the noses of the French, and brought back to Britain, where they were held, under wartime laws and without anyone's knowledge, in a former Intelligence safe house – Farm Hall, near Cambridge. The intention seems to have been partly to prevent their passing on any atomic secrets to either of our other two allies, the Russians and the French; partly to forestall any discussion of the possibility of nuclear weapons until we had completed and used our own; and partly, perhaps, to save Heisenberg and the others from the alternative solution to these problems proposed by one American general, which was simply to shoot them out of hand.

They were detained at Farm Hall for six months, during which time they were treated not as prisoners but as guests. Hidden microphones, however, had been installed, and everything they said to each other was secretly recorded. The existence of the transcripts from these recordings was kept as secret as that of the prisoners. General Groves, the head of the Allied bomb programme, quoted from them in his memoirs (1962), and Goudsmit plainly had access to them, which he drew upon in his book on Alsos, but the British Government, perhaps to protect the feelings of the former detainees, some of them now prominent in post-war German science, perhaps merely out of its usual pathological addiction to secrecy, continued to block the release of the papers themselves. Even Margaret Gowing was refused access when she wrote her official history of British atomic policy in 1964, and David Irving was refused again, in spite of strenuous efforts, for *The Virus House* in 1967. The ban was maintained until 1992, when the Government finally gave way to a combined appeal from leading scientists and historians.

The German originals are lost, and the translation was plainly done under pressure, with little feeling for colloquial nuance, but the transcripts are direct evidence of what Heisenberg and the others thought when they were talking, as they believed, amongst themselves. The ten detainees represented a wide range of different attitudes. They ranged from Walther Gerlach, the Nazi Government's administrator of nuclear research, and Kurt Diebner, who had been a member of the Nazi party, to Max von Laue, who had been openly hostile to the regime, who had never worked on the atomic programme, and whose inclusion in the party seems on the face of it mysterious. Their conversations over the six-month period reflect a similarly wide range of attitudes and feelings. The general tone is pretty much what one might expect from any group of academics deprived of their liberty without explanation and cooped up together. There is, as one might suppose, quite a lot of complaining, scheming and mutual friction.

One thing, though, seems to me to emerge quite clearly: for all practical purposes German thinking had stopped at a reactor, and there had been no eagerness at all to look beyond this to the possibility of weapons. Their shocked comments in the moment of unguarded horror that followed the announcement of Hiroshima are particularly revealing. The internees had been given the news by their (almost) endlessly sympathetic and urbane gaoler-cum-host, Major Rittner, at dinner-time, but Heisenberg had not believed it until he had heard it with his own ears on the BBC nine o'clock news. 'They were completely stunned,' reported Rittner, 'when they realised that the news was genuine. They were left alone on the assumption that they would discuss the position . . . '

'I was absolutely convinced,' says Heisenberg, in the conversation that followed, 'of the possibility of our making an uranium engine [reactor] but I never thought that we would make a bomb and at the bottom of my heart I was really glad that it was to be an engine and not a bomb. I must admit that.' Weizsäcker says that he doesn't think that they should make excuses now for failing, 'but we must admit that we didn't want to succeed.' Gerlach: 'One cannot say in front of an Englishman that we didn't try hard enough. They were our enemies, although we sabotaged the war. There are some things that one knows and one can discuss together but that one cannot discuss in the presence of Englishmen.'

In a letter written fourteen years later von Laue complained that, during their conversations at table in the following weeks, 'The version was developed that the German atomic physicists really had not wanted the atomic bomb, either because it was impossible to achieve it during the expected duration of the war or because they simply did not want to have it at all.' Von Laue's account of the elaboration of this sanitised 'version' (*Lesart* in German) has been seized upon by unsympathetic commentators, and contrasted with the encouraging prospects for atomic weapons that some of the physicists had undoubtedly held out to the Nazi authorities at various times during the earlier part of the war.

Well, we all reorganise our recollections, consciously or unconsciously, as time goes by, to fit our changed perceptions of a situation, and no doubt Heisenberg and his fellow detainees did the same. But Bernstein locates the origins of the *Lesart* in those immediate reactions to the announcement of Hiroshima on the nine o'clock news. If this is so then I can only say that the team began to get their story together with quite remarkable spontaneity, speed, presence of mind and common purpose. If they all thought as fast as this, and co-operated as closely, it's even more surprising that they didn't get further with the bomb.

To me, I have to say, those immediate and unprepared reactions suggest quite strongly that the first part of Powers's thesis, at any rate, is right, and that there *had* been the 'fatal lack of zeal' that he diagnosed. Perhaps Gerlach's claim, unchallenged by the others, that they had actually 'sabotaged the war' suggests at the very least a consciousness that quite a lot of stones had been left unturned.

*

But do the transcripts support Powers's contention that Heisenberg 'cooked up a plausible method of estimating critical mass which gave an answer in tons, and that he well knew how to make a bomb with far less, but kept the knowledge to himself?'

One preliminary point needs to be cleared out of the way first: the question whether Heisenberg understood an even more fundamental point, the difference between a reactor (which is operated by slow neutrons in natural uranium, or some other mixture of U-238 and U-235) and a bomb (which functions with fast neutrons in pure U-235 or plutonium). Goudsmit, who plainly had access to the transcripts when he wrote his book on Alsos, seems to have thought they supported his view that Heisenberg didn't. Before the transcripts were published Rose shared Goudsmit's dismissive view.

But, according to the transcripts, what Heisenberg tells Hahn that same night, when Gerlach has retired to sob in his room, and they are finally alone together, is that 'I always knew it could be done with 235 with fast neutrons. That's why 235 only [presumably = "only 235"] can be used as an explosive. One can never make an explosive with slow neutrons, not even with the heavy water machine [the German reactor], as then the neutrons only go with thermal speed, with the result that the reaction is so slow that the thing explodes sooner, before the reaction is complete.'

Bernstein (unlike Goudsmit) reads this and what follows as showing that Heisenberg *did* understand the difference between a reactor and a bomb, 'but that he did not understand either one very well – certainly not the bomb'. Rose now seems to accept that Heisenberg's remarks do indicate that he realised the bomb would have to be fissioned with fast neutrons (though he shows that in the past Heisenberg had been toying with the idea of some kind of vast exploding reactor).[1]

This same conversation between Heisenberg and Hahn, when they were alone together on that terrible night, seems to me also to resolve the question of Heisenberg's understanding of the critical mass beyond any reasonable doubt. He takes Hahn through what he believes to be the relevant calculation and tells him that the answer is 'about a ton'. I can't see any earthly reason why he should be rehearsing a fabricated calculation or a fabricated answer at this stage, in a private conversation with someone he seems to have trusted, after the German team are out of the race and in custody, and after someone else has in any case already built the bomb. If he had had the right calculation and the right answer up his sleeve all the time, now would surely have been the moment to produce them. I find it much more plausible that he was telling the simple truth when he said to Hahn just before this that 'quite honestly I have never worked it out as I never believed one could get pure 235'.

Earlier on in the evening, it's true, when everyone was present during the conversation immediately after the news bulletin, Hahn says to Heisenberg: 'But tell me why you used to tell me that one needed 50 kilograms of 235 in order to do anything.' (To which Heisenberg replies that he wouldn't like to commit himself for the moment.) This does seem to suggest that he *had* made a calculation of some sort earlier, as von Ardenne claimed – though it also surely destroys once and for all the improbable proposition that Hahn had been involved in it, or had made some kind of estimate of his own. Perhaps Heisenberg had made not so much a calculation as some kind of guess or estimate. Even if it *was* a serious calculation, it seems most unlikely that it was the right calculation, or that it was one he had adhered to.

---

1. Bernstein takes the trouble to explain in his book what few other commentators do – the difference between slow and fast neutrons: 'By definition, slow neutrons move with speeds of the order of a few kilometers a second, about the speeds that molecules at room temperature move in a gas. That is why these neutrons are also referred to as thermal. Fast neutrons, the kind that are emitted in many nuclear processes, move at speeds of tens of thousands of kilometers a second.'

This is made clear to me (at last) by Jeremy Bernstein. I should explain that when I first read the Farm Hall transcripts, before I wrote the play, I was using the bare uncommented text published in Britain, unaware that there was also a completely different edition published in the US, incorporating Bernstein's detailed commentary. After the play was produced and published he was kind enough to send me it, and it illuminated a great many matters that I had not understood before. These are after all scientists talking to scientists, and they are reported verbatim with all the ellipses of spoken conversation, and with a further haze cast over the proceedings by translation. Bernstein is both a distinguished journalist and a professor of physics, and he has a long acquaintance with the history of atomic research. (He recalls being given the bare plutonium core of a bomb to hold on the Nevada test site in 1957: 'It was slightly warm to the touch, since plutonium is marginally radioactive.') He has a thorough understanding of the scientific issues involved, and is the ideal guide to the physics – though a slightly less percipient one, I think, to the psychology of the physicists.

I'm pleased to discover for a start that he takes the same view of Heisenberg's admission to Hahn about never having worked out the critical mass. He believes that it has to be taken at its face value, and he asks how it can be reconciled with the figure of 50 kg recalled by Hahn. He demonstrates that when Heisenberg attempts to do the calculation for Hahn he 'gets it wrong at every level' – he does the arithmetic wrong, and is in any case doing the wrong arithmetic. 'Knowing how scientists work,' says Bernstein, 'I find it implausible that he ever did the calculation correctly before. One can imagine even a Heisenberg forgetting a number – he was, in any case, not very good with numbers – but it is very difficult to imagine his forgetting a general method of calculation, a method that once led him to a more reasonable answer.'

The calculation of the critical mass is not the only thing that Heisenberg got wrong that night. Even when he revealed to Hahn that he understood how the critical mass could be reduced by the use of a reflective shield he suggested a material, carbon, that would have had the opposite effect to the one intended. Carbon is a good moderator for a reactor, and Heisenberg's proposing it for the 'tamper' in a bomb, says Bernstein, 'shows he was thinking like a reactor physicist, which, for the last two years, he was'.

These were of course Heisenberg's first thoughts off the top of his head in the wake of Hiroshima. A week later, with the help of what few details the newspapers had given of the two bombs, Heisenberg offered all his fellow-internees a lecture in which he presented a complete and considered account of how the Allies had done it. The inclusion in the lecture of quite fundamental matters, argues Powers, together with the questions which his hearers asked, make it clear that it was all news to everyone present except his closest associates. 'What the Farm Hall transcripts show unmistakably,' he says, 'is that Heisenberg did not explain basic bomb physics to the man in charge of the German bomb program [Gerlach] until after the war was over.' They 'offer strong evidence that Heisenberg never explained fast fission to Gerlach'. At the end of the lecture, says Powers, 'the German scientists, given a second chance, would have been ready to start building a bomb'.

Bernstein sees the lecture very differently. He demonstrates that Heisenberg's exposition is still marred by quite fundamental misconceptions. Heisenberg now seems to have 'the first inkling' of how to calculate the critical mass (though he still does the arithmetic wrong), but is not much nearer to the practicalities of building a bomb than his audience. What the novelty of a lot of this material suggests to Bernstein is simply that communications between the different sections of the German project were very poor.

As a non-scientist I can't offer any opinion on the physics. To my eyes, I have to say, Heisenberg does seem to have come a remarkably long way in a week – if, that is, he was starting more or less from scratch. And he surely must have been. It's really not plausible that he hadn't recollected more by this time if he actually had done the work. The conclusion seems to me inescapable: he hadn't done the calculation. If he had kept the fatal knowledge of how small the critical mass would be from anyone, as Powers argues, then it was from himself.

*

In the end, it seems to me, your judgment of Heisenberg comes down to what you make of his failure to attempt that fundamental calculation. Does it suggest incompetence or arrogance, as his detractors have claimed? It's possible. Even great scientists – and Bernstein agrees that Heisenberg was one of them – make mistakes, and fail to see possibilities that lesser men pick up; Heisenberg accepted that he had made a mistake in the formulation of uncertainty itself. And I think we have to accept Bernstein's judgment that, although he was the first person to be able to grasp the counter-intuitive abstraction of quantum mechanics, he was not so good at the practicalities of commonsense estimates and working arithmetic.

Or does the failure suggest something rather different? An unconscious reluctance to challenge the comforting and convenient assumption that the thing was not a practical possibility? Comforting and convenient, that is, if what he was trying to do was *not* to build a bomb. Is it all part of a general pattern of reluctance, as the first and more plausible part of Powers's thesis suggests? If so, you might wonder whether this reluctance was a state definite enough to be susceptible of explanation. Heisenberg was trapped in a seamless circle which explains itself: he didn't try the calculation because he didn't think it was worth doing – he didn't think it was worth doing because he didn't try it. The oddity, the phenomenon that requires explaining, is not this non-occurrence but its opposite – the escape of Frisch and Peierls from that same circle. It seems almost like a random quantum event; in which case, of course, it is no more explainable than its not happening.

After the war, certainly, Heisenberg was not just passively reluctant about any military application of nuclear power, but very actively so. In the 1950s, when there was a proposal to arm Federal Germany with nuclear weapons, he joined forces with Weizsäcker and others to fight a vigorous campaign that entirely and permanently defeated it.

There is also one small piece of evidence about his attitude during the war that Powers rather curiously doesn't comment on: the question of the cyclotron.

At the crucial meeting between Heisenberg and Speer in 1942, which seems finally to have scuppered all possibility of a German bomb, Heisenberg is reported to have emphasised the need to build a cyclotron. A cyclotron could have been used, as the cyclotrons in America were, for isotope separation, the great sticking point in the German programme. In the account of this meeting in his memoirs Speer says: 'Difficulties were compounded, Heisenberg explained, by the fact that Europe possessed only one cyclotron, and that of minimal capacity. Moreover, it was located in Paris and because of the need for secrecy could not be used to full advantage.' Powers mentions this, but does not go on to the obvious corollary: that if Speer's recollection is accurate, then Heisenberg was plainly lying, because he knew perfectly well that there was a second cyclotron to hand – at Bohr's Institute in Copenhagen. This would suggest that his apparent anxiety to lay his hands on a machine that might actually separate some U-235 was not quite what it seemed. Or, at the very least, that he placed Germany's war aims below his desire to protect Bohr's Institute.

Perhaps Speer is simply wrong. It seems uncharacteristic of Heisenberg to have risked such a blatant falsehood, and he makes no mention of it in his own accounts of the meeting. All the same, when he went back to Copenhagen in 1944, after Bohr had fled, to adjudicate a German proposal to strip the Institute of all its equipment, presumably including the cyclotron, he seems to have contrived to leave it even then still in Danish hands.

*

One of the forms of indeterminacy touched upon in the play is the indeterminacy of human memory, or at any rate the indeterminability of the historical record. There are various examples which I left out, for fear of making the play even more tangled than it is. Some, such as the difficulties about the amazingly realistic figure for the critical mass that von Ardenne recollected being given by Heisenberg and Hahn in 1941, I have already mentioned in this Postscript. There were

others. A minor one concerns whether there were two ships
sent to load the Jews of Copenhagen for deportation, as some
witnesses recall, or a single one (named as the *Wartheland*).
A more significant point of dispute is the drawing which
Heisenberg did or didn't make for Bohr during their meeting
in 1941.

According to Hans Bethe, who was one of the team at Los
Alamos, Heisenberg drew a rough sketch to show Bohr the
work that was being done in Germany. Bohr evidently took it
to Los Alamos with him when he went, because Bethe (and
others) recall it being passed around at a meeting there. Bethe
told Powers that Bohr believed it represented a bomb; but the
consensus of opinion at the meeting was that it was a reactor.
However, Aage Bohr, Niels's son, a physicist himself (and
another Nobel prizewinner), who was with his father in
Copenhagen during Heisenberg's visit, and with him again in
Los Alamos, was absolutely insistent that there was no drawing.

If the story is true it might help to explain Goudsmit's
insistence, in the teeth of the evidence from Farm Hall, that
Heisenberg couldn't tell the difference between a reactor
and a bomb. It would certainly cast doubt on Heisenberg's
recollection that the entire discussion with Bohr in 1941 took
place during the walk, and that Bohr broke off the conversation
almost as soon as it was broached. It seems improbable to me
that Heisenberg would have risked putting anything down on
paper, and if even so he had, then I can't see why he didn't
seize upon it after the war, to support his claim that he had
hinted to Bohr at the German research on a bomb. I suppose
it's possible that Bohr made the sketch himself, to illustrate to
his colleagues at Los Alamos what he thought Heisenberg was
getting at, but the truth of the matter seems to be irretrievable.

*

I have had many helping hands with this play, both before it
was produced in London and since. Sir John Maddox kindly
read the text for me, and so did Professor Balázs L. Gyorffy,
Professor of Physics at Bristol University, who made a number
of corrections and suggestions. I am also indebted to Finn

Aaserud, the Director of the Niels Bohr Archive in Copenhagen, and to his colleagues there, for much help and encouragement. Many scientists and other specialists have written to me after seeing the play on the stage. They have mostly been extraordinarily generous and supportive, but some of them have put me right on details of the science, for which I am particularly grateful. They also pointed out two mathematical errors so egregious that the lines in question didn't make sense from one end to the other – even to me, when I re-read them. All these points have now been addressed, though I'm sure that other mistakes will emerge. So much new material has come to hand, in one way or another, that I extensively overhauled and extended this Postscript to coincide with the production of the play in New York.

One matter of dispute that I have not been able to resolve completely concerns the part played by Max Born in the introduction of quantum mechanics. The matter was raised (with exemplary temperance) by his son, Gustav Born, who was concerned about the injustice he felt I had done to his father's memory. I was reluctant to make the play any more complex than it is, but I have since made adjustments both to the play itself and to this Postscript which go at any rate some way to meeting Professor Born's case. We are still at odds over one line, though, in which Heisenberg is said to have 'invented quantum mechanics'. I am quoting the judgment of other physicists here (including one not especially sympathetic to Heisenberg), but I realise that it is a huge over-simplification, and that it seems to compound the original injustice committed when Heisenberg was awarded the Nobel Prize in 1932 'for the creation of quantum mechanics', while Born had to wait another 22 years to have his part acknowledged in the same way. The trouble is that I have not yet been able to think of another way of putting it briefly enough to work in spoken dialogue.

The American physicist Spencer Weart, in a letter to Finn Aaserud, very cogently pointed out that the calculation of the critical mass was much harder than I've made it seem for Heisenberg once Bohr has suggested it to him. 'Perrin failed to get it and his publication of a ton-size critical mass subtly misled everyone else, then Bohr and Wheeler failed, Kurchatov failed, Chadwick failed, all the other Germans and Russians and French and British and Americans missed it, even the greatest of them all for such problems, Fermi, tried but missed, everyone except Peierls . . . Physics is hard.'

Some correspondents have also objected to Heisenberg's line about the physicists who built the Allied bomb, 'Did a single one of them stop to think, even for one brief moment, about what they were doing?', on the grounds that it is unjust to Leo Szilard. It's true that in March 1945 Szilard began a campaign to persuade the US Government not to use the bomb. A committee was set up – the Committee on Social and Political Implications – to allow the scientists working on the project to voice their feelings, and Szilard also circulated a petition among the scientists, 67 of whom signed it, which mentioned 'moral considerations', though it did not specify what exactly these were.

But the main stated reasons for Szilard's second thoughts were not to do with the effects that the bomb would have on the Japanese – he was worried about the ones it would have on the Allies. He thought (presciently) that the actual use of the bomb on Japan would precipitate an atomic arms race between the United States and the Soviet Union. The Committee's report (which Szilard himself seems to have written) and the petition stressed the same points. By this time, in any case, the bomb was almost ready. It had been Szilard who urged the nuclear programme in the first place, and at no point, so far as I know, while he worked for it (on plutonium production) did he ever suggest any hesitation about pursuing either the research or the actual manufacture of the bomb.

I think the line stands, in spite of Szilard's afterthoughts. The scientists had already presented their government with the bomb, and it is the question of whether the German scientists were ready or not to do likewise that is at issue in the play. If Heisenberg's team *had* built a bomb, I don't think they would have recovered very much moral credit by asking Hitler to be kind enough not to drop it on anyone – particularly if their objection had been the strain it might place upon post-war relations among the Axis powers.

*

One looming imponderable remains. *If* Heisenberg had made
the calculation, and *if* the resulting reduction in the scale of
the problem had somehow generated a real eagerness in both
the Nazi authorities and the scientists, could the Germans
have built a bomb? Frank believes that they could not have
done it before the war in Europe was over – 'even the
Americans, with substantial industrial and scientific advantage,
and the important assistance from Britain and from ex-
Germans in Britain did not achieve that (VE-Day, 8 May
1945, Trinity test, Alamogordo, 16 July 1945).' Speer (who as
Armaments Minister would presumably have had to carry the
programme out) suggests in his memoirs that it might have
been possible to do it by 1945, if the Germans had shelved all
their other weapons projects, then two paragraphs later more
cautiously changes his estimate to 1947; but of course he needs
to justify his failure to pursue the possibility. Powers makes
the point that, whatever the timetable was, its start date could
have been much earlier. Atomic energy in Germany, he
argues, attracted the interest of the authorities from the first
day of the war. 'The United States, beginning in June 1942,
took just over three years to do the job, and the Soviet Union
succeeded in four. If a serious effort to develop a bomb had
commenced in mid-1940, one might have been tested in
1943, well before the Allied bomber offensive had destroyed
German industry.'

If this 'serious effort' had begun only after Heisenberg's
visit to Copenhagen, as the play suggests might have happened
if the conversation with Bohr had gone differently, then
even this timetable wouldn't have produced a bomb until late
1944 – and by that time it was of course much less likely that
German industry could have delivered. In any case, formidable
difficulties remained to be overcome. The German team were
hugely frustrated by their inability to find a successful technique
for isolating U-235 in any appreciable quantity, even though
the experimental method, using Clusius-Dickel tubes, was of
German origin. They could have tried one of the processes
used successfully by the Allies, gaseous diffusion. This was

another German invention, developed in Berlin by Gustav
Hertz, but Hertz had lost his job because his uncle was
Jewish. (It was, incidentally, the delays in getting the various
American isotope-separation plants to function which meant
that the Allied bomb was not ready in time for use against
Germany.)

The failure to separate U-235 also held up the reactor
programme, and therefore the prospect of producing
plutonium, because they could not separate enough of it
even for the purposes of enrichment (increasing the U-235
content of natural uranium), so that it was harder to get the
reactor to go critical. The construction of the reactor was
further delayed because Walther Bothe's team at Heidelberg
estimated the neutron absorption rates of graphite wrongly,
which obliged the designers to use heavy water as a moderator
instead. The only source of heavy water was a plant in Norway,
which was forced to close after a series of attacks by
Norwegian parachutists attached to Special Operations
Executive, American bombers, and the Norwegian Resistance.
Though perhaps, if a crash programme had been instituted
from the first day of the war, enough heavy water might have
been accumulated before the attacks were mounted.

If, if, if . . . The line of ifs is a long one. It remains just
possible, though. The effects of real enthusiasm and real
determination are incalculable. In the realm of the just
possible they are sometimes decisive.

*

Anyone interested enough in any of these questions to want
to sidestep the fiction and look at the historical record should
certainly begin with:

Thomas Powers: *Heisenberg's War* (Knopf, 1993; Cape, 1993)

David Cassidy: *Uncertainty: The Life and Science of Werner Heisenberg*
(W.H. Freeman, 1992)

Abraham Pais: *Niels Bohr's Times* (OUP, 1991) – Pais is a
fellow nuclear physicist, who knew Bohr personally, and

this, in its highly eccentric way, is a classic of biography, even though Pais has not much more sense of narrative than I have of physics, and the book is organised more like a scientific report than the story of someone's life. But then Bohr notoriously had no sense of narrative, either. One of the tasks his assistants had was to take him to the cinema and to explain the plot to him afterwards

Werner Heisenberg: *Physics and Beyond* (Harper & Row, 1971) – in German, *Der Teil und das Ganze.* His memoirs

Jeremy Bernstein: *Hitler's Uranium Club, the Secret Recordings at Farm Hall,* introduced by David Cassidy (American Institute of Physics, Woodbury, New York, 1996)

or the British edition of the transcripts:

Operation Epsilon, the Farm Hall Transcripts, introduced by Sir Charles Frank (Institute of Physics Publishing, 1993)

Also relevant:

Heisenberg: *Physics and Philosophy* (Penguin, 1958)

Niels Bohr: *The Philosophical Writings of Niels Bohr* (Oxbow Press, Connecticut, 1987)

Elisabeth Heisenberg: *Inner Exile* (Birkhauser, 1984) – in German, *Das politische Leben eines Unpolitischen.* Defensive in tone, but revealing about the kind of anguish her husband tended to conceal from the world; and the source for Heisenberg's ride home in 1945

David Irving: *The German Atomic Bomb* (Simon & Schuster, 1968) – in UK as *The Virus House* (Collins, 1967). The story of the German bomb programme

Paul Lawrence Rose: *Heisenberg and the Nazi Atomic Bomb Project* (U of California Press, 1998)

Records and Documents Relating to the Third Reich, II: German Atomic Research, Microfilms DJ29–32. (EP Microform Ltd, Wakefield) – Irving's research materials for the book, including long verbatim interviews with Heisenberg and others. The only consultable copy I could track down was in the library of the Ministry of Defence

Archive for the History of Quantum Physics, microfilm. Includes the complete correspondence of Heisenberg and Bohr. A copy is available for reference in the Science Museum Library. Bohr's side of the correspondence is almost entirely in Danish, Heisenberg's in German apart from one letter

Leni Yahil: *The Rescue of Danish Jewry* (Jewish Publication Society of America, Philadelphia, 1969)

There are also many interesting sidelights on life at the Bohr Institute in its golden years in:

French & Kennedy, eds: *Niels Bohr, A Centenay Volume* (Harvard, 1985)

and in the memoirs of Hendrik Casimir, George Gamow, Otto Frisch, Otto Hahn, Rudolf Peierls, and Victor Weisskopf.

For the subsequent challenges to the Copenhagen Interpretation:

David Deutsch: *The Fabric of Reality* (Allen Lane, 1997)

Murray Gell-Mann: *The Quark and the Jaguar* (W.H. Freeman, 1994; Little, Brown, 1994)

Roger Penrose: *The Emperor's New Mind* (OUP, 1989)

The actual 'two-slits' experiment was carried out by Dürr, Nonn, and Rempe at the University of Konstanz, and is reported in *Nature* (3 September 1998). There is an accessible introduction to the work in the same issue by Peter Knight, and another account of it by Mark Buchanan (boldly entitled 'An End to Uncertainty') in *New Scientist* (6 March 1999).

Post-Postscript

I made a number of changes to the text of the play, as I have
explained above, in response to suggestions and criticisms
I received during the run of the play in London, and to new
material I came across. The production in New York,
however, opened up a much broader and more fundamental
debate. A number of commentators expressed misgivings
about the whole enterprise. Paul Lawrence Rose, the most
outspoken of the play's critics, even managed to detect in it
a 'subtle revisionism . . . more destructive than Irving's self-
evidently ridiculous assertions – more destructive of the
integrity of art, of science, and of history'.

One of the most frequent complaints about the play in
America was that I should have laid more stress on the evils
of the Nazi regime, and in particular upon the Holocaust;
it was pointed out that Heisenberg's visit to Copenhagen in
1941 coincided with the Wannsee Conference. It was argued
that I should have put the visit in the context of a number of
subsequent trips he made during the course of the war to
other occupied countries. It was also felt that I should have
laid more stress than I did on Heisenberg's stated view that
Germany's conquests, at any rate in Eastern Europe, were
justified, and that her victory over Russia was to be welcomed.

With hindsight, I think I accept some of these criticisms.
I should perhaps have had Heisenberg justify Germany's war
aims on the Eastern front direct, instead of having Bohr refer
to his arguments in one angry but passing aside. I should
perhaps have found some way to make the parallel with all
the other trips that were found offensive, and about whose
purpose there was none of the mystery which had seemed to
attach to the one to Copenhagen.

About a greater stress on the evil of the Nazi regime I'm
not so sure. I thought that this was too well understood to
need pointing out. It is after all the *given* of the play; this was
precisely why there was (or should have been) a problem
facing Heisenberg, and us in understanding him. In any case,
the play returns to the persecution of Jews in Nazi Germany
again and again, from the suppression of so-called 'Jewish

physics' (relativity) to the enforced flight of all the Jewish physicists, the death of Goudsmit's parents in Auschwitz, and the attempt by the SS to deport the Jewish population of Denmark to the death camps, which Margrethe Bohr describes as 'that great darkness inside the human soul . . . flooding out to engulf us all'.

Some of the criticisms were even more radical. The play turns on the difficulty of determining why Heisenberg made his trip. For a number of commentators there was no problem at all – they knew the correct explanation for certain; though what that explanation was varied from one to another. For some it was Heisenberg's desire to persuade Bohr of the rightness of Germany's war aims and of its inevitable victory; for Rose and others, he was on a spying mission, to find out through Bohr if the Allies were also working on an atomic bomb.

I agree that Heisenberg may have wished to present the German case to Bohr; but he surely didn't go all the way to Copenhagen *just* to do that. I also agree about the spying. But then so does my Heisenberg. He tells Bohr that he wanted 'some hint, some clue' about whether there was an Allied nuclear programme. This seems to me to be common sense; he would have had to be insanely incurious not to seize any chance he could to find out whether the Allies might drop atomic bombs on his country. There is surely no contradiction at all with what he himself claimed his purpose was – to discuss whether the German team were justified in working on a German weapon. Any information he could get about the other side's intentions would have been a prerequisite for deciding what to do.

Some criticisms I reject, and I should like to put the record straight. Professor Rose suggested that I had 'fantasised' Heisenberg's fear that he was in danger of his life from the Gestapo for talking to Bohr. Not so – I was simply expanding upon what the real Heisenberg said. Jonothan Logan, a physicist writing in *American Scientist*, dismissed as misleading the fictitious Bohr's assertion that in June 1942 Heisenberg had been slightly ahead of Fermi in Chicago. The context makes plain that this was in terms of neutron multiplication, and the claim was based on what David Cassidy says in his biography of Heisenberg. The correctness of Cassidy's assessment was verified for me, after much inquiry on my part, by Al Wattenberg, one of the editors of Fermi's *Collected Papers*.

All these are at any rate debatable points. Other criticisms I found extremely difficult to make sense of – some even to credit. Professor Rose, who detected the subtle revisionism of the play, found a particularly sinister significance in one detail – the fictitious Heisenberg's remarking upon the neatness of the historical irony whereby the crucial calculation (of the critical mass), which persuaded the Allies of the possibility of building a nuclear weapon, was made by a German and an Austrian, driven into exile in Britain because they were Jewish. Professor Rose saw this as an attempt to blame 'the Jews' for the bomb's invention.

A little more extraordinary still was the view of the play taken by Gerald Holton, Professor of Physics and Professor of the History of Science Emeritus at Harvard. He saw it as being 'structured in good part' to reflect the thesis advanced by Powers, that Heisenberg had correctly calculated the critical mass, but concealed it by 'cooking up' a false result. By the time the play was produced in New York, he believed, I had been forced (by Bernstein) to lay this idea aside, so that I now had an 'unsolvable problem' with the motivation of the play.

I can only suppose that Professor Holton was misled because in the Postscript I speak warmly and gratefully about Powers's book. It has been much attacked, but I continue to admire the generosity of its tone, and the range of Powers's research. I also agree with the first part of his thesis (lack of zeal). But then so does Holton himself, and so, he says, does everyone else who has studied the matter. In the Postscript, however, I make abundantly clear that I don't accept Powers's view about the 'cooking up' and never did.

But you don't even need to read the Postscript to discover this, because it's all over the play itself. The central argument turns on Heisenberg's confession to Otto Hahn that he had *not* attempted the calculation. By my count, there are something like thirty-five speeches devoted to establishing this, to asking why he hadn't attempted it, and to suggesting what might have happened if he had. How anyone could give the play even the most cursory glance and fail to notice this is difficult to understand.

Even harder to credit was the reaction in some quarters to the 'strange new quantum ethics' proposed by the fictitious Heisenberg. I suppose I should have erected a flashing 'IRONY' sign in front of it. The allusion is to his insight, in his original introduction of quantum mechanics, that physics should be limited to the measurement of what we could actually observe – the external effects of events inside the atom. We should need a similar kind of ethics, he suggests in my play, if we judged people purely on the external effects of their actions, without regard to their intentions. According to Professor Holton, Heisenberg 'exults' that under the new dispensation there would be a place in heaven even for him. Professor Holton fails to mention that Heisenberg also 'exults' that, under the new quantum ethical rules, there would also be a place in heaven for the SS man who seemed ready to murder him in 1945, simply because in the end he settled for a pack of American cigarettes instead. Jonothan Logan manages to believe that I am seriously proposing even the SS man's assumption into heaven.

Let me make it absolutely unambiguous: my Heisenberg is saying that we *do* have to make assessments of intention in judging people's actions. (The epistemology of intention is what the play is about!) He is saying that Bohr will continue to inspire respect and love, in spite of his involvement in the building of the Hiroshima and Nagasaki bombs; and that he himself will continue to be regarded with distrust in spite of his failure to kill anyone. The reaction of Holton, Rose, and others to the play is perhaps an oblique testimony to the truth of this judgement.

*

One of the most striking comments on the play was made by Jochen Heisenberg, Werner Heisenberg's son, when I met

him, to my considerable alarm, after the premiere of the play
in New York. 'Of course, your Heisenberg is nothing like my
father,' he told me. 'I never saw my father express emotion
about anything except music. But I understand that the
characters in a play have to be rather more forthcoming
than that.'

This seems to me a chastening reminder of the difficulties
of representing a real person in fiction, but a profoundly
sensible indication of the purpose in attempting it, which is
surely to make explicit the ideas and feelings that never quite
get expressed in the confusing onrush of life, and to bring out
the underlying structure of events. I take it that the nineteenth-
century German playwright Friedrich Hebbel was making a
similar point when he uttered his great dictum (one that every
playwright ought to have in pokerwork over his desk): 'In a
good play everyone is right.' I assume he means by this not
that the audience is invited to approve of everyone's actions,
but that everyone should be allowed the freedom and
eloquence to make the most convincing case that he can for
himself. Whether or not this is a universal rule of playwriting,
it must surely apply to this particular play, where a central
argument is about our inability, in our observation of both
the physical world and the mental, ever to escape from
particular viewpoints.

I suppose that this is what sticks in some people's throats –
that my Heisenberg is allowed to make a case for himself –
even to criticise others. His claims about his intentions are
strongly contested by another character in the play, Margrethe
Bohr. Neither Heisenberg nor Margrethe Bohr, so far as I can
see, is presented as winning the argument. I don't see why my
Margrethe shouldn't be allowed to express her suspicions of
Heisenberg much more sharply and woundingly than the real
Margrethe's habitual courtesy would ever have permitted,
and I don't see why my Heisenberg shouldn't be free to
express the deeper feelings that the real Heisenberg remained
silent about. Why shouldn't he have the same conflicting
loyalties and the same mixed motives and emotions that we
all have? Why shouldn't he try to juggle principle and
expediency, as we all do? Why shouldn't he fear his country's

defeat, and its destruction by nuclear weapons? Why shouldn't he lament its ruin and the slaughter of its citizens?

I can imagine it being asked how far I think this principle should be carried. Do I believe that a fictitious Hitler should be accorded the same privileges? I can see all the problems of exhibiting Hitler on the stage, but I can't see any point in attempting it at all if he is to be simply an effigy for ritual humiliation. Why should we be asked to endure a represen-tation of his presence if he doesn't offer us some understanding of what was going on inside his head from his own point of view? The audience can surely be trusted to draw its own moral conclusions.

*

The most surprising result of the debate set off by the production of the play, though, has been the release of the Bohr documents.

I was told privately about the existence of at any rate one of the documents at a symposium on the play organised in Copenhagen by the Niels Bohr Archive in the autumn of 1999. Heisenberg had made public his own version of the 1941 meeting with Bohr, chiefly in two places: a memorandum written in 1957 to Robert Jungk, who was preparing the material for *Brighter Than a Thousand Suns,* and his memoirs, published in 1969. Bohr, however, had never publicly given his side of the story, and historians had been obliged to rely upon what other people (chiefly his son Aage – also a physicist, and later a Nobel prizewinner himself – and his colleague Stefan Rozental) recalled him as saying about it.

In 1957, however, Bohr had apparently been so angered by Heisenberg's version, when he read it in Jungk's book, that he had written to Heisenberg, dissenting and giving his own account. He had never sent the letter, though, and at his death in 1962 it had been placed in the Archive by his family, not to be released for another fifty years. This was all my informant was prepared to tell me.

I said nothing about this because I believed that I had been told in confidence. The existence of the letter was first publicly mentioned, so far as I know, by Professor Holton, at a further symposium on the play organised in New York in March 2000 on the occasion of its production there. He said that he had actually seen the letter – he had been shown it by the Bohr family. He felt bound not to divulge its contents, but I recall him as promising that when it was finally made public, in 2012, it would entirely change our view of the meeting.

Now the cat was out of the bag, and at yet another symposium on the play, at the Niels Bohr Archive in September 2001, it was announced that the Bohr family had decided to release the letter early. It also turned out that there was not just the one letter but various alternative drafts and notes relating to it. When they were finally published on the web in February 2002, the whole question of the visit was accorded even wider attention in the press than ever before.

The documents seem to me to bear out remarkably well the very detailed reconstruction made of Bohr's attitude by Powers from other sources. The most surprising thing to me in Bohr's first attempt at the letter is its remarkably sharp tone – particularly coming from a man so celebrated for his conciliatoriness:

> I think that I owe it to you to tell you that I am greatly amazed to see how much your memory has deceived you . . .
>
> Personally, I remember every word of our conversations, which took place on a background of extreme sorrow and tension for us here in Denmark. In particular, it made a strong impression both on Margrethe and me, and on everyone at the Institute that the two of you spoke to, that you and Weizsäcker expressed your definite conviction that Germany would win and that it was therefore quite foolish for us to maintain the hope of a different outcome of the war and to be reticent as regards all German offers of cooperation. I also remember quite clearly our conversation in my room at the Institute, where in vague terms you spoke in a manner that could only give me the firm impression that, under your leadership, everything was being done in Germany to develop atomic weapons

and that you said that there was no need to talk about
details since you were completely familiar with them and
had spent the past two years working more or less exclusively
on such preparations. I listened to this without speaking
since [a] great matter for mankind was at issue in which,
despite our personal friendship, we had to be regarded as
representatives of two sides engaged in mortal combat.

It is a revelation to have all this in Bohr's own voice, and I
wish it had been available when I wrote the play. I recognise
that the real Bohr remained much angrier for much longer
than my character, that he claimed to have paid much closer
attention to what Heisenberg said, and that he claimed to
recall it much more clearly.

Does it really modify our view of what Heisenberg said,
though, and of what his intentions were?

Slightly, I think, but not fundamentally. There has never
been any disagreement, for a start, that Heisenberg publicly
told various people at the Institute that Germany was going
to win the war, and that her aims, at any rate in the East,
were justified. Then again, Aage and Rozental were both
already on record as recalling Bohr's saying that Heisenberg
had talked about the military applications of atomic energy.
According to Aage, 'My father was very reticent and expressed
his scepticism because of the great technical difficulties that
had to be overcome, but he had the impression that Heisenberg
thought that the new possibilities could decide the outcome of
the war if the war dragged on.' According to Rozental: 'I can
only remember how excited Bohr was after that conversation
and that he quoted Heisenberg for having said something
like, "You must understand that if 1 am taking part in the
project then it is in the firm belief that it can be done."'

The letter, however, is the first direct confirmation that
Bohr believed he was being urged to accept German 'offers
of co-operation', which is what Weizsäcker suspected he may
have understood Heisenberg to be suggesting. It's not clear
from the letter what Bohr thought this 'co-operation' would
entail, and the recollection may not be entirely at odds with
what Weizsäcker recalls Heisenberg as telling Bohr – that he

ought to establish contact with the staff of the German Embassy for his own safety.

Some of the differences between Bohr's account of the meeting and Heisenberg's are less clear-cut than Bohr's indignation makes them appear. According to Heisenberg, in his memorandum to Jungk, he told Bohr he knew that the use of uranium fission for making weapons was 'in principle possible, but it would require a terrific technical effort, which one can only hope cannot be realised in this war'. Bohr, he said, was shocked, 'obviously assuming that I had intended to convey to him that Germany had made great progress in the direction of manufacturing atomic weapons'. This is not all that different in substance, it seems to me, from what Bohr recalls.

The same is true when Bohr goes on to dispute Heisenberg's interpretation of his reaction:

> That my silence and gravity, as you write in the letter, could be taken as an expression of shock at your reports that it was possible to make an atomic bomb is a quite peculiar misunderstanding, which must be due to the great tension in your own mind. From the day three years earlier when I realised that slow neutrons could only cause fission in Uranium 235 and not 238, it was of course obvious to me that a bomb with certain effect could be produced by separating the uraniums . . . If anything in my behaviour could be interpreted as shock, it did not derive from such reports but rather from the news, as I had to understand it, that Germany was participating vigorously in a race to be the first with atomic weapons.

The difference between the 'shock' that Heisenberg diagnosed and the more dignified 'silence and gravity' that Bohr himself recalled dissolves a little in a later draft of the letter, where Bohr refers to his reaction as 'alarm'. His assertion that he already understood about the possibility of producing a weapon based on fission is moreover a simplification which is not quite supported by his subsequent behaviour. He had in fact up to that moment believed that it was a practical impossibility, because of the difficulty of separating the fissile U-235, and Heisenberg could not tell him why the balance of probability had now changed – because of the German team's realisation that a reactor, if they could get one going, would produce plutonium as an alternative. After Heisenberg's visit, according to Rozental, he was sufficiently shaken by Heisenberg's confidence to go back to the blackboard and rework all his calculations. Even so, he seems to have remained unconvinced when he got his guarded report on the meeting through to Chadwick, his contact with British intelligence, and said: 'Above all I have to the best of my judgment convinced myself that in spite of all future prospects any immediate use of the latest marvellous discoveries of atomic physics is impracticable.'

The real kernel of the apparent disagreement about the meeting emerges only in later drafts of the letter, where Bohr says that 'there was no hint on your part that efforts were being made by German physicists to prevent such an application of atomic science'. This appears to be a rebuttal of some claim made by Heisenberg. The belief that Heisenberg made some such claim seems to be widespread. Professor Holton suggests that my play is 'based in large part on Heisenberg's published claim that for him an impeding moral compunction may have existed about working on atomic energy'.

But nowhere, so far as I know, did Heisenberg ever make the claim that Bohr seems to have attributed to him. There is no mention of it in the memorandum to Jungk. Even in the expanded account of the meeting that he gave in his memoirs he remained extremely cautious:

> I hinted that . . . physicists ought perhaps to ask themselves whether they should work in this field at all . . . An enormous technical effort was needed. Now this, to me, was so important precisely because it gave physicists the possibility of deciding whether or not the construction of atom bombs should be attempted. They could either advise their governments that atom bombs would come too late for use in the present war, and that work on them therefore

detracted from the war effort, or else contend that, with the utmost exertions, it might just be possible to bring them into the conflict. Both views could be put forward with equal conviction . . .

One might think this sounds a quite implausibly judicious rendering of anything he might have said. The fact remains, however, that he is not claiming to have made any efforts to prevent work on weapons. He is not even claiming that up to this point the German team had exercised the option of offering discouraging advice, only that they might at some point if they so chose. In any case, Heisenberg says that Bohr 'was so horrified by the very possibility of producing atomic weapons that he did not follow the rest of my remarks'.

Some reports on the release of the documents have suggested that they refute a claim made by Heisenberg to have offered Bohr a 'deal', whereby the German physicists would discourage their government from proceeding with nuclear weapons if Allied physicists would do likewise. I suppose the implication of Heisenberg's indeterminate phrase 'the physicists' is that this applied to the physicists on both sides, but the only evidence I can find for Heisenberg having made any more definite suggestion than this is in a part of the memorandum to Jungk which is quoted by Powers: 'I then asked Bohr once again if, because of the obvious moral concerns, it would be possible for all physicists to agree among themselves that one should not even attempt work on atomic bombs . . . ' This might perhaps be interpreted as a tentative hint at some possible arrangement, though in the interview he gave to David Irving for *The Virus House* in 1965 he seems to be retreating even from this, and says merely that Bohr 'perhaps sensed that I should prefer it if physicists in the whole world would say: we will not make atom bombs'. The remark to Jungk was not quoted by him in his book, and so presumably not seen by Bohr in 1957. In his letter, in any case, Bohr makes no reference to any such claim, or to having understood any such offer at the time.

There are discrepancies in every other aspect of the evidence relating to this meeting, and it is scarcely surprising that there are some to be found between the two participants' own accounts. In both cases they are attempting to recollect something that happened sixteen years earlier, and their perceptions are inevitably coloured by strong feelings and conflicting loyalties. On the whole, I think, what's surprising is how slight the differences of substance are, and how readily most of them can be understood in the circumstances.

The most remarkable point of agreement, it seems to me now that I have had time to reflect upon it, was missed by everyone who wrote about the letters at the time of their release, myself included: Bohr's confirmation of Heisenberg's claim to have overriden all normal obligations of secrecy. Heisenberg did indicate to him, he agrees, that there was a German atomic programme; that he himself was involved in it; and that he now believed it in principle possible to build atomic weapons.

Whatever Heisenberg was officially licensed or ordered to do in Copenhagen, I cannot believe that it included revealing the existence of one of the most secret research programmes in Germany – least of all to an enemy alien who was known to be in contact with Allied scientists (Bohr was at this point still contributing to the US journal *The Physical Review*), and also to be under observation because of his hostile attitude to Nazism and his extensive help for its victims. Heisenberg must have done this of his own initiative, and he must have been aware that Bohr would pass the information on, if he possibly could, to his contacts in Britain or the US. This, it seems to me, goes a considerable way to supporting the account that Heisenberg subsequently gave of his intentions.

*

The only really clear-cut disagreement between the two accounts is about a circumstantial detail – where the meeting took place. Bohr talks about 'our conversation in my room at the Institute'. Heisenberg, on the other hand, recalls in his memoirs visiting the Bohrs' home in Carlsberg, and finally broaching 'the dangerous subject' on their evening walk. This version is reinforced by what he recalls of his attempt to reconstruct with Bohr the 1941 meeting when he returned to Copenhagen in 1947. He was convinced, he said, that the conversation had taken place during 'a nocturnal walk on Pile Alle', which is very close to Carlsberg, and four kilometres from the Institute. (Bohr at the time, according to Heisenberg, thought it had been in his study – but in his study at home in Carlsberg.)

Bohr himself lends some colour to the Carlsberg version by his remark in the letter that 'every word of our conversation . . . made a strong impression both on Margrethe and me'. It seems highly unlikely that Margrethe would have been present at any of the various meetings in the Institute; I don't think that any of the other participants mention her. Jochen Heisenberg recalls his father showing him the street where he said he had walked with Niels Bohr in 1941, though he can't now remember the name of it, only that it was tree-lined (which Pile Alle is).

There is a secondhand account of the meeting given to Thomas Powers by Ruth Nanda Anshen, Heisenberg's American editor, who said that she was told it by Bohr, and that his assistant Aage Petersen confirmed it. According to Powers, in *Heisenberg's War*, Bohr told Anshen that 'the invitation had cost him much agony – he wanted to sit down to dinner with Heisenberg, but his wife, Margrethe, objected, and Bohr couldn't make up his mind what to do. Finally his assistant Aage Petersen suggested that Bohr should write down his objections to Heisenberg's visit, then read them carefully a day or two later, and decide. This Bohr did; the old friendship seemed to him stronger than the objections, and he told his New York friend that he finally obtained Margrethe's agreement with a solemn promise to discuss only physics with Heisenberg – not politics.'

On the other hand Abraham Pais, Bohr's biographer, after making inquiries among Bohr's surviving colleagues just before his own death in 2000, concluded that Heisenberg had never been to the Bohrs' home. Even Heisenberg's own testimony is not entirely consistent. According to his biographer, David Cassidy, he made an earlier statement in which he 'remembered that his most important talk with Bohr occurred one evening as they strolled along a tree-lined path in the large and secluded Faelledpark, just behind Bohr's Institute'. Weizsäcker, who recalled that he met Heisenberg only ten minutes after the meeting with Bohr was over (the two men had parted company, he said, 'in a friendly way', but Heisenberg had immediately told him: 'I'm afraid it's gone completely wrong') agreed that it had taken place in the open air, but introduced another location altogether – Langelinie, the raised walk beside the harbour, miles from either Carlsberg or the Institute.

*

Some further light on this question was cast, nine months after the release of the Bohr documents, by the emergence of yet another letter. This one was written by Heisenberg, and revealed by Dr Helmut Rechenberg, the director of the Werner Heisenberg Archive in Göttingen.[1] The Heisenberg family, who released it, seem not to have taken in its implications earlier.

It makes no direct reference to the disputed conversation itself, but is a much more reliable guide to the circumstances surrounding it than the accounts we have had so far, because it was written not sixteen years after the event but during the week that Heisenberg was actually there. In fact it's in three sections, dated respectively to three different evenings – Tuesday (16 September, the day after he arrived), Thursday, and Saturday – and it was posted to his family in Leipzig as soon as he got back to Berlin.

The letter clears up one small point of dispute completely. Heisenberg *did* go to the house – and more than once. He also records various visits to the Institute, and the sheer number and variety of meetings that the two men had during the week supports the claim that Heisenberg's chief reason for making the trip was to see Bohr. The conflation of the different

1. In a Heisenberg Centenary Festschrift issued by the Sachsische Akademie der Wissenschaften. The letter was published in 2003 in a collection of his correspondence edited by his daughter Maria Hirsch.

occasions in the participants' memories also probably explains some of the later discrepancies.

The first visit to the Bohrs was late on the Monday evening, as soon as Heisenberg had got off the train from Berlin. The sky, he recorded, was clear and starry, but in the Bohrs' house he found rather darker weather. 'The conversation swiftly turned to the human questions and misfortunes of our time; about the human ones there was spontaneous agreement; on the political questions I found it difficult to cope with the fact that even in a man like Bohr, thoughts, feelings, and hatred cannot be completely separated.'

It is just possible that the fateful conversation occurred at this first meeting, either in the house – where, said Heisenberg, 'later I sat for a long time alone with Bohr' – or later still, after midnight, when Bohr saw him to the tram. But they were accompanied to the tram stop by Hans, one of Bohr's sons, who would surely have remembered and remarked upon it if it had happened then. And if Weizsäcker's recollection is even remotely accurate then the conversation can't have occurred at any point during this first meeting, because he himself arrived in Copenhagen only on the Wednesday.

The most likely occasion was two days later, during Heisenberg's second visit, on the Wednesday evening. (This time there was a young Englishwoman present, who 'decently withdrew' during 'the unavoidable political conversations, in which the role of defending our system of course automatically fell upon me'.) Dr Rechenberg suggests plausibly that Bohr accompanied Heisenberg alone part of the way back to his hotel, where Weizsäcker was waiting for him.

The real surprise of the letters, though, is that Heisenberg was invited back to the Bohrs' home for a *third* time, on the Saturday evening, three days after this (and the conversation can't have occurred during this visit, because this time Weizsäcker was accompanying him). 'It was in many ways particularly nice,' wrote Heisenberg later that same night. 'The conversation turned for a great part of the evening around purely human problems. Bohr read something aloud, I played a Mozart sonata (A major).'

The immediate rupture of the two men's friendship is almost the only aspect of the story which has up to now seemed reasonably unambiguous (I certainly take it for granted in the play). Now even this turns out to be as clouded as everything else.

Rechenberg suggests that it may have been at this farewell meeting that Heisenberg and Weizsäcker urged Bohr to maintain contact with the German Embassy. If so it could have been Bohr's anger at this that coloured his recollection of the earlier conversation. It is in any case clear that the quarrel took the form it did only later, in the recollection of the participants, as they reflected upon it – probably also as the circumstances of the war got worse, as the deepest horrors of the Nazi period were uncovered, and as the actual development of nuclear weapons called into question the two men's participation.

History, in other words, is not what happens when it happens, but what seems to people to have happened when they look back upon it.

*

In 2005 there was another development that changed the historical record on which the play was based – the publication of *Hitlers Bombe*, by the German historian Rainer Karlsch. This, unlike the release of the Bohr and Heisenberg letters, was not occasioned by the play, and its revelations have no direct relevance to its content. They do change its perspective, though, because Karlsch demonstrates that in addition to the two German fission programmes, Heisenberg's and Diebner's, there was a third, about which the historians of the period seem to have known nothing – and that this was into an even more terrifying possibility, fusion, the process involved in a hydrogen bomb.

Fusion can occur only in conditions of intense pressure and heat. These are produced in a hydrogen bomb by a preliminary fission explosion. The two German teams, as we know, never got close to producing a fission bomb, but according to Karlsch some other scientists in the field believed that the necessary conditions could be produced by a particular configuration of conventional explosives.

Karlsch had access to some previously unavailable sources, in Soviet and East German archives. He also found a great deal of other material which must have been available before, but which seems to have been missed by previous investigators, and he shows that fusion research was carried out at various institutions all over Germany. It involved Diebner, who was running a fusion programme in parallel with his known fission programme, and it was coordinated by the SS under the direction of Walter Gerlach. Both Diebner and Gerlach were among the internees at Farm Hall. They were evidently more devious – and more effective – than they emerge from the transcripts. They seem to have kept all knowledge of the fusion programme not only from their interrogators (or they would hardly have been released before the first American hydrogen bomb was tested in 1952), but also from their fellow internees (though one of them, Paul Harteck, may have been supplying them, or attempting to, with enriched uranium).

Karlsch believes that the programme produced a number of weapons that were actually tested, and he quotes disturbing evidence of events which seem to have caused radioactive contamination, and in one case many deaths through radiation sickness. These claims have been intensively discussed by American and British nuclear physicists since the book was published. The consensus of their opinions is that there is no way in which the conditions for fusion could ever have been produced by conventional explosives, however configured, and that the explosives in the tests simply scattered the radioactive components, as in a 'dirty' bomb.

The book does reveal, though, the astonishing lacunae that have persisted in the record of a subject that seemed to have been exhaustively researched. And if Nazi leaders believed, as Karlsch suggests, that the programme was just about to deliver a *Wunderwaffe* that could be launched (on one of Wernher von Braun's rockets) and with one blow stop the Soviet advance on Berlin in its tracks, then it could help to make sense of Germany's apparently self-destructive refusal to surrender when everything was plainly lost. It might also explain the

otherwise inexplicable efforts of the SS to move personnel
and equipment out of Berlin during the last days of the war,
not to the *Alpenfestung*, the 'Alpine redoubt', where a last stand
against the Allies was supposed to be mounted, but to Ohrdruf,
an apparently undefendable small town in Thuringia, whose
only other claim upon history is that it was the site of a
particularly notorious concentration camp. And of at least
one of the supposedly successful tests.

*

But it is really the drafts of Bohr's letter to Heisenberg,
and the letter that Heisenberg sent to his wife, that affect the
record relating to the play, and if I had known about them
before I should have shaped it somewhat differently.

I can't help being moved, though, by the picture that the
new documents give of Bohr drafting and redrafting the
text of the letter over the last five years of his life – and still
never sending it. He was famous for his endless redrafting
of everything he wrote, and here he was trying not only
to satisfy his characteristic concern for the precise nuance,
but also to reconcile that with his equally characteristic
consideration for Heisenberg's feelings. There is a sad parallel
with the account which Professor Hans-Peter Dürr gave, at
the Heisenberg Centenary symposium in Bamberg in 2001,
of Heisenberg's rather similar efforts to understand what had
happened.

Professor Dürr, who worked for many years with
Heisenberg in Göttingen after the war, said that Heisenberg
had continued to love Bohr to the end of his life, and he
recalled his going over the fatal meeting again and again,
trying to work out what had happened. Professor Dürr
offered what seems to me the most plausible commonsense
estimate of Heisenberg's intentions that has yet been advanced.
He thought that Heisenberg had simply wanted to have a
talk. Heisenberg and Bohr had been so close that they could
finish each other's sentences, and he assumed that he would
have only to hint at what was on his mind for Bohr to grasp
the significance of it. What he had entirely failed to grasp

was that the situation had changed, and that Bohr's anger about the German occupation would make the old easy communication entirely impossible.

Whatever was said at the meeting, and whatever Heisenberg's intentions were, there is something profoundly characteristic of the difficulties in human relationships, and profoundly painful, in that picture of the two ageing men, one in Copenhagen and one in Göttingen, puzzling for all those long years over the few brief moments that had clouded if not ended their friendship. It's what their shades do in my play, of course. At least in the play they get together to work it out.

Electrons
1895 Thomson discovers the electron, the extremely light, negatively charged particles orbiting inside the atom which give it its chemical properties.

Quantum Theory
1900 Planck discovers that heat energy is not continuously variable, as classical physics assum There is a smallest common coin in the currency quantum, and all transactions are in multiples o

The Nucleus
1910 Rutherford shows that the electrons orbit around a tiny nucleus, in which almost the entire mass of the atom is concentrated.

Photons
1905 Einstein realises that light, too, has to be understood not only as waves but as quantum particles, later known as photons.

The Quantum Atom.
1913 Bohr realises that quantum theory applies to matter itself. The orbits of the electrons about the nucleus a limited to a number of separate whole number possibilities, so that the atom can exist only in a number of distinct and definite states. (The incomplete so-called 'old quantum theory'.)

Quantum mechanics
1925 Heisenberg abandons electron orbits as unobservable. Max Born finds instead a mathematical formulation terms of matrices for what can be observed - the effects they produce upon the absorption and emission of ligh

Uncertainty
1927 Heisenberg demonstrates that all statements about the movement of a particle are governed by the uncertainty relationship: the more accurately you know its position, the less accurately you know its velocity, an vice versa.

Matter as Waves
1924 De Broglie in Paris suggests that, just as radiation can be treated as particles, so the partic of matter can be treated as a wave formation.

The Wave Equation
1926 Schrödinger finds the mathematical equatio for the wave interpretation, and proves that wave a matrix mechanics are mathematically equivalent.

The Copenhagen Interpretation
1928 Bohr relates Heisenberg's particle theory and Schrödinger's wave theory by the complementarity principl according to which the behaviour of an electron can be understood completely only by descriptions in both wav and particle form. Uncertainty plus complementarity become established as the pillars of the Copenhagen (or 'orthodox') interpretation of quantum mechanics.

Neutrons
1932 Chadwick discovers the neutron - a particle which can be used to explore the nucleus because carries no electrical charge, and can penetrate it undeflected.

Into the Nucleus
1932 Heisenberg opens the new era of nuclear physics by using neutron theory to apply quantum mechanics to the structure of the nucleus.

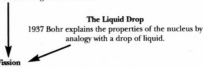

Transmutation

1934 Fermi in Rome bombards uranium with neutrons and produces a radio-active substance which he cannot identify.

Identification

1939 Hahn and Strassmann in Berlin identify the substance produced by Fermi's bombardment as barium, which has only about half the atomic weight of uranium.

The Liquid Drop

1937 Bohr explains the properties of the nucleus by analogy with a drop of liquid.

Fission

1939 Lise Meitner and Frisch in Sweden apply Bohr's liquid drop model to the uranium nucleus, and realise that it has turned into barium under bombardment by splitting into two, with the release of huge quantities of energy.

The Neutrons Multiply

1939 Bohr and Wheeler at Princeton realise that fission also produces free neutrons. These neutrons are moving too fast to fission other nuclei in U-238, the isotope which makes up 99% of natural uranium, and will fission only the nuclei of the U-235 isotope, which constitutes less than 1% of it.

The Chain Reaction

1939 Joliot in Paris and Fermi in New York demonstrate the release of two or more free neutrons with each fission, which proves the possibility of a chain reaction in pure U-235.

The Critical Mass

1940 Frisch and Peierls in Birmingham calculate, wrongly but encouragingly, the minimum amount of U-235 needed to sustain an effective chain reaction.

The War

1939 The Second World War begins, and Germany at once commences research into the military possibilities of fission.

The Manhattan Project

1942 The Allied atomic bomb programme begins.

Germany Defeated

1945 The Allied advance into Germany halts the atomic programme there.

The Reactor

1942 Fermi in Chicago achieves the first self-sustaining chain reaction, in a prototype reactor.

The Bomb

1945 The bomb is successfully tested in July, and in the following month used on Hiroshima.

Democracy

Democracy first premiered at the National Theatre, London, on 9 September 2003 with the following cast:

Günter Guillaume	Conleth Hill
Arno Kretschmann	Steven Pacey
Willy Brandt	Roger Allam
Horst Ehmke	Jonathan Coy
Reinhard Wilke	Paul Gregory
Ulrich Bauhaus	Paul Broughton
Herbert Wehner	David Ryall
Helmut Schmidt	Glyn Grain
Hans-Dietrich Genscher	Nicholas Blane
Günther Nollau	Christopher Ettridge

Director Michael Blakemore
Set Designer Peter J. Davison
Costume Designer Sue Wilmington
Lighting Designer Mark Henderson
Sound Designer Neil Alexander

Characters
in order of speaking

Günter Guillaume
Arno Kretschmann
Willy Brandt
Horst Ehmke
Reinhard Wilke
Ulrich Bauhaus
Herbert Wehner
Helmut Schmidt
Hans-Dietrich Genscher
Günther Nollau

Setting

A complex of levels and spaces; of desks and chairs; of files and papers; also of characters, who mostly remain around the periphery of the action when not actually involved in it, listening or unobtrusively involved in their work.

Act One

Darkness. The expectant murmur of an audience, silenced by a handbell.

Voice   Ladies and gentlemen, I declare the result of the vote to be as follows. Those in favour: 251. Those against: 235.

Applause, excitement. Lights up on **Brandt***.*

I therefore declare . . . I therefore declare, according to article 63 paragraph 2 of the Basic Law, that the proposed Member has received the votes of the majority of Members of the Bundestag. Herr Brandt, do you accept election as Chancellor of the Federal Republic of Germany?

Guillaume (*with* **Brandt** *and* **Kretschmann**)   And for a moment time seemed to hold its breath. The world was about to change in front of our eyes. A Chancellor from the left again, after nearly forty years!

Kretschmann   Twelve years of Hitler. Four years of military government. Twenty years of conservatism and Cold War. And now a hope at last of ending the long stalemate in Europe.

Guillaume   Eleven twenty-two a.m., on the twenty-first of October, 1969 . . .

Brandt   Yes, Herr President. I accept the election.

Guillaume   Congratulations, tears. Willy Brandt had finally done it!

Kretschmann   And you were there in the Bundestag to see it.

Guillaume   An ordinary party worker from a humble district office in Frankfurt, up in Bonn for the day with a spectator's ticket. I shed a tear myself, I have to confess.

Brandt   I am grateful for the confidence that has been reposed in me. I am also a little proud. Almost forty years have passed since any member of the Social Democratic Party of Germany has held this office. Years during which this great party of ours, founded by a poor turner in Leipzig exactly a century ago to bring strength and hope to the oppressed, was brutally crushed by the Nazi state; years during which so many of our members underwent unspeakable sufferings in prisons and concentration camps, and so many of them met a violent death; years during which, after the end of the horror, we played our part, in city after city, in the resurrection of our nation from degradation and destruction, and in the miracle of its rebirth as a stable and decent society. No one can ever belittle what has been achieved in this country by people in all parties and of all persuasions. But on this day the war that Hitler waged, against the peoples of Europe and against so many of our own people, has finally been lost. We have a chance at last to create the Germany glimpsed by that ordinary Leipzig working-man a hundred years ago – a fatherland of love and justice.

Kretschmann (*with* **Guillaume**)   The most extraordinary thing of all, though, is what's happened to *you*. No one back home can believe it.

Guillaume   I can't quite believe it myself.

Kretschmann   You never seriously expected to see Willy Brandt elected Chancellor. Not in your wildest dreams, though, can you have imagined that three weeks later they'd be sending for you to join him.

Ehmke (*with* **Guillaume**)   Ehmke. Horst Ehmke. Willy's chief of staff. Running the Chancellor's office for him. Getting the whole enterprise up and running . . . (*With* **Wilke** *and* **Bauhaus**.) Thank you, Uli. Very helpful. Over there, if you would, on the desk . . .

Wilke   Not over there, if you please, Herr Bauhaus! Not on the desk!

Ehmke (*with* **Guillaume**)   Good of you to come in at such short notice. Listen, we need some fresh blood in here. And not just academics like me who learnt their politics at university. – Over here, Uli! Don't take any notice of Reinhard. – What we need is some of the lads from the party. People who can talk to people. Our colleagues in Frankfurt say you're just the type for us. Done wonders down there. Work all the hours God made. And I'm told you have a lively appreciation of our young friends on the left. All the idealistic young folk who've just put us into power. I believe you would describe them as . . .

Guillaume   Well . . .

Ehmke   Arseholes?

Guillaume   Arseholes.

Ehmke   Right – job for you. – The key to the drinks cupboard, Uli. I'm going to put it in your safe hands. – Chancellor's office. Liaison with the trade unions. Start Jan. 1. Yes?

Guillaume   Chancellor's office? Work there? You mean . . . with Willy?

Ehmke   Department III. Economic, Financial, and Social Policy. Federal salary scale IIa. Accept?

Guillaume   Yes, Herr Ehmke. I accept the appointment.

Kretschmann (*with* **Guillaume**)   So, you and Willy! Under the same roof! Starting your new jobs together!

Guillaume   I joined the party the year Willy became Governing Mayor of Berlin. Our stars are linked!

Kretschmann   You can't help laughing, though. Willy Brandt talks about the achievements of West Germany. Twenty years it's taken West Germany just to get its first mildly leftish government. Not a word about us over there in East Germany. No mention of what *we've* done in those same twenty years. We've actually built the socialist society they used to dream about!

Guillaume   Including the best foreign intelligence service the world has ever seen.

Kretschmann   Mischa Wolf asked me to give you his personal congratulations. This is the biggest feather in his cap yet. Our own man in the Federal Chancellor's office!

Guillaume   As long as Mischa's happy. That's all I want . . . And now here I am at work. A little room all to myself, up in the attics of the Palais Schaumburg. My first morning!

Ehmke (*with* **Guillaume**)   Would you step into my office for a moment, Herr Guillaume? One or two things we need to talk about.

Guillaume   – Personal welcome from the boss, even. Very charming.

Ehmke   Security want some questions answered. You left East Germany thirteen years ago. They've gone very carefully through your career in the West.

Guillaume   – Not a speech of welcome. A security vetting.

Ehmke   Freelance photography . . . photocopy shop . . . party work – it all seems to check out. Lot of unanswered questions, though, about what you were doing in East Berlin before you left.

Guillaume   – I wondered when it was coming. But out of the blue like that! Fright of my life. Somebody's obviously been telling tales. Two solid hours it goes on! Where? When? Who? In the end I have to lose my temper. – Herr Ehmke, escaping from East Germany means that you have to abandon everything you ever had in life. Your home, your friends, your family. For ever. And then you have to start life again from nothing, as nobody. You haven't had to do that, if I may say so. You can't begin to understand what it means. But now comes the bitterest part of all. You find you're going to spend the rest of your life in your new homeland under a black cloud of distrust and suspicion. Thirteen years I've been here! The last nine of them working night and day for this party! – Etcetera, etcetera. I could hear the choke in my voice. And in the end . . .

Ehmke   Sorry. Have to put you through the hoops, though. I have actually been doing a bit of checking with your old boss in Frankfurt. Says he'd put his hand in the fire for you. So what are we wasting each other's time for, Günter? Let's get cracking!

Kretschmann (*with* **Guillaume**)   Your initiation rite.

Guillaume   And now of course he's my friend for life.

Kretschmann   So there you are, in the Palais Schaumburg! What's it *like*? I'm blind, I'm deaf. You're my eyes, you're my ears. I've got to paint the picture for Mischa! You've got to paint it for me.

Guillaume   Towers, casements. A nineteenth-century ironmaster's dream of the aristocratic life. Ghosts, of course. From the Kaiser's time, from the Nazis. From the Occupation. From Adenauer. And every now and then in my office I hear a tiny ticking in the roof timbers.

Kretschmann   Deathwatch beetle. Symbolic, perhaps.

Guillaume   And every now and then Willy hears faint sounds over *his* head. Footsteps. The scrape of a chair.

Kretschmann   That's you?

Guillaume   My office is directly above his.

Kretschmann   His own weevil in the woodwork. Can you hear him?

Guillaume   Not a sound.

Kretschmann   Ear to the floor?

Guillaume   Nothing. He works very quietly. And when I come downstairs . . .

Wilke (*with* **Guillaume**)   Herr Guillaume.

Guillaume   Günter! Please! Call me Günter!

Wilke   Settled in up there, are you, Herr Guillaume?

Guillaume   Snug as a bug, thank you, Reinhard. – Dr Reinhard Wilke. My immediate superior. The dragon guarding Willy's door. – Anything I can do for you, Reinhard? Filing? Copying? Watering the plants?

Wilke   Thank you, Herr Guillaume. We do have secretaries.

Guillaume   Extra pair of hands always available if you need them. No job too big or too small.

Wilke   I'm sure you have plenty to do upstairs.

Guillaume   – He's a little resistant to my charms. I'm not a prof or a doctor of anything, like all the others. – Just popping down to Party Headquarters. Anything you want me to take? Files? Papers?

Wilke   We have messengers, Herr Guillaume.

Guillaume   – I'll wear him down in the end.

Kretschmann   – Take your time. Don't rush it. We've waited thirteen years. We can wait a few more weeks.

Wilke (*with* **Ehmke**)   This Herr Guillaume of yours.

Ehmke   Good man. Just the type we need.

Wilke   Everyone in the office finds him a most surprising appointment.

Ehmke   Reinhard, we need to broaden our horizons in here. You're a lawyer, I'm a professor. We've all got dust in our hearts!

Wilke   But this wretched man has no professional training or experience of any sort whatsoever!

Ehmke   He's a trained photographer.

Wilke   So if we should need a souvenir of the staff outing . . .

Ehmke   He's also got practical experience of management.

Wilke   Management? Of what?

Ehmke   Of a photocopying shop.

Wilke   Horst, can we be serious for a moment?

Ehmke   Times have changed, Reinhard. We have to embrace the whole of society. Photographers. Managers of copy-shops. Women! We have to find some women, Reinhard, and embrace *them*!

Wilke   There's no shortage of secretarial staff. And as I understand it, Horst, they have been embraced by every government since the foundation of the Federal Republic.

Guillaume   – And now – the big day!

Kretschmann   – You met Willy?

Guillaume   – I'd just come downstairs and put my helpful smiling face round the door . . . – Would you like me to slip out for a sandwich, Reinhard? Oh, hello, Horst. How are things on your side of the corridor? Sandwich for you?

Wilke   Herr Guillaume, we must come to some understanding about access to this office . . .

Guillaume   – And suddenly, before he could push me out again . . .

Brandt   Capitalism stands on the brink of the abyss!

Wilke   Herr Chancellor . . .

Ehmke   Willy . . .

Brandt   And what's it doing there? Looking down on the Communists. And this is . . . ?

Ehmke   Herr Guillaume. Our contact with the unions.

Brandt   Oh yes. The owner of the footsteps.

Guillaume   – He knew who I was!

Kretschmann   – He knows who everyone is. Politician's trick.

Brandt   Another member of the Berlin Mafia, I believe. We Berliners have to stick together. They don't like us here in Bonn, Herr Guillaume.

Guillaume   No. When the Wall went up in sixty-one no one in Bonn lifted a finger. The only one who fought for us was you. We're never going to forget that. Particularly those of us who come from the other side. Those of us who know what it's like over there. – Sorry. Live with the wolves – howl with the wolves.

Brandt   East Berliner goes to the Stasi. 'My parrot's escaped.' Stasi: 'We don't do Lost and Found – we're the political police.' 'Exactly. I want it put on record that I don't share the parrot's political views.'

Guillaume   – He loves jokes. Particularly East German ones. – Why do the Stasi go round in threes? One who can read, one who can write . . .

Brandt   . . . And one to keep an eye on the two intellectuals.

Kretschmann   – You'll need fresher ones than that.

Guillaume   – I'm out of touch! Rush me the latest!

Brandt   My speech. Has it been typed?

Wilke   I'll send a messenger across.

Guillaume   *I'll* go! – And here I am! Fetching Willy's speech for him!

Brandt   Guillaume?

Ehmke   Günter Guillaume.

Guillaume   – I think I've caught his eye!

Brandt   He looks like the manager of a pornographic bookshop.

Wilke   He was in fact the manager of a photocopying shop.

Guillaume   Herr Chancellor . . .

Brandt   Thank you. Run off a few copies, will you, Reinhard?

Guillaume   I'll do it, Herr Chancellor.

Brandt   Oh yes. Your speciality.

Guillaume   Virtuoso of the Xerox machine. Confidentiality assured.

Kretschmann   – So we've got our foot in the door. Well done. Mischa's very pleased.

Brandt   I don't think I shall be able to stand very much of Herr Guillaume's company.

Ehmke   Willy, it's not good for you to be surrounded by professors and politicians. You need to keep some contact with the grass roots. You need some ordinary human being around who can tell you what people are thinking.

Brandt   Herr Guillaume, however, carries ordinariness a little too far. Find me someone else, will you, Horst?

Kretschmann (*with* **Guillaume**)   Now, here's how we're going to work. We're living in a goldfish bowl in Bonn – and if one of the goldfish keeps vanishing from sight people are going to notice. So we'll carry on meeting like this, quite openly, in the restaurants and bars where everyone goes. Two old friends having a drink together, where everyone can see us. Nothing passing between us. All photographs or photocopies of documents you'll hand over to your wife. She'll be your courier.

Guillaume   Poor Christel. She was the star of the show, not me!

Kretschmann   She did very well.

Guillaume   A job in the Hesse State Chancellery in Wiesbaden! What more could anyone hope for?

Kretschmann   One in the Federal Chancellery in Bonn.

Guillaume   Pure blind chance, Arno! A gift from the gods!

Kretschmann   Even the gods are working for Mischa.

Guillaume   It was her life, you know.

Kretschmann   Nevertheless, all written material to Christel. What Mischa really wants from you, though, is all the things that politicians and civil servants *don't* write down. The gossip. The background. The smell of things. The way they think. Who's in, who's out. Who's got their knife into whom. Copier and camera, certainly. But, above all, eyes and ears.

Guillaume   Willy keeps saying he wants to open their working procedures to public scrutiny.

Kretschmann   Here's how we can help him. And of course what we want to know about most of all is . . .

Guillaume   The Eastern Policy.

Kretschmann   The Eastern Policy. Any scrap of information that helps us judge his intentions towards the socialist block. Reconciliation, he says. Peace. But can we trust him? Is he really going to risk everything on such a gamble? 'Small steps', he says. How small? As small as the space he gives it in his speeches, slipped in below security and a lot of pious platitudes about 'daring more democracy'?

Brandt   – It was the historical achievement of my predecessors in this office to establish an understanding between Germany and its former enemies in the West. This understanding remains the basis of our political life and the guarantee of our security. But the division of the world into two great power blocs has torn Europe apart. It has split our country and our capital, and undermined our relationship with the peoples to the East of us. Our reconciliation with them is, as we all know, especially difficult. And yet it is as essential for peace as our reconciliation with the West.

Kretschmann   But will he really pay the price, when he comes right down to it? Is he really going to persuade people here to take their head out of the sand at last and recognise that we exist? You and me? The other Germany? Will he pay the final bill for the war: a quarter of Germany's lands lost to Poland and Russia – another quarter, us seceded and free. Half the nation, gone for ever!

Brandt   – Those who have been separated from their families, those whose homeland has been taken, will never forget what they have lost, and we can only try to understand and respect their grief.

Kretschmann   Twelve million people who have taken refuge here will never forgive him. Can any democratic politician simply write off a fifth of the population? He chooses his words so carefully. What do they mean?

Brandt   – Even if it is true that two separate states exist in Germany they can never be foreign to each other. We are bound by our language and our history, by our glory and our woe. We have even now common tasks and common responsibilities: for the peace between ourselves and for peace in Europe. Our unity is gone, and there is no way back. Step by step we must seek to ease the pain of separation. We must draw a line under the evils of the past. This government, then, will venture to open direct negotiations with Moscow, with Warsaw, and with East Berlin . . .

Kretschmann   But can we really trust him?

Guillaume   You can't help trusting him. When you're there in the audience. You look up at him – and there he is looking straight back at you. You personally. Talking to you alone. One human being to another.

Brandt – Dear friends, we must be at one with our neighbours. With all our neighbours – in the East just as much as in the West, within the German lands just as much as without. We must at last be reconciled.

Kretschmann   And then when you remember him in his Berlin days. When you think of all his efforts to stop West Berlin being reunited with the East. When he trots out his ancient East German jokes . . . Has he really changed? Or has he simply noticed that the young people in West Germany are all suddenly turning against capitalism and militarism? That the world is going our way? What does he say in private? In the office. Talking to his own people.

Brandt (*with* **Ehmke**, **Wilke** *and* **Guillaume**)   Can we trust them, though, Horst? When you look at their record. When you think of their total cynicism. What would people here say if they knew how East Germany tries to balance its trade deficit with us?

Wilke   I believe we may be about to venture onto rather sensitive ground here. Herr Guillaume . . .

Guillaume   Going, going!

Ehmke   No, let's try it on him. Ordinary voter. Our man in the street. Günter, this is something our new friends over there in the East don't want you to know about, for some strange reason. They have to find something to export to us. What's their one successful industry? The manufacture of political prisoners. So that's what they sell us. They arrest as many as they need, and we buy them out. A thousand or so a year at 40,000 Deutschmarks a head. Oh, and they also charge us for letting people out to be reunited with their families. So what do you think, Günter? Can we trust these new friends of ours?

Guillaume   – Yes? No? What do I say? Which one of me's going to answer?

Kretschmann − I leave it to you, Günter.

Guillaume − Leave it to which of me?

Brandt A difficult decision, evidently.

Guillaume Half of me wants to say one thing. Half of me wants to say another.

Brandt The position of the electorate as a whole on almost everything.

Ehmke I told you, Willy! Our man in the street!

Guillaume (*with* **Kretschmann**) *Do* we sell them political prisoners, though? Do we charge for family reunions?

Kretschmann Never mind about traitors and dissidents. What's worrying us now is the effect Willy's having on the rest of our people.

Wilke (*with* **Ehmke**) His visit to East Germany.

Brandt − The most moving day of my life.

Wilke It starts as soon as his special train crosses the border.

Kretschmann Suddenly there he is amongst us. The first West German leader ever to set foot on East German soil.

Wilke Suddenly there it is all around us. The other Germany. The Germany we've never recognised. The Germany that doesn't exist.

Kretschmann Our people have never seen anything like it before. A living, breathing West German leader!

Wilke It's never happened before! In every town and village along the line − people with their hands outstretched towards him, people waving tablecloths and bedsheets. Armed police everywhere with orders to stop any demonstrations, but there's nothing they can do.

Kretschmann   This is why we need to make up our minds about Willy so urgently. Because we can't hold the lid on all this much longer.

Wilke   He gets to Erfurt for his meeting with his East German counterpart and they break through the police lines outside his hotel.

Kretschmann   It's terrifying, Günter.

Wilke   'Willy! Willy!' they shout. 'Come to the window!'

Kretschmann   There's only one person who can control them.

Wilke   'Willy! Willy!' they chant. 'The window!' He comes to the window . . .

Kretschmann   He looks down on all those upturned faces.

Wilke   What can he say that won't pour petrol onto the flames?

Brandt *gestures.*

Wilke   Silence. One of the greatest speeches of his career. Not a word. Just that one little gesture. That one characteristic little gesture.

Ehmke   I've seen him make it in Cabinet.

Wilke   'Calm down, calm down.'

Ehmke   Willy the peacemaker.

Wilke   A silent speech to a non-existent nation – and each person in the crowd feels he's being spoken to like a human being. Spoken to personally. One small gesture.

Ehmke   'Easy now! Easy does it!'

Wilke   But everyone understands another meaning altogether.

Ehmke   'Patience, patience. The time will come.'

Kretschmann   We're taking a huge risk here. Every word and gesture of Willy's raises the stakes. Every word and gesture of ours raises them again. He's going to sign treaties with Moscow, with Warsaw, with us. But can he get them through the Bundestag?

Guillaume   Majority of twelve.

Kretschmann   Twelve, yes. But only if the coalition holds together. It's all very well for Willy to cobble a government together by making a coalition with the Liberals, but how does he keep them in it?

Wehner (*with* **Brandt**, **Ehmke** *and* **Guillaume**)   Only thirty of them in the House to start with – and half of them don't want the Eastern treaties at any price.

Kretschmann   – This is the man who's got to make the coalition work?

Guillaume   – Herbert Wehner. Willy's party leader in the Bundestag.

Wehner   Three of them definitely going over. According to my private information. Three of them who find even desertion to the Christian Democrats preferable to the Eastern treaties.

Kretschmann   – Three of them going? Only take another three and the treaties are dead in the water. The whole Eastern Policy will have vanished like the morning mist.

Wehner   My sources tell me there's three more tender souls examining their consciences. Or the size of the offers they've had.

Kretschmann   – You're there? In the room with them?

Guillaume   – They've stopped noticing me.

Kretschmann   – So what does Willy say?

Guillaume   – Nothing. He won't look at Uncle Herbert. Uncle Herbert won't look at him. Long silences while Uncle sucks his pipe and rolls his thick wet lower lip.

Kretschmann   – 'Uncle Herbert.' They call Wehner that to his face?

Guillaume   – They don't dare. One look at that face and you can't say anything. It's like eating a persimmon. Your mouth dries. He appears on television and all the cats in Germany run under the sofa.

Wehner   Any fool could have seen this coming. We had a good stable coalition with the Christian Democrats.

Ehmke   As junior partners! Tied to a party that totally rejects any accommodation with the East!

Wehner   We were learning to govern. We're still learning. The party's not ready for office yet. But we pick up a few more votes, and what happens? Without consulting anyone our great captain cuts the tow and lashes us to the Liberals instead. To a leaking old tub of a party that's sinking in front of our eyes. We all knew this government wouldn't last for six months. So then what happens? Fresh elections? The Liberals drop one more point at the polls and they're out of the Bundestag altogether. Then we haven't got a coalition at all.

Guillaume   – You're getting all this? The man who's responsible for keeping the coalition going – and he's against it.

Ehmke   Herbert treats the party like a china teacup that's too precious ever to drink tea out of.

Wehner   Coalitions come and go. Parties remain. A coalition has no roots and no loyalties. A party has members and funds, offices and officers, patronage and punishments. We know we can rely on the loyalty of Herr Guillaume here because we know he's devoted his life to the party – and we know he's going to go on devoting his life to it because his job depends on it. And if any of our lads down there in the parliamentary party begin examining their consciences I'll begin examining their records.

Guillaume – He's got files on all of them.

Wehner I'll get Karl after them. They usually see sense.

Kretschmann – Karl Tromsdorf?

Guillaume – His private security service.

Kretschmann – A highly reliable one. Learnt his trade with us. Old double agent.

Wehner We've told the world we're going to 'dare more democracy.' Whatever that means. Let me tell you what I've learnt from bitter experience about democracy. The more of it you dare, the tighter the grip you have to keep on it. Not something that Number One wants to know about. He likes to look down at the end of a hard day's work and see two clean hands folded on the desk in front of him. But if the plumbing needs fixing someone's got to put their hands down the toilet. Never for one moment do I forget what finished representative government in this country in the thirties. Unstable coalitions, collapsing one after another like soap bubbles. It could happen again. Parliamentary democracy in Germany is still in its infancy. Without two strong legs to stand on it will go down to its enemies. One of those legs, whether we like it or not, is the Christian Democratic Party. The other one is this party of ours. Slowly, slowly, in these last twenty years, we've persuaded the electors to trust us. And now we've put our future into the hands of a dwindling band of dilettantes over whom we have no control at all. The Liberals. The name alone makes my blood run cold.

Kretschmann – Old Communist himself, of course, Wehner. What would Willy's party do without us?

Brandt (*with* **Ehmke**) He's never forgiven me for becoming Chancellor. Too spiritually disfigured to show his own face, because every cat in Germany would be up the curtains, and hates anyone who isn't. The puppetmaster who's jealous of his own puppets. He wanted to keep a Christian Democrat in the Palais Schaumburg just to keep me out of it. An old Nazi! But then he knew how to pull his strings. What a pair. The old Communist pulling the strings. The old Nazi dancing on the end of them.

Ehmke   Discipline, Willy. That's what Uncle craves. Someone to take the stick to him. That's what maddens him about you, Willy. You won't take the stick to him. And whatever you think about him, he's given his heart and soul to this party.

Brandt   He gave his heart and soul to the Communist Party. He also gave all his comrades away to the Russian secret police.

Ehmke   He's still tormented by it.

Brandt   He's still as thick as thieves with his old mates in East Berlin.

Ehmke   They've never forgiven him. They hate him.

Brandt   They understand each other, though.

Guillaume   – Do they?

Kretschmann   – Of course.

Ehmke   Anyway, he's a sentimental old thing, underneath it all. The night you were elected he threw his arms round you.

Brandt   With all the grace of someone's maiden aunt making a drunken lunge at the postman.

Ehmke   He travels all over Germany visiting sick and dying party members.

Brandt   Sits on their beds praying over them. First he's a Communist, now he's a religious maniac.

Ehmke   Just as well there's no one can hear what you're like when you're like this.

Brandt   Only Herr Guillaume.

Ehmke   Oh – still here, Günter?

Brandt   How does Uncle know so precisely when people are dying, Herr Guillaume? Because, even if you're not dying when he arrives, after half-an-hour of his company you are.

Ehmke   Come on, Willy. These things get back to him.

Brandt   It's the only legal form of euthanasia.

Kretschmann   – I think you were a little soft on Willy when you started this job. What did I tell you, though? Wehner's not the only one with another side to him.

Guillaume   – No. Then there's Helmut.

Schmidt (*with* **Wehner**)   I revere Willy. You know I do. I always have. He's my political idol. I'd put my hand in the fire for him.

Kretschmann   – Helmut Schmidt. The heir to Willy's throne.

Schmidt   But his attitude to you is frankly ridiculous. Our majority's fast approaching zero. He knows he can't keep the party together without you.

Wehner   He also knows we can't get re-elected without him.

Schmidt   We all need each other! It's we three who made this party electable! You and Willy and I. We dumped the Marxism. We fought and fought. The three of us together. The Three Musketeers of modern socialism! I was so proud to be one of them!

Kretschmann   – Crown Prince Helmut. Waiting in the wings.

Guillaume   – And waiting there for ever. He's only five years younger than Willy. Unless Willy gets run over by a tram he'll be too old to inherit. That's his tragedy. That's what makes him so edgy. That and his thyroid. He can't eat. He's living on ice-cream and Coca-cola.

Kretschmann   – Ice-cream, Coca-cola, and the hope of a runaway tram.

Schmidt   Willy always seems to be closeted with Horst Ehmke these days.

Wehner   Herr Ehmke has a talent that some of the rest of us lack: he appreciates the great man's jokes.

Schmidt   Most of them are about you, of course. You've heard the one about you and the Virgin Mary?

Wehner   Yes. Thank you.

Schmidt   Meanwhile I have to sit there in Cabinet each week and watch Willy let everything we fought for slip through his fingers. He won't exercise any control! Won't or can't. He claims to be interested in defence, but he won't give me any support in preserving the department's budget! He sits there saying nothing while Karl Schiller lectures us by the hour on economics. It's like being back in college. All those long silences of Willy's! All those compromises, all that indecision. Anything to avoid confrontation or conflict. (*With* **Brandt**.) So, Willy, yes or no? This draft or that draft? My proposal or Karl Schiller's proposal?

Brandt   Let's talk about it. See if we can't find a solution that keeps everyone happy.

Schmidt   You *can't* keep everyone happy, Willy! Not if you're running a government! We've got to come to a decision!

Brandt   Thank you, Helmut. What do the rest of us feel . . . ?

Wehner (*with* **Schmidt**)   The great peacemaker.

Schmidt   And I honour him for it, like the rest of the world. If only he wouldn't do it in private as well. I'm not the most patient of men, I accept that. But to sit there in Cabinet and *know* that I have the answer to a problem – and then to watch Willy piddle it away – it's more than flesh and blood can bear!

Wehner   And then suddenly, out of nowhere, some great gesture. Rushes us all into a new coalition without a word to any of us. All very fine, this wonderful spontaneity of his. But spontaneity's like democracy – it needs to be kept firmly under control . . . Can we help you, Herr Guillaume?

Guillaume   Sorry. Just looking for something. Don't mind me.

Schmidt   No, hand in the fire for him, it goes without saying. Hand in the fire.

Kretschmann   – The old Communist and the old Wehrmacht officer. Both yearning for long-forgotten discipline.

Guillaume   – Funny sort of discipline they practise, though. All they do is niggle away behind Willy's back.

Wehner (*with* **Ehmke** *and* **Guillaume**)   The great man at home again last night, I gather, to all his fashionable friends. Camelot-on-the-Rhine, by all accounts.

Ehmke   You should have been there.

Wehner   Curious, isn't it. Scarcely have we got the grimy old cloth cap off this party's head and wrenched the oily spanner out of its hands than the big chief's got us all into white tie and tails, drinking champagne out of actresses' slippers. No wonder they all love him. All the champagne-growers, at any rate. All the firms that rent out evening dress.

Schmidt (*with* **Wilke** *and* **Guillaume**)   Berliners! Not one of them who knows the value of money! We give them three billion marks a year to keep the city going, so they chuck it

around as if it came out of the taps. And now of course
Willy's letting them take over the whole government. It's
like some kind of infestation!

Wilke   Even got them in here. Union business, Herr
Guillaume?

Guillaume   Party business.

Wilke   Oh, yes, you've been promoted.

Schmidt   Not that Willy's even a real Berliner. He was
born in Lübeck! So of course he has to be more Berlinish
than all the rest of them.

Ehmke (*with* **Brandt** *and* **Guillaume**)   The problem with
Uncle is very simple. He doesn't like you and you don't like
him. The problem with Helmut is more complex. He loves
you – and you don't love him back. He's like a sixth-former
with a crush on the teacher. So he has to keep proving to
her how much cleverer than her he is.

Wehner (*with* **Schmidt** *and* **Guillaume**)   Horst Ehmke
closeted away with Number One again.

Schmidt   He's rapidly becoming Willy's Lord High
Chamberlain. We're all going to end up taking our orders
from him.

Wehner   He's certainly stepped in *your* light.

Ehmke (*with* **Brandt** *and* **Guillaume**)   Willy, what you
need to do with both of them is to make them feel secure
and appreciated. And the way to do that, Willy, if I may put
it plainly, is to give them both the most colossal boot up the
backside.

Guillaume   – And then underneath it all, gnawing away
like rats at the foundations of the whole enterprise – the new
left.

Genscher (*with* **Brandt**, **Ehmke**, **Nollau** *and*
Guillaume)   This is our Achilles heel. People look at the
government and what do they see? A lot of long-haired

radicals from the universities. People didn't like them when they were rampaging round the streets in '68, and they don't like them now.

Guillaume   – Genscher. Minister of the Interior. He's the one who's got to control the demonstrations. He's the one who's got to deal with the terrorists.

Genscher   Every time people turn on the television – yet more violence by the left. They've held up a bank. They've murdered a judge.

Ehmke   That's Baader-Meinhof! The Red Army Fraction! Nothing to do with our lot! Our lot wouldn't put their thumb on a bedbug!

Genscher   The left's the left. As far as most people are concerned.

Brandt   It was the young radicals who put us in office.

Ehmke   We shove the old left off the raft before it finally sinks under their weight, and as soon as the new left see it's afloat they all scramble aboard and sink it again.

Genscher   Then the next item on the news is the Chancellor in East Germany having some kind of love-in with the Communists.

Ehmke   The Communists? What have the Communists got to do with the left?

Genscher   The left's the left! In any case Herr Nollau tells me that East Berlin is giving active support to the terrorists.

Nollau   We believe that the East German Ministry of State Security is offering them refuge and training facilities. We have evidence that it has been providing passage to the Fatah camps in Syria and South Yemen.

Guillaume   – Günther Nollau. The head of West German Security . . . *Do* we support the terrorists?

Kretschmann – Another of our defectors, Herr Nollau. Inspired choice for the job. Wanted for murder when he did his bunk.

Nollau   Nor, I may say, have the present negotiations with East Germany led to any abatement in the Ministry's campaign of espionage against us. We believe that East Berlin currently has something like a thousand agents active here.

Kretschmann – Keep very still, Günter!

Guillaume – They've forgotten about me. I'm the hatstand in the corner.

Nollau   There are almost certainly several hundred agents operating in government offices as this very moment . . . I understood this to be a private meeting.

Ehmke   Herr Guillaume. Works upstairs. One of us. Hates the left.

Brandt   Anyway, we no doubt have similar arrangements over there. Why not? We all speak the same language. I see the whole of Germany, East and West, as one gigantic glass palace.

Genscher   We must take security issues rather more seriously, Herr Chancellor. One more spy scandal and it could be the finish of this government.

Kretschmann (*with* **Guillaume**)   It could, Günter, it could. Keep very, very still under all those hats and coat.

Guillaume   In fact what finishes this government may well be Genscher.

Kretschmann   Genscher?

Guillaume   Liberal.

Kretschmann   Perfectly tame one.

Guillaume   Some of the more reactionary members of the Liberal Party don't think so. They want to make him party leader. The first thing he'd do would be to abandon Willy and go into coalition with the Christian Democrats.

Wehner (*with* **Nollau** *and* **Guillaume**)   The Foreign Ministry. That's what his pay-off would be. That's what he's got his eye on, and he knows Willy's never going to let him near it. Trips to Paris and New York. Interviewed every time he steps off a plane. If he appears on television often enough he thinks one or two of the more observant voters might start to notice his existence.

Guillaume   – Wehner and Nollau.

Kretschmann   – Always been as thick as thieves. Both from Dresden, of course.

Wehner   So, what's the word inside the Liberal Party? Is Herr Genscher taking over or isn't he?

Nollau   I've no idea. I'm not a Liberal.

Wehner   He's your Minister.

Nollau   You want me to spy on my own Minister?

Wehner   What's wrong with that? Equality before the law. Just as long as Willy doesn't know. Clean hands! And don't forget, you're not just an official of the government – you're also a member of the party. You have a duty to uphold the party's interests. Anything you get hold of, on Genscher or anyone else – let me know. We have to stick together, you and I. Two simple Saxons trying to survive in a world full of cocksure Bavarians and devious Rhinelanders. Two babes in the wood from Dresden, with a wolf from Berlin lurking behind every bush.

Nollau   I'm very grateful for everything you've done for me . . .

Wehner   So keep me informed.

Nollau   I always do.

Wehner   First. Yes?

Kretschmann (*with* **Guillaume**)   West Germany,
Günter! The Federal Republic! Not just one so-called
democracy – eleven separate democracies tied up in a
federation like ferrets in a bag! Eleven separate talking-shops
all talking at the same time, with the Federal talking-shop in
Bonn trying to make itself heard above the rest of them!
Three political parties, in and out of bed with each other
like drunken intellectuals, fifteen warring Cabinet Ministers
in Bonn alone, and sixty million separate egos. All making
deals with each other and breaking them. All looking round
at every moment to see the expression on everyone else's
face. All trying to guess which way everyone else will jump.
All out for themselves, and all totally dependent on everyone else. Not one Germany. Sixty million separate
Germanies. The tower of Babel! With not just one weevil in
the rafters, but weevils in every timber in the house. We have
our defects in the East, God knows we do. But at least we all
speak with one single voice. We all sing the one same song.
This is our strength. This is why we shall endure when this
whole ramshackle structure finally comes tumbling down.

Nollau (*with* **Wehner**)   One thing that might interest
you . . .

Guillaume   – Nollau to see Wehner this time. Something
about Genscher?

Kretschmann   – Leave it, Günter! Not twice running!

Guillaume   – Hatstand. No one notices it.

Kretschmann   – Hatstand keeps walking into the room
and they will.

Nollau   The security services are looking for a sleeper.
Someone inside our own party. I thought you might wish to
institute a few discreet inquiries of your own.

Wehner   A sleeper? What do we know about him?

Nollau   Not much. Planted at least a dozen years ago.
That was when we intercepted a radio transmission to him.

Ended with a personal message. Birthday greetings and congratulations on the arrival of his second son.

Wehner   Two sons? That's all we know?

Nollau   Also his name begins with G.

Guillaume   – Don't worry, Arno! The sky's clear!

Kretschmann   – A clear sky – that's just what the thunderbolt falls out of.

Ehmke (*with* **Guillaume**)   Could I have a private word, please, Günter?

Kretschmann   – I knew it!

Guillaume   – Hold on. Keep calm.

Ehmke   Party Conference next week in Saarbrücken. I'm setting up a temporary office for the Chancellor. You'll be running it. All right?

Guillaume   Of course. Anything. Always happy.

Ehmke   Going to be short-staffed, I'm afraid – you'll have to look after liaison with the security services. Sorry about that.

Guillaume   No – I've always had a secret interest in security. – You see? Just tossing another hat on the poor old hatstand.

Kretschmann   – Unbelievable. Only it's making me even more nervous.

Ehmke   Consolation prize, though, Günter. Egon Bahr's going to be negotiating in Moscow. You can have the use of his official car and chauffeur.

Kretschmann (*with* **Guillaume**)   Something's going to go wrong somewhere.

Guillaume   Don't worry! Willy's got the first treaty signed.

Kretschmann   Still Poland to go before he gets to us.

Guillaume   The Soviet one was the hard one. And it's the one that unlocks the door to all the others.

Kretschmann   It's not ratified yet. His majority's down to four. And if we lost Willy for any reason. A tram . . . a bus . . . a thunderbolt . . . A scandal of some sort . . . His private life, for instance. All these women he has . . .

Guillaume   Secretaries, journalists. Nothing serious these days. I've given you the list.

Kretschmann   If it got out, though . . .

Guillaume   Everyone knows!

Kretschmann   But doesn't say.

Guillaume   *We're* not going to mention it. Are we?

Kretschmann   Not us. We're trying to keep him on his feet. If ever Willy *did* lose his shine, though, Wehner would have him out like a bad tooth. Half a chance, that's all he and Helmut need . . .

Brandt (*with* **Schmidt**, **Wilke**, **Ehmke**, **Guillaume** *and* **Bauhaus**)   Uli!

Bauhaus   Chief?

Brandt   Bottles, glasses!

Kretschmann   – Drinking. He hasn't started drinking again?

Guillaume   – Not spirits this time. Only wine. They all do. By the bucket. Just wine, though, always wine. And always red, for some reason.

Kretschmann   – The last traces of their socialism.

Guillaume   – End of the working day they all get together with glasses in their hands. Relax. Forget their differences. Even Helmut. Even Wehner. And for an hour or two all our problems are behind us. A little circle of upturned faces, and after all that listening Willy talks at last.

Brandt   1945. Every city in Germany reduced to rubble. So what did we start rebuilding with? The rubble. It was all we had. Lines of women patiently sorting the usable bricks out one by one. Passing them from hand to hand, cleaning them, storing them . . . Who knows what buildings those bricks had been part of? The cellars of the local SS . . . the factories where the slave labourers suffered and died . . . They cleaned up the bricks as best they could, and out of them we built the plain straightforward cities we all live in today. It was the same with the people. Who were the people we rebuilt our shattered society with? Some of them were survivors of the camps and prisons. Some of them were exiles. But most of them had been the ordinary citizens of the Reich. They were our building materials. We had no other. And with those people we built the plain straightforward institutions of the society we're all part of. Now what confronts us? Two Germanies, broken apart like the old shattered masonry. This is the material out of which we have to build the world we're going to be living in tomorrow. This is the only material we possess – the two Germanies as they actually are. Riddled with doubts and suspicions on both sides. If the building we're creating is going to stay up, we have to make sure that this fragile stuff will bear the load we're placing upon it. We have somehow to find ways for the doubtful and the fearful on both sides to accept what we're doing.

Schmidt   Willy's dream. Life without conflict.

Brandt   Conflict resolved.

Schmidt   Irreconcilables reconciled.

Brandt   Even the irreconcilables inside our own party.

Ehmke   Now there's a really solemn thought.

Brandt   One more solemn thought to carry with you into the night, gentlemen, as you go back to your pining wives and children, if you can still remember where they live: under capitalism man is oppressed by man – under socialism it's the other way round . . . Clear the desk, will you, Uli. Work to be done.

Guillaume (*to* **Bauhaus**)   I'll help you.

Schmidt   Yes, where *do* our wives and children live . . . ?

Brandt   East Berlin sends one of its functionaries to the West to report back on the death of capitalism. He goes to London, he goes to Paris, he goes to New York. Gets back to East Berlin. 'It's a beautiful death,' he says.

Wilke   Didn't try Bonn, I notice . . .

Wilke *and* **Schmidt** *go.*

Wehner   I wonder if Number One has ever asked Herr Bauhaus what he feels about being used as his butler and bottlewasher.

Brandt   Uli?

Ehmke   He's your bodyguard, Willy.

Brandt   No one's going to shoot me at this time of night.

Bauhaus   If there's nothing else, Chief . . .

Brandt   Wife and children, Uli.

Bauhaus   I'll be waiting with the car. (*Goes.*)

Ehmke   Does he *have* a wife and children, Willy?

Wehner   He probably can't remember any more.

Ehmke   Or Günter. Does *he*? You don't know, do you, Willy. You've never talked to him.

Brandt   I asked you to get rid of Herr Guillaume.

Ehmke   Talk to him, Willy. He's devoted to you. All those upturned faces gazing at you adoringly from the hall – he's one of them. Talk to him. Find out what they're thinking down there.

Brandt   He always reminds me of another Berlin speciality: meatballs cooked in fat. Very leaden and very greasy.

Wehner (*to* **Guillaume**)   Wives and children, yes . . . Grabert. G. Grabert would fit the bill. Horst Grabert. He a family man? You know all about us, Herr Guillaume. Does Horst Grabert have any children?

Guillaume   A boy and a girl. Why?

Wehner   Idle curiosity. Like to keep abreast of my colleagues' personal lives. Gaus. How about Herr Gaus?

Guillaume   Günter Gaus? One daughter.

Wehner   One daughter? Less trouble, perhaps, than a couple of sons . . . (*Goes.*)

Ehmke (*to* **Brandt**)   Talk to him!

Kretschmann   – So, now you're alone with him.

Brandt   No wife to go home to, then, Herr Guillaume? No children?

Guillaume   I'll wait till you've finished, thank you, Herr Chancellor. Make sure the spoons are locked up for the night.

Brandt   Though I gather you still find time to make yourself agreeable to one or two of the secretaries.

Guillaume   Oh . . . Just trying to be friendly . . .

Brandt   The Frankfurt party?

Guillaume   Me? Yes, I was.

Brandt   Know this man? Standing for party office down there.

Guillaume   Communist.

Brandt   Thank you. Helpful to know . . .

Guillaume   A wife, yes. I have a wife. You asked.

Brandt   In the same line of business as yourself, I believe?

Guillaume   She's transferred from Wiesbaden. We've found a flat in Bonn at last . . . You know there's something you and I have got in common, Herr Chancellor? You have a son called Peter – I have a son called Pierre. Fourteen. Somewhat different political views, though. Great lefty, your Peter, I know. Every time you open the newspaper – there he is, out on the streets again with his chums, protesting against his Dad's government. You must feel very . . . very proud of him . . . Whereas my Pierre is a tremendous fan of yours. Plastered 'Vote Willy' stickers all over the house.

Brandt   In bed by now. You never see him.

Guillaume   On Sundays. I try to make it up to him then. Our Sunday morning ritual – we jump in the car and drive out to the airport to fetch the papers. Wander round the airport together. Chat. I don't know what about. Watch the planes taking off. Imagine we're on one of them. Lifting away through the clouds. Up into the sunlight. Where are we going? No idea. Somewhere warm. Somewhere where the skies are blue and life is simple.

Brandt   Midnight, and a rather different Herr Guillaume begins to emerge. Something of a romantic, this one.

Guillaume   Another thing we have in common, Herr Chancellor.

Brandt   So, every Sunday morning. You and Pierre.

Guillaume   That's what I live for. Sunday mornings. Fetching the papers with Pierre.

Kretschmann   – You're not falling for him, like all the others?

Guillaume   – He listens! That's his trick. He listens to what other people say. Anyway, how can you see into someone's heart if you don't fall a little in love with them? And suddenly, out of nowhere, I hear my own voice speaking. – Herr Chancellor, you asked me once if you could trust them. The East Germans . . .

Brandt   You were in two minds, I recall.

Guillaume   – Midnight. No one but him and me, talking quietly together . . . – We have to trust each other, Herr Chancellor. There's no other way we can live.

Brandt   Thank you.

Guillaume   – Yes?

Kretschmann   – If you got away with it.

Guillaume   – I trusted him. And he trusts me. Then two days later . . . it's over.

Kretschmann   – Over? What's over?

Guillaume   – Everything! The whole project! The whole adventure!

Ehmke (*with* **Wilke** *and* **Guillaume**)   We're out! We're done for! There's no way we can win! Motion of no confidence, and five of our own people are going to rat!

Wilke   I believe Herr Wehner has turned one of them round again.

Ehmke   We're still going to lose. Out goes Willy. Out go all of us. In comes Barzel. In come the Christian Democrats.

Guillaume   Out go the Eastern treaties.

Ehmke   It's a squalid little procedural swindle. There are people out on the streets right the way across Germany.

Schmidt (*with* **Wehner** *and* **Guillaume**)   It was an accident waiting to happen. You set up a coalition like an egg balanced on the end of a billiard cue and sooner or later you have broken egg over the carpet. Not something that either of us would wish to remind Willy of now, but I have to say to you privately that this is precisely what you and I saw coming. I assume you've got one or two cards up your sleeve?

Wehner   Everyone waits for kind Uncle Herbert to do one of his party tricks. Even Number One. Just so long as I do it by magic. Just so long as he doesn't have to see the hidden springs and levers.

Guillaume   – Not for me to tell my masters what to do. But you said Mischa wanted me to use my political judgement, yes? My understanding of human psychology? I'll give it you in one word.

Schmidt   Money?

Guillaume   – Money.

Wehner   Is that what they call the stuff?

Guillaume   – Crisp crackling Deutschmarks.

Schmidt   You'd only need to pay two or three of that lot to abstain.

Guillaume   – Nearly two hundred and fifty of them to choose from.

Kretschmann   – Günter, you're becoming a little cynical.

Guillaume   – Why not, though? Mischa's done it before. What's wrong? We buy, we sell. Sell political prisoners – buy politicians. What's the difference?

Kretschmann   – Sixteen years of living in this place.

Guillaume   – *Do* we sell political prisoners?

Wehner   Clean hands. An interesting obsession for the man who claims to represent this country's manual workers.

Ehmke (*with* **Schmidt**, **Wehner**, **Wilke**, **Nollau**, **Genscher**, **Guillaume** *and* **Bauhaus**)   I've started shredding the files. I want every file of ours out of the office by the time Barzel moves in.

Wilke   He's already sent us the timetable. Fourteen hundred – result of the vote . . .

Schmidt   And it's late, it's late. What's the trouble? What's the hold-up?

Wilke   Fifteen hundred – he's appointed Chancellor; sixteen hundred – sworn in; seventeen hundred – moves into the Palais Schaumburg.

Ehmke (*to* **Guillaume**)   Here, Günter – grab. Dynamite. Handle them with your eyes shut.

Genscher   Here they come, here they come!

Nollau   We've lost.

Wehner   Wait.

Nollau   I happen to know.

Wehner   Wait, wait.

Nollau   I have my sources . . .

Schmidt   Look at Willy.

Genscher   On the scaffold.

Schmidt   As calm as a king . . .

Ehmke   Come on, come on . . .

Guillaume   They dragged people out of hospital!

Genscher   Poor old Guttenberg looks at the point of death.

Nollau   He is . . .

Ehmke   I don't think I can bear this . . .

Schmidt   Look, look! Sepp Woelker! He's signalling!

Wilke   Two! Two! He's signalling two!

Ehmke   They've done it!

Nollau   I told you.

Schmidt   By two votes!

Wehner   Wait . . . wait . . .

Schmidt   By two votes they've brought down the greatest leader this country ever had!

Wilke   Look at Willy.

Ehmke   He's *smiling* . . .

Guillaume (*with* **Kretschmann**)   And the whole party went mad! Not lost by two – *won* by two! Those bastards were so sure they'd got it in the bag! They had it all planned! Sworn in at four! Into the Palais Schaumburg by five! *We* thought they'd won! Got half the files shredded! Then out comes Sepp Woelker. Two, two, he signals. Oh *no* . . . !

Kretschmann   Well . . . congratulations.

Guillaume   Never mind football! Try parliamentary democracy! Sorry. Howling with the wolves.

Kretschmann   Howling with them? Or hunting with them?

Guillaume   Hunting with them, eating with them. Laughing with them, crying with them. No other way, if you're half man and half wolf.

Kretschmann   You won't forget the human half?

Guillaume   Don't worry. I shall remain the perfect servant of two masters. Mischa and Willy. Willy and Mischa. My two great masters. Tell me one thing, though. To satisfy my curiosity. How much did it cost?

Kretschmann   You're howling again, Günter.

Guillaume   Sorry. As long as Mischa's happy. That's all I want in life.

Kretschmann   And Willy.

Guillaume   And Willy.

Kretschmann   Back to work, then.

Wilke (*with* **Schmidt**, **Wehner** *and* **Guillaume**)   The Chancellor? Indisposed, I'm afraid, Herr Guillaume.

Schmidt   Another of his feverish colds.

Wehner   As they are known technically.

Schmidt   The doctor suspects that this one was brought on by the prospect of new elections.

Wehner   The doctor's with him now.

Wilke   Dr Ehmke.

Schmidt   Administering the usual medicine.

Wehner   Wielding the therapeutic corkscrew.

Schmidt   So do please take a seat. We're all waiting urgently for signs of recovery, and if past experience is anything to go by we may have to wait for some considerable time.

Guillaume   New elections?

Schmidt   Who knows?

Wehner   Ask Number One.

Schmidt   Join the queue.

Wilke   There *have* to be new elections. We've lost our majority in the House. We can't even pass the Budget.

Guillaume   We'll pick up votes.

Schmidt   The Liberals, however, will drop them. Will go below the five per cent mark. Will vanish altogether.

Wehner   And this misbegotten coalition with them.

Guillaume   So the Chancellor feels . . . ?

Schmidt   Ill, apparently, at the mere thought.

Wehner   Someone ought to take him another bottle of medicine.

Wilke   I suppose it should be me.

Schmidt   I think our little friend is already on his way.

Ehmke (*with* **Brandt** *and* **Guillaume**)   Come on, Willy. You're the Chancellor. Remember? So up you get and chancel.

Guillaume   Election candidate: 'If we win you'll get a new hospital – a new school – a new bridge over the river!' Voice from the crowd: 'We haven't got a river.' Candidate: 'You'll *get* a river . . . !'

Brandt   I can't face them, Horst. They look at me, and I see the perpetual question in their eyes. 'Why you? Why not me? Why *you*?'

Ehmke   They know the answer. Because you're the man you are.

Brandt   Whoever that is.

Ehmke   The man who's done all the things you've done.

Brandt   Done is done.

Ehmke   The man who's going to do all the things you're going to do.

Brandt   The man they hope I am, in spite of everything. The man they hope their hope will make me. The man they know they'll sooner or later find I'm not.

Ehmke   Up you get, Willy.

Brandt   All those expectant faces gazing up at me. I look down at them and I see always the same question, the same hope, the same dawning disappointment . . .

Kretschmann   – Shocked?

Guillaume   – Surprised. Never seen him in one of his depressions before.

Kretschmann – Disillusioned?

Guillaume – Disarmed.

Brandt And when I think of the jibes that come out at
every election. The sneers about my illegitimacy. The taunts
about being a traitor. What was I doing during the war,
eating smorgasbord in Scandinavia while all the rest of them
were trapped inside the charnel-house? I came back with
clean hands! That's what they cannot bear.

Ehmke It's themselves they demean, Willy, not you.

Brandt I think the time has come for me to step down.

Schmidt (*with* **Wilke**, **Wehner** *and* **Guillaume**)
Resigning?

Guillaume Talking about it.

Wehner Of course.

Schmidt Talking, though. Talking's a good sign.

Wehner I have some sympathy with him, I have to
admit. They skinned *me* alive for my exile.

Schmidt You were a Communist. You got your hands
dirty. You were part of the great train-wreck of German
history like all the rest of us. Even our chirpy friend here
from Berlin, no doubt. What, seventeen at the end of the
war, Herr Guillaume?

Guillaume Eighteen.

Schmidt Hitler Youth? Boy soldier?

Guillaume Of course. Anti-aircraft. Like you.

Wehner All of us on the train, except the great man
himself.

Schmidt On the boat to Norway instead.

Wehner He leaves here each night and he turns back into a Norwegian. The German Chancellor – and he speaks Norwegian with his wife and children.

Schmidt He came back in 1945 wearing Norwegian uniform.

Wehner Those beloved Berliners of his scrabbling like pigs in the dirt for scraps, and where was the great man? Sitting at table with the Occupation forces, eating with commandeered silverware off commandeered china. His hands as clean as ever.

Schmidt This is Willy's great strength. He's not quite one of us. He doesn't quite understand what all the rest of us understand.

Kretschmann (*with* **Guillaume**) You look as if you could do with a spoonful or two of the red medicine yourself.

Guillaume They've got Karl Schiller out of Economics and Finance. Trapped him into resigning. Helmut's taken them both over.

Kretschmann One step closer to the throne.

Guillaume Also things are a little bleak at home.

Kretschmann Christel?

Guillaume Silences. Tears.

Kretschmann I'm so sorry.

Guillaume She seems to have been doing a little spying on her own account.

Kretschmann This is the secretaries?

Guillaume Etcetera.

Kretschmann You've told her it's purely professional?

Guillaume   Etcetera, etcetera. It's the profession that's finished us. She gets homesick, Arno. Don't you ever feel a sudden longing to be over there again?

Kretschmann   Of course.

Guillaume   It comes at the oddest moments.

Kretschmann   Those quiet grey streets. That blessed dullness.

Guillaume   That simplicity.

Kretschmann   We smuggled you back a couple of times.

Guillaume   Like a returning ghost. Sworn to silence and invisibility. Eavesdropping on my own absence.

Kretschmann   So West Germany has not proved to be the paradise that so many of our fellow-citizens think it is.

Guillaume   She wants a divorce, Arno.

Kretschmann   She can't have one. Mischa won't let her. We need you as a couple. And think about Pierre.

Guillaume   I think about him all the time.

Kretschmann   Your Sunday mornings at the airport together.

Guillaume   Even that's just the cover for a letter drop.

Kretschmann   Every coin has two faces.

Guillaume   If I'm arrested . . .

Kretschmann   Why should you be?

Guillaume   It can't go on, Arno! Not for ever! And when they arrest me they'll arrest Christel.

Kretschmann   Pierre would be looked after. I promise you.

Guillaume   He's only fifteen. He wouldn't understand.

Kretschmann   It would all be explained to him.

Guillaume   I wake sometimes at night, and I feel a sick dread creeping through my body.

Kretschmann   You and Willy. You're like some old couple who've been married for forty years. He goes down so you go down. He comes up again and . . .

Ehmke (*with* **Guillaume**)   Günter! A little light bedtime reading!

Guillaume   The railway timetable?

Ehmke   Elections in November. Willy's going to be out campaigning in his special train.

Guillaume   The train? It's his personal assistant who organises the train. Peter Reuschenbach.

Ehmke   Standing for election. You'll have to take over.

Guillaume   As Willy's . . . personal assistant?

Ehmke   Bit of a killer, I'm afraid. Train, files, his dispatch-boxes, all incoming and outgoing correspondence – the whole works. Sorry, but *someone's* got to do it, and – there you are.

Kretschmann   – Pinch me, will you?

Guillaume (*with* **Brandt**)   – And now everything changes. For days at a time our home becomes this luxurious suite of softly rolling rooms. They're fitted out in rosewood and teak, in walnut and mahogany and cherry, and they once bore Reichsmarschall Göring around the Nazi empire. Now they're bringing Willy to ask the electors of Germany for their votes.

Brandt   Dear friends, I say to you and I say to all our people: have the courage to show compassion.

Guillaume   – Compassion. This is the party's election slogan. But on the hoardings everywhere he goes there's a simpler message: Willy!

Brandt   Compassion for those nearest to you!
Compassion, too, for those who are not so close!

Guillaume   – 'Willy must stay Chancellor! Willy! Willy!'
And always, in the shadows at Willy's side – Günter. The
master of the timetables – the high priest of the holy book.
The major-domo of our little travelling court. The personal
valet. The bearer of the official dispatch-case.

Brandt   Where's this?

Guillaume   Berneburg, Chief. – 'Chief', you notice. Not
'Herr Chancellor'. Not on the train. Picked it up from Uli.

Brandt   And we arrive Hildesheim . . . ?

Guillaume   1207. Seven minutes handshaking Town
Hall – ten minutes discussion Mayor – three minutes
Register Office spontaneous with bride and groom . . .

Brandt   This is where I feel at home, Herr Guillaume. On
the move. Fourteen years I spent in exile. Fourteen years of
travelling for the cause and eluding the Nazis. Norway,
Sweden. Spain, France. Then nearly twenty years going
back and forth between Berlin and Bonn. Going round and
round the world, telling everyone 'Berlin, Berlin'. Thirty or
forty years of my life looking out of trains and planes at
other lands and other lives.

Guillaume   Speech Town Hall . . . Unemployment
figures . . . Federal investment . . . Local anecdote . . .

Brandt   I get so much more done on the train. No Uncle
to suck his pipe at me. No Helmut to lecture me.

Guillaume   – No Wilke to keep me away from Willy. No
Ehmke to listen to his stories.

Brandt   No wife. No family.

Guillaume   – Just me. Getting his suit pressed. Laying it
out with the matching shirt and tie. Taking the telexes back
and forth to the wireless car.

Brandt   These two are urgent. This one's confidential.

Guillaume   I'll get it ciphered. Never know who's going to see these things in transit. – Every communication he has with the outside world – it passes through me. The knight errant and his loyal squire. The travelling magician and the assistant who knows all his tricks. Everything he sees – I see it, too.

Brandt   All those other worlds! That little factory on the industrial estate. I could be working in there . . . And already it's gone . . . The bent old man in that village street, turning to glance up at the passing train . . . That could have been me instead of him . . . I could be in that silver Mercedes on the autobahn, vanishing into another distance altogether . . . We're stopping.

Guillaume   Nordstemmen. Three minutes. A few words from the window. – And there they are, the good people of Nordstemmen.

Brandt   Not a bad house.

Guillaume   – The same sort of dutiful supporters we've seen waving and smiling in Northeim and Freden and Alfeld.

Brandt   Dear friends! Have the courage to show compassion . . . !

Guillaume   – Which of the women has he got his eye on this time? Is it that one at the front gazing up at him with very slightly parted lips? Or the one over there smiling that strange dark half-smile? Or both of them at once? Or all of them? Each one of them knows he's looking at her, and her alone . . .

Brandt   I can see you, Herr Guillaume. Eyeing the girls.

Guillaume   What is it about women, Chief?

Brandt   The way they look at you . . . The way they look straight into your eyes and you look straight into theirs. The way you can't understand them. The way you can.

Guillaume   The way they smile.

Brandt   The way they look seriously at you. The way they make fun of you.

Guillaume   The way they're not like men.

Brandt   The way they are. The way they touch your hand. The way they touch your face. The softness of their touch on your skin. The softness of your own on theirs . . . All the different people you can be with them. All the different ways your life might go . . .

Guillaume   – But already they're slipping away from us. All those sweet possibilities – vanishing for ever . . . And when the evening comes . . .

Brandt   Uli! Where are you?

Bauhaus   Chief. (*Offers wine.*) Red or red?

Guillaume   – He relaxes and he talks, the way he does at the end of the working day in Bonn. But now there's no Uncle Herbert, no Crown Prince Helmut, no faithful Ehmke. Only the journalists travelling with us. Only Uli. And sometimes – only me. Nobody. An upturned face like all the others.

Brandt   I've been trying to remember a boy I used to know when I was growing up in Lübeck. Strange lad. Always rather solemn and serious. Not much fun in his life. Never quite enough to eat. No money. No friends. No father. Not much of a mother, for that matter. Brought up by his grandparents . . .

Guillaume   And this boy was called Herbert Frahm?

Brandt   Herbert Frahm. The name's as odd as everything else about him . . . Then one day, when he was nineteen years old, he vanished off the face of the earth. He set out from Lübeck to go to Dresden, and he never arrived. Well, this was 1933, and my celebrated predecessor with the little moustache had just taken office. People had a habit of vanishing then, in one way or another. Not a good time to be a member of a left-wing party, as Herbert Frahm was. Not a good time to be going to its annual conference. Only one bit of Herbert Frahm ever arrived in Dresden. His old student cap. But now it was perched on the head of a young man no one had ever seen or heard of before.

Guillaume   Willy Brandt.

Brandt   That's the strangest thing of all about Herbert Frahm. The fact that I was him, and he was me. What was it like, being him? I look back, and all that time has vanished behind a thick grey veil, like the old Lübeck waterfront in the fog on a winter morning. What became of him, when Willy Brandt took over his body and his student cap? Sometimes I catch a glimpse of him. Out of the window of the train. In a waiting crowd. A solemn boy, glancing up at me with a speculative look in his eye. What does he make of me? But then he turns, and goes away into some other life where I can never follow . . . You had a father, Herr Guillaume?

Guillaume   Café pianist.

Brandt   An honourable vocation.

Guillaume   He was also a Nazi. And when he came back at the end of the war and found my mother with another man he jumped out of the window. It was a high window.

Brandt   Two fatherless boys, wandering the world looking for . . . what are we looking for?

Guillaume   I don't know, Chief. Women?

Brandt   Günter! I'm shocked!

Guillaume   – 'Günter', though! 'Günter'!

Bauhaus   Sorry, Chief . . .

Brandt   What is it, Uli?

Bauhaus   One of the journalists is getting a bit impatient. Says you promised to do an interview before we get to Kassel.

Brandt   Günter and I are talking. Tell him I'll do it tomorrow.

Bauhaus   Her.

Brandt   Her? Oh, yes. *Her*. Well . . . I suppose we have to keep the press happy.

Guillaume   I'll be just the other side of the wall, Chief, if you need me.

Brandt   I think I can manage a press briefing on my own, thank you, Günter. So she's . . . ?

Bauhaus   In your compartment. I've taken the files off the bed.

Brandt   And we arrive Kassel . . . ?

Guillaume   In forty-five minutes. Witzenhausen first, though.

Brandt   Word from the window?

Guillaume   And . . . jacket and tie, Chief!

Brandt   Trousers?

Guillaume   Certainly. (*With* **Bauhaus**.) Pretty, this one?

Bauhaus   I wouldn't know.

Guillaume   Eyes closed while you searched her?

Bauhaus   You find all this very amusing.

Guillaume   You did give her a full body-search?

Bauhaus   *I* find it pretty distasteful.

Guillaume   I sympathise. Terrible job.

Bauhaus   I've got a wife and children.

Guillaume   *He's* got a wife and children.

Bauhaus   Oh, really?

Guillaume   So for all we know she may be wired? May even be working for *them*?

Bauhaus   Wouldn't put it past them.

Guillaume   – *Not* one of ours, is she?

Kretschmann   – Not my department, women. I'm pleased to say.

Guillaume   Or Baader-Meinhof. Gun in her knickers. Put your ear to the wall, Uli!

Bauhaus   Note the time in, note the time out. That's all I'm required to do.

Guillaume   Just take the dispatch-case into my compartment for me, then. And, Uli . . . Any more young ladies who want a briefing – any hour of the day or night – my compartment is next door to the Chief's. – And on we go. Trip after trip. Week after week. Kiel, Karlsruhe . . . Bremen, Brunswick . . .

Brandt   Dear friends. Have courage . . .

Guillaume   – Everywhere, as the campaign goes on, the upturned faces become more radiant, the outstretched hands more clamorous to touch him. Willy passes among them like a Messiah. Smiling, smiling . . . Speaking, speaking . . .

Brandt   The courage to show compassion . . .

Guillaume   – And always, a few discreet paces behind him, his loyal servant, his faithful friend.

Brandt   The courage to love your neighbour . . .

Guillaume   – He asked Horst Ehmke to get rid of me. I found the memo. My personality was one of the things that depressed him, he said. I was hurt. Naturally. But I put it behind me. It was the depression speaking. I've forgotten all about it. So has Horst, by the look of it – because here we are, the Chief and I, together still, closer than ever.

Brandt   The courage to find your own true self . . .

Guillaume   – Willy and Günter. The noble hero and his comic servant. Don Quixote and his Sancho Panza. Over and over again he gazes down on those upturned faces. Over and over again he speaks, until his throat's raw.

Brandt   Dear friends . . . dear friends . . .

Guillaume   – Some of the older women weep, and press amulets and rosaries into his hands for him to bless. And as for the younger women . . .

Bauhaus (*with* **Guillaume**)   Look at them out there! It's worse than a rock concert! How am I supposed to cope with that mob? Soon as he shows his face they're going to rush him.

Guillaume   I'll help you, Uli. They won't get past us! Only one or two of the very prettiest ones, perhaps.

Bauhaus   Supposing they were *your* daughters.

Guillaume   We're public servants, Uli. We have to respect the voters' wishes.

Kretschmann   – Don Quixote and Sancho Panza? Or Don Juan and Leporello?

Guillaume   – You sound almost as sour as Uli.

Kretschmann   – The free society, Günter. Enjoy it while you may.

Guillaume (*with* **Brandt**)   – The softness of their skin. The light in their eyes. Or the warmth in their hearts. Something that got left behind in the mists of Lübeck all those years ago . . . No? No, very well. Just a thought. Forget it. He's a bit of a lad, that's all. We're two lads together. Two fellows on the loose. Two travelling salesmen away from their wives. But what a product we have to sell! Willy Brandt, the saviour of Europe, the greatest statesman in the world, with the Nobel Peace Prize to certify it. The Moscow treaty – signed and ratified. The Warsaw treaty – signed and ratified. Yes, and in Warsaw he achieved immortality. He left a single image in the memory of the world that no one will ever forget . . .

Ehmke – Another of his unspoken speeches, and the greatest of them all.

Guillaume – He lays his official wreath at the monument to the murdered Jews of the Warsaw Ghetto. He steps back. And then . . .

Schmidt – Something else. He's going to do something else . . .

Guillaume – For a moment once again time seems to hold its breath. Once again the world is about to change in front of our eyes. And out of nowhere . . .

Brandt *kneels.*

Guillaume – For a moment I think, 'No, no, no! This time he's gone too far!' But I'm wrong, and he's right, because this is what the world remembers. That long moment when the German who has no cause to kneel went back down into the lowest depth of German history and knelt for all of us. The one unspoken word that said everything he longed to say. The one simple gesture that embodied everything he was loved for and everything he was loathed for.

Wehner – Something speaks in him, and he hears it.

Schmidt – Some small voice that speaks to him, and to none of the rest of us.

Guillaume – I wept, Arno.

Brandt *rises.*

Kretschmann   – Perhaps at last the wounds are beginning to heal. Perhaps the irreconcilables are beginning to be reconciled.

Guillaume   – Ten days before the election and they sign the treaty between the two Germanys. The keystone of the Eastern policy locked into place.

Kretschmann   – Because you helped us to trust him.

Guillaume   – And on election night, who is it who brings the good news to Willy? – (*with* **Brandt**, **Wehner**, **Schmidt**, **Ehmke**, **Genscher**, **Wilke**, **Nollau** *and* **Bauhaus**.) May I be the first to offer my congratulations, Chief? They're saying two hundred and seventy-one seats! They're saying a clear forty-six-seat majority!

Wehner   Our best result ever!

Genscher   Even the Liberals have picked up another eleven seats!

Wehner   Right across the board! Swing voters in the middle. Catholic workers. Old ladies. The young.

Genscher   Willy, we've had our differences, and we'll have more in future. But let's make no mistake about it. This is your victory.

Schmidt   We planted the seed of this when we reformed this party ten years ago. You and Herbert and I. And now we harvest the golden fruit.

Wehner   Here – a hug from your wicked Uncle.

Wilke   Congratulations, Herr Chancellor. On behalf of everyone in the office.

Nollau   And everyone in Federal security.

Bauhaus   Also from your barman and bouncer.

Guillaume   May I say, Chief, that working with you has been the best thing that ever happened to me, or ever will?

Ehmke   Willy, your long exile is over at last.

All   Speech! Speech!

Wilke   He can't speak!

Ehmke   He's spoken himself hoarse!

Schmidt   Come on, Willy!

Ehmke   Make the most of it, Willy! It's all downhill from now on!

Brandt   Dear friends . . .

Ehmke   He can still say *that*!

All   Listen! Listen!

Brandt   This is of course a victory for all of us here who have worked so hard together. But it is more than that. It is the German people's endorsement of the great reconciliation that we have begun. Never before, never before, has a German state lived in such harmony both with the free spirit of its citizens and with its neighbours.

Guillaume (*with* **Kretschmann**)   And on into the night the celebration goes. Parliamentary democracy, Arno! One unending wild party! You're on your feet – you're on the floor! They've thrown you out – you've got back in! Now everyone's singing – now they're fighting. Now they're weeping – now they're laughing. Now someone's passed out behind the sofa – and it may be you.

Kretschmann   Now someone certainly needs a strong black coffee.

Guillaume   I'll be sober enough in the morning, never you fear. We'll all be sober.

Wehner (*with* **Schmidt**)   So, what does the world look like in the cold grey light of day? I'll tell you what I see. Another four years of indecision. Another four years of compromise and drift. Another four years of Willy.

Schmidt   Another four years of sudden unscheduled gestures. There'll be no holding him now. He'll be more intoxicated with success than he ever was on red wine or schnapps.

Wehner   He needed his old friends before to control the party and hold the coalition together. Now he won't need us any more.

Ehmke (*with* **Schmidt** *and* **Wehner**)   Listen, jobs in the new government. Who gets what. The usual horse-trading. You two gentlemen are going to have to stand in for Willy and preside over the negotiations.

Wehner   Not another feverish cold?

Ehmke   His throat. The doctors won't allow him to speak. On his way into hospital for tests. Here – letter from him. This is how he wants you to do it.

Wehner (*with* **Schmidt**) So, the game begins once more.

Schmidt   Only now ministers are handed their instructions by the Lord High Chamberlain.

Wehner   I shall put them carefully away in the inmost chamber of my briefcase.

Schmidt   Better look first. See who's in, who's out.

Kretschmann   – *You're* in, are you?

Guillaume   – I'm waiting for Ehmke to tell me.

Kretschmann   – He told Ehmke to get rid of you.

Schmidt   So, what does Willy say?

Wehner   Not much, I imagine, if he can't speak.

Schmidt   In the letter. The letter Ehmke gave you.

Wehner   Ehmke, yes . . . I know you've always felt he might benefit from a change of job himself.

Schmidt   Broaden his experience. Give him a new perspective.

Wehner   Which department do we feel would suit his talents best?

Schmidt   The Post Office needs reorganising. He might find that an interesting challenge.

Wehner   He knows a lot about carrying messages.

Schmidt   Does Willy say anything about him in the letter?

Wehner   What letter?

Schmidt   You put it in your briefcase.

Wehner   Oh, dear God, I've lost it. Can't find it for the life of me.

Schmidt   So . . . Ehmke gets the Post Office, then?

Kretschmann   – And what *does* Ehmke say?

Guillaume   – Nothing. No Ehmke. – Have *you* seen him? Horst Ehmke?

Wehner   Taking a little well-deserved holiday, perhaps. Oh, and Herr Guillaume. Your family. Are they well?

Guillaume   In rude health, thank you.

Wehner   Two sons, is it?

Guillaume   Just one.

Wehner   Of course. I'm glad to hear it.

Kretschmann   – No Ehmke? What does that mean?

Guillaume   – It means that Willy will have to look me in the eye and tell me himself. (*With* **Brandt**.) So what's been decided, Chief? Am I staying with you? – Not a word! He simply . . . hands me the dispatch-case. Another of his silent gestures! And what this one means is: 'Yes! On we go! To the bitter end! Together!'

Darkness.

Act Two

Guillaume (*with* **Brandt** *and* **Kretschmann**)   Nothing in this world turns out the way anyone expects. Nothing! I look at Willy sometimes and it breaks my heart. Everything he ever wanted he gets. The election. The treaties. Even the treaty with us that crowns the whole enterprise. And at once everything goes wrong. Everything! Inflation, rising prices, impossible wage demands, industrial chaos . . .

Kretschmann   Democracy, Günter! Sixty million separate selves, rolling about the ship like loose cargo in a storm.

Guillaume   They've hauled the monument into place. And now they've dropped the ropes there's nothing to keep them together. They're like tired children at the end of the holiday, with nothing left to do but squabble.

Schmidt (*with* **Wilke** *and* **Wehner**)   Will someone kindly tell me how the Cabinet can discuss the Foreign Ministry's proposals for arms reduction when the Foreign Ministry still hasn't tabled them?

Wilke   There seems to have been some slight confusion over the date . . .

Schmidt   No doubt on the part of the same nameless person who arranged for the Chancellor to give a press conference on tax-reform the day before we decided what the policy was.

Wehner   On the other hand we've launched a major new policy initiative. Or so I read in the press.

Wilke   A leak, I'm afraid.

Wehner   A pilgrimage to find the New Middle.

Schmidt   The New Middle? What happened to the old one? Which is where Herbert and I have been struggling to keep this party for the last ten years.

Wilke   I believe the idea originated with the Press Office. As I understand it, the intention is to provide some sort of counterpoise to the left.

Wehner   We shouldn't need a counterpoise if Number One hadn't got them worked up by all his talk about daring more democracy.

Schmidt   What is happening to this government? We casually launch into wild schemes without any proper consultation. We take on new commitments without any idea how they're going to be funded. When Horst Ehmke was running the Chancellor's office he used to co-ordinate this kind of thing.

Wehner   The great man in his wisdom decided to dispense with Horst Ehmke's services.

Schmidt   But Grabert's in charge here now! Why can't he do it?

Wilke   Dr Grabert is away this week.

Guillaume   In Siberia.

Schmidt   *Siberia?*

Wilke   On his way to Tokyo.

Schmidt   A treaty with Japan?

Wilke   A study of airline development.

Guillaume   A freebie.

Schmidt   Another Berliner, of course.

Wehner   This government is falling apart in front of our eyes.

Schmidt   Because Willy does nothing! Nothing, nothing, nothing!

Guillaume (*with* **Brandt** *and* **Kretschmann**)   Nothing. It's true. I wait in the shadows at his back on provincial railway stations, willing him to speak, as if he were Pierre,

five years old still and standing dumbstruck in the school
nativity play. He gazes out over the expectant faces, and –
not a word. Not a gesture. Not a smile or a frown. His face
is a mask. A mask with no one behind it. The people gaze at
the effigy of their Chancellor. The effigy gazes back. His
famous silence. But this time what it says is – nothing.

Schmidt (*with* **Wehner**, **Wilke**, *and* **Guillaume**)   Where
is he now? Not another feverish cold?

Wehner   Or still brooding about his operation?

Schmidt   *Other* people have medical problems. They
manage not to let it affect their behaviour . . . What?

Guillaume   I didn't speak.

Schmidt   I'm perfectly prepared to subscribe to the
general belief that Willy is God. What I find a little
confusing, though, is not knowing which Person of the
Trinity he's going to be from one moment to the next – God
the Father or Christ crucified. Saving your presence,
Herbert.

Wehner   Our great leader's jibes have inured me to any
insult to my beliefs.

Schmidt   Most of them you never even heard when Horst
Ehmke was around to control things.

Ehmke (*with* **Brandt**)   We won. That was our great
mistake, Willy. Defeat is the only thing that this party
understands. Defeat is a testimony to high ideals. Defeat
makes no demands. Victory means you have to *do*
something – and *doing* something always involves dissent and
compromise and making mistakes.

Brandt   Even you seem to have abandoned me.

Ehmke   I'm reorganising the Post Office. The job you
gave me. You sacked me, if you remember, Willy.

Brandt   I saw a boy watching me the other day. In the
crowd on a station somewhere. Fifteen, sixteen. Very

solemn and unsmiling. Some kind of cap on his head, like an old-fashioned student's cap. I couldn't take my eyes off him. He just gazed back at me. Gazed and gazed, and never a smile. He didn't like what he saw.

Ehmke   Don't worry about the radicals.

Brandt   I watched him. He watched me. Until we vanished from each other's sight again.

Guillaume   Shall I send Uli out for a packet of cigarettes, Chief? – He's trying to give up smoking, on top of everything else.

Brandt   That operation, Horst . . .

Ehmke   Operations are like everything else, Willy. They sometimes go wrong.

Brandt   I thought I was going to die. I came round in the middle. I couldn't breathe . . . Solve everything, wouldn't it. Helmut would take over. Uncle would come back into the party leadership. Genscher would become Foreign Minister, and be kissed by the television lights and changed into a prince.

Guillaume   – He nearly died again in Israel in that helicopter on top of Masada. A sudden gust of wind, and it slides away like a fallen leaf. Stops at the very edge of the drop. Uli shouts 'Everybody out!' And the Chief just sits there, not moving, looking down into the Dead Sea valley four hundred metres below.

Brandt   It's waiting so quietly and patiently, the earth down there. Smiling, arms outstretched, like a mother waiting for her child to run to her . . . I don't fear death. Only the agonising struggle to breathe until death comes, only the long fall . . . Only opening my eyes in some bleak hospital ward and finding Herbert Wehner praying over me.

Guillaume (*with* **Kretschmann**)   Let me go, Arno. Let me go home. You don't need me any more. What more do you want to know?

Kretschmann   Whether the treaties are going to be implemented. Whether Willy is going to survive long enough to make sure they are. You're closer to him than ever before, Günter! You practically live in his dispatch-case!

Guillaume   I could give Christel back her life. I could explain to Pierre.

Kretschmann   No more official cars, Günter! No more private train. No more upturned adoring faces. No more respectful attention from me at our little lunches. No more grateful appreciation from Mischa. No more sweet quiet Sundays, cruising out to the airport with Pierre. Or is it Willy you're worrying about?

Guillaume   If I resigned now he'd never find out about me. Let me go, Arno!

Kretschmann   We need you, Günter! We need you more than ever. Not just to tell us whether he's going to survive but to help him to. Who else can he depend upon, now that Ehmke's gone? Who else works the hours that you work? Never condemns him for his faults? Never takes offence at his indifference, or hurt at his slights? This is why *we* need you – because *he* needs you. Howl with him, Günter. Help him.

Wehner (*with* **Nollau**)   Guillaume?

Nollau   The name keeps jumping out of the files at us. Three separate espionage cases where Herr Guillaume seems to have known the defendants. So we looked up his birthday. The first of February. The date of the birthday greetings for G. I'm sorry to add to your troubles, which I know are legion.

Wehner   That's the complete case against him?

Nollau   So far.

Wehner   An initial and a date? And one son too many?

Nollau   We need more evidence. But getting more evidence means watching him. Leaving him in place and watching him.

Wehner   Make the big man look a bit small if it's true. He trusts him completely. Lets him see everything.

Nollau   Lets him see what? He *is* only union liaison? He won't be handling anything too sensitive?

Wehner   If they catch you hounding someone in Number One's office and you're wrong . . .

Nollau   They'll crucify me. Sorry, Herbert.

Wehner   You're in a difficult position, my friend.

Nollau   So how do we play this? What do we tell Willy?

Wehner   Nothing. We can't have him unsettled any further just at the moment. In any case he usually prefers to hear about problems after they've been solved.

Nollau   We can't just leave him in the dark! We'll have to tell him *something*!

Wehner   If we can't manage to be discreet we're going to find all kinds of nasty creatures coming out of the woodwork. Matters that we all hoped everyone had forgotten about.

Nollau   Oh, not that nonsense again! You don't really believe I committed a murder?

Wehner   Of course not.

Nollau   It was a pure fabrication! You know that!

Wehner   *I* know that.

Nollau   I was completely cleared!

Wehner   Let's keep you that way.

Nollau   I'll have to tell Genscher, at any rate. My own Minister!

Wehner   He'll immediately run bleating to Willy.

Nollau   I'm sorry, but if I don't get Genscher's authorisation I'll be . . .

Wehner   Crucified.

Nollau   Crucified.

Wehner   Question of how you put it. No need to go shouting 'Fire' at the top of your voice. Something more like a passing remark on the warmth of the weather. Then you're in the clear – and nobody panics.

Nollau   They just get burnt to death.

Wehner   Drawbacks to every policy.

Nollau   And he *is* only union liaison . . .

Wilke (*with* **Brandt** *and* **Guillaume**)   Herr Wehner? Gone to East Berlin?

Brandt   Private summit. Little chat with Honecker himself.

Wilke   Prisoners and families?

Brandt   Trying to get the trade going again.

Guillaume   – Another unforeseen consequence of success. We normalise our relations – and it turns out that normal relations between two countries don't include buying and selling human beings.

Brandt   I gather East Berlin's full of people sitting on their bags. They can't leave – they can't go back.

Guillaume   – I don't know how much I've managed to find out about *this* country, but I've certainly found out a few things about my own.

Wilke   When was this trip arranged, Herr Chancellor?

Brandt   This afternoon, apparently. At an hour's notice. No unworthy suspicions, Reinhard! This is something he takes very seriously. The priest in him emerging from hiding once again.

Wilke   With something of a rush.

Brandt   He can scarcely have had time to pack the holy oil.

Guillaume   – It *is* prisoners and families, is it, Arno?

Kretschmann   – I've no idea.

Brandt   Only another month, anyway, and we shall be on holiday. Out of all this mess. In the moist green depths of Norway, where remarkably little ever occurs.

Guillaume   Nothing makes the Chancellor happier about being where he is than the prospect of being somewhere else.

Brandt   No Uncle. No Helmut. No one at all except Uli to protect my privacy and Reinhard to intercept my messages.

Wilke   I have a slight personal problem, Herr Chancellor. There is an unfortunate clash with the dates of my own family holiday.

Guillaume   So who immediately steps forward to fill the breach?

Wilke   Oh, I see . . . But *your* holiday, Herr Guillaume?

Guillaume   Take it another time.

Wilke   Your family, though . . .

Guillaume   Glad to see the back of me! And the Chancellor and I are old travelling-companions.

Brandt   Many a weary mile have I gone with Herr Guillaume at my side.

Kretschmann (*with* **Guillaume**)   You see? We all need you! We all depend upon you!

Guillaume   A whole month. Howling in the wilderness together.

Kretschmann   Where should *I* be without you? Back in East Berlin, eating Bratwurst in the office canteen! Where would *Mischa* be? You're the jewel in his crown, Günter! Even if you never told us anything, simply having you there at God's right hand would still be the justification of Mischa's whole career!

Brandt (*with* **Genscher**)   Guillaume? My little meatball?

Genscher   The usual nonsense. Nollau didn't even think it was worth mentioning to you. I said, 'Look, we can't have your people crawling round the Chancellor's office without getting his authorisation.'

Brandt   So what am I to do?

Genscher   Nothing. Carry on exactly as before. Nollau says not to change anything by a hairsbreadth.

Brandt   Same access to documents?

Genscher   Exactly the same.

Brandt   He's coming to Norway with me. He's going to have sole charge of all my communications with the outside world.

Genscher   Excellent chance for Nollau's people to watch him at work.

Brandt   I don't know where they can hide themselves. Middle of nowhere. Have to dress up as cows.

Genscher   Keep an eye on him yourself, perhaps.

Brandt   Provide a little entertainment. Nothing much else there to watch except the grass growing and Norwegian television.

Genscher   His wife's also under observation, incidentally.

Brandt   Whole family of spies!

Genscher   I don't know about their two sons.

Brandt   One son.

Genscher   Two, according to my information.

Brandt   One, according to Herr Guillaume.

Genscher   Nollau's obviously got the wrong man. In any case even the East Germans are hardly likely to be spying on someone who's just inscribed their wretched little state on the map of Europe for them.

Brandt   The merest possibility that Guillaume's not what he seems makes him infinitely more tolerable. (*With* **Guillaume**.) You have a moment, Herr Guillaume?

Guillaume   Chief. – Something odd about the way he's looking at me. As if I were someone else.

Brandt   Herr Guillaume, I've been having second thoughts about your kind offer to come to Norway with us.

Guillaume   – Genscher was here! Genscher's told him something!

Brandt   On reflection I feel it would be quite unforgivable of me to separate you from your family.

Guillaume   – I feel the wave of alarm go through me. And then the hollow behind the wave. Disappointment. Sheer childish disappointment. The party's over! He's never going to take me anywhere with him again!

Brandt   So why don't you bring them with you?

Guillaume   Why don't I . . . ? I'm sorry . . . ?

Brandt   Bring your wife! Christine, yes?

Guillaume   Christel.

Brandt   And your son. Pierre. Like my Peter. A great supporter of mine, I seem to remember. Rut and I will have one of our boys there. Not Peter – Matthias. Otherwise – perfect holiday symmetry. Us two and our son. You two and yours.

Guillaume   Chief, this is astonishingly kind . . .

Brandt   Pack your raincoats, Herr Guillaume. And a good supply of fresh jokes.

Kretschmann   – So you're happy again.

Guillaume   – He suddenly looks at you as if he's seen you for the first time. It's like a ray of sunlight striking down from the clouds, shining on you and you alone out of all the world. At once all the cold greyness of the day dissolves. You can feel the warmth in your bones.

Brandt   It *is* just the one boy?

Guillaume   Just the one, Chief.

Brandt   You should have persisted, Herr Guillaume. Two would have been even more fun.

Guillaume   – And it turns out to be the best family holiday we've ever had. They put us up in a charming little green wooden house just downhill from the Chief, and we all have the time of our life, all six of us. – Real holiday for Christel, Chief, yattering away to Rut. No idea where those two boys are, though. Vanished into the woods together again.

Brandt   Cops and robbers. Secret agents.

Guillaume   Getting on like a house on fire, anyway.

Brandt   Nice boy, your Pierre. You must be proud of him.

Guillaume   Light of my life.

Brandt   So different for them. Peace. Freedom.

Guillaume Fathers.

Brandt Who should we have turned out to be, if things had been different? You might have been standing here. I might have been standing there.

Guillaume Freedom, though. That's what's so relaxing about this place, Chief. You can leave all the doors unlocked and let the kids run wild.

Brandt You know why that is, Günter?

Guillaume Because the whole area's been sealed off by the local police.

Brandt Our own little police state to make you feel at home.

Guillaume – Time to think, time to talk. A little work, of course, at our respective jobs. Outgoing messages . . .

Brandt Negotiating points for Egon Bahr. Bit of a dog's breakfast. You'd better type them out before you send them.

Guillaume – Incoming telexes. Two copies of each. One for the Chief . . . – Personal message from Richard Nixon. – The other one for me. But we also spend hours out in the woods, like the boys, rambling around with Uli Bauhaus looking for mushrooms. (*With* **Bauhaus** *and* **Brandt**.) Makes a change to see you enjoying your work, Uli.

Bauhaus Makes a change to end up with some tangible results.

Brandt That's what I like about mushrooms, Uli. You pick them, you pickle them, you eat them; they stay picked, they stay pickled, they never try to eat you back. Spread them out on the table, then, and let's see what we've got. You're sloping off, are you, Günter? Not an initiate into the mycological mysteries?

Guillaume Too frightened of getting a wrong 'un.

Brandt   We can always spot a wrong 'un, can't we, Uli.

Guillaume   – So while the Chief and Uli sort their trophies I sort mine.

Bauhaus   Some real beauties.

Guillaume   – One or two quite attractive specimens.

Brandt   Sparassis. Rather uncommon.

Guillaume   – The British privately encouraging us to be nasty to the Americans.

Brandt   Wonderful sweet fragrance.

Guillaume   – Charmingly indiscreet tone.

Bauhaus   Look at this whopper!

Guillaume   – Oh, and a real corker here!

Brandt   Parasol. *Lepiota procera*.

Guillaume   – The French Foreign Minister in person, being even nastier about the Americans.

Brandt   Ask Rut to fry it in butter with a little chopped onion and chervil.

Guillaume   – Mischa should be able to cook up something rather tasty with this . . . I even get on well with Uli. In fact I get on well with the entire security team. Christel and I give a little drinks party for them, and Pierre takes snaps of them all. Then in the evening we stroll across and have drinks on the verandah with Willy and Rut.

Brandt   Fetch us out another couple of bottles, Uli. Then we shan't have to trouble you again.

Guillaume   – It's like one of those sessions in the office in the old days. Except there's no Uncle and no Helmut. Just Rut and Christel and the boys. Uli, waiting with gun in holster and corkscrew in hand. The Chief and me. Also one or two old friends who emerge from Willy's Norwegian past as the long northern twilight wears on.

Brandt   Willy Brandt isn't the only person I was when I was here in Norway in the thirties. I was also Willy Flamme. I was Karl Martin. I was Felix Franke. Each of them writing articles for a different paper, each of them with a slightly different viewpoint. You must learn English, Günter, and read Walt Whitman. 'Do I contradict myself? Very well then I contradict myself. I am large, I contain multitudes.'

Guillaume   Your first experience of presiding over a Cabinet, Chief.

Brandt   I must have been rather better at it then. I don't recall any major splits or betrayals. What about you? Being our good familiar Günter Guillaume can't have exhausted all your possibilities.

Guillaume   Only name I've ever had.

Brandt   People kept taking me for a spy. Not something anyone's ever accused you of?

Guillaume   Being a spy? No.

Brandt   The Norwegians thought I was spying for the Finns. The Swedes arrested me for spying for the Russians.

Guillaume   Can't see you as a spy.

Brandt   No?

Guillaume   Too noticeable. Too, if I may say so, Chief, secretive.

Brandt   I knew all the tricks of the trade. Learnt them when I was on the run from the Gestapo. Suitcases with false bottoms. Invisible ink.

Guillaume   Invisible ink? You have actually written messages in invisible ink?

Brandt   Useful training. It's what politicians do all the time. No, I could have been a spy, Günter. Might be one, for all you know. Might be spying now.

Guillaume   – And for a moment I wonder . . .

Kretschmann – Wonder what?

Guillaume – Nothing. Ridiculous. The Chief could no more spy than fly.

Brandt All right, it's 1936. Yes? For six months I'm back in Nazi Germany. In Berlin, working underground for the party. Who am I? Willy Brandt? Obviously not. Willy Flamme – Karl Martin – Felix Franke? No – I'm not even a German . . . May I introduce myself? My name is Gunnar Gaasland. I was born and brought up in Oslo, as I'm afraid is only too clear from my accent! A very exciting time to be in Berlin, and to see all the wonderful new political developments here!

Guillaume I believe you, Chief. Gunnar Gaasland, from Oslo!

Brandt And always, always, at the back of your mind, the fear that you'll be taken by surprise. Suddenly – another Norwegian. What will your Norwegian sound like to a Norwegian? – *Vi må sørge for å møtes en gang. Det ville være en lettelse å snakke norsk igjen noen timer . . . !* – Will you pass or won't you? What if he's an old friend of Gunnar Gaasland's? Or what if you find yourself face to face with an old friend of Willy Brandt's? Or you're sitting talking with someone. Someone you've got to know quite well, perhaps. Feeling at ease with them. Feeling that everything's going well. And then you realise he's looking at you in a slightly odd way. At once you think . . .

Guillaume 'He knows!'

Brandt 'He knows . . . He knows . . .' It takes courage to live like that.

Guillaume I can imagine.

Brandt Courage and endurance.

Guillaume Yes.

Brandt   More courage and endurance than I could muster. I fled, Günter. I fled. So perhaps you're right – I'm not a spy. Just a suitcase with a series of false bottoms. Willy Flamme, Karl Martin . . . Felix Franke, Gunnar Gaasland . . . And somewhere among them the most secret compartment of them all. The one that you can remember finding once, and that you can never quite find again.

Guillaume   The one called Herbert Frahm.

Brandt   Or is it someone else altogether? Another little boy. A rather cheerful, ordinary one, not solemn or serious at all. Someone rather like your Pierre. The little boy that Herbert Frahm might have been if his father had brought him up and told him stories and played with him. Or even acknowledged his existence and given him his name. Herbert Möller. The boy I might have been, and never was.

Guillaume   – We sit there through the long Norwegian evenings, and in that unfamiliar northern light everything begins to seem strange and uncertain. I've become transparent to him, and he's playing with me, just as I am with him. Or is it only the possibility he's playing with? Or is that what I'm doing? Is it him I'm seeing in the half-light, or is it a reflection of myself?

Kretschmann   – You're still handling the telexes?

Guillaume   – Yes.

Kretschmann   – And not being watched?

Guillaume   – No.

Kretschmann   – Certain?

Guillaume   – Certain. Then one night he asks me the same question he asked me before.

Brandt   And you still think I can trust them?

Guillaume   – It's almost dark. I can't see the expression on his face. – I hope they haven't been listening in to some of the things you've been telling me, Chief, or they might start to have a few doubts about *you* . . .

Kretschmann   – He can't see *your* face.

Guillaume   – No. But in the end the time comes to leave, and I have to show you the collected fruits of all my labours. So I simply get two of our dispatch-cases . . .

Bauhaus   These two?

Guillaume   Thank you, Uli. – I pack up all my copies of the incoming and outgoing messages in *that* one, and put it in the boot of my car. *This* one I fill up with the little souvenirs that the Chief hands out on our travels. Then . . . – Uli!

Bauhaus   If you're going to ask me to carry something back to Bonn for you . . .

Guillaume   Classified documents, Uli.

Bauhaus   I've got all the Chief's bags already. I've got five jars of pickled mushrooms.

Guillaume   Uli, you're a trained security officer.

Bauhaus   Yes. Not a porter.

Guillaume   You're flying. I'm driving.

Bauhaus   Certainly not *your* porter.

Guillaume   Uli, if anything should happen to these papers while they were in the boot of my car . . .

Bauhaus   It wouldn't be *my* responsibility.

Guillaume   I'll tuck it under your arm, look. Now, don't let that box out of your sight, Uli. Not for an instant. Thanks, Uli. You're a pal.

Bauhaus   I can't even draw my gun!

Guillaume   If you need to draw your gun, Uli – drop the mushrooms. – And my fears are fully justified. We stop for the night at a hotel in Sweden, and I lock the box of souvenirs in our room while Christel and I go dancing. I have a strong suspicion when we get back that somebody has let themselves in and photographed the entire collection.

Kretschmann   – Worked like a charm. Thank you.

Guillaume   – So now we're back in the Palais Schaumburg. And even if any suspicions crossed the Chief's mind up there in Norway they've soon vanished into the autumn mist, because everything's even worse than it was before. There are wildcat strikes in the metalworking industry. The dustmen aren't emptying the dustbins.

Kretschmann   – Sixty million Germanys!

Guillaume   – Helmut's raging away.

Schmidt   Someone's got to stand up to these people! Someone's got to *do* something! Make some decisions! Give this government a sense of purpose and direction!

Guillaume   – And where's Uncle off to?

Ehmke (*with* **Wilke** *and* **Guillaume**)   Can you believe he actually said it? Even Herbert Wehner?

Wilke   'What the present German government lacks is a head.'

Ehmke   At a press-conference! In *Moscow*, of all places! We've only just established normal relations! The entire world waiting to hear what he's going to say!

Wilke   'The Chancellor's asleep on his feet. He's lost in a world of his own . . . Quite frankly I have never taken this government seriously as a government . . .'

Ehmke   Who put him up to it, though? You know the Russians are telling us in private that he's having more secret meetings with his friends in East Berlin?

Wilke   What East Berlin is telling us in private is that the Russians are lying.

Ehmke   Two old friends make a new friend – and at once they get jealous of each other. Another unforeseen consequence of our success. Life's such a tangle, Reinhard! Everyone looking at everyone else. Everyone seeing something different. Everyone trying to guess what everyone else is seeing. It's such an endless shifting unreliable indecipherable unanalysable *mess*!

Wilke   I think that what Herr Wehner is saying is comparatively simple. 'Sack me. Or sack yourself.'

Ehmke   And this time Willy will have to do it. He'll have to nerve himself to pick up the pistol and pull the trigger. It's either Willy or Uncle. They can't both survive.

Wehner (*with* **Ehmke**, **Wilke** *and* **Guillaume**) Banished! Exiled! Shut out from the sunshine of our great leader's smile!

Ehmke   Sacked?

Wehner   Sacked? Dear God, no. Made to sit in the corner at lunch. Firmness tempered with mercy, as always. The great peacemaker at work once again. Hands as unspotted as ever.

Ehmke (*with* **Wilke** *and* **Guillaume**)   So now of course it's Helmut's turn again to chisel away at him.

Schmidt (*with* **Brandt**)   'No.' That's the word, Willy. You must learn to say it! 'No . . . no . . . no . . .' They want a fifteen per cent pay rise? No. 'No' meaning no.

Brandt   'No' will mean no buses or trains, of course. No post. No hospitals.

Schmidt   It will also mean no lack of support from me as your Minister of Finance.

Guillaume   – So that's what he says. No. And what does it mean? It means no.

Ehmke   No buses or trains. No post. No hospitals. And no support from Helmut, because – no Helmut!

Wilke (*with* **Brandt**)   He's in Washington, Herr
Chancellor.

Brandt   And no word?

Wilke   He says – just do whatever you think best.

Brandt   Thank him, will you, Reinhard?

Ehmke (*with* **Guillaume**)   So when the employers
collapse and 'no' turns out to mean 'yes', who's to blame?

Guillaume   Willy.

Ehmke   When the world's oil producers force prices up,
and suddenly there's no petrol in the pumps and no cars on
the autobahn,who's the guilty party?

Guillaume   Willy.

Ehmke   Who made the sun shine for them yesterday?

Guillaume   Willy.

Ehmke   So who's making it rain today?

Guillaume   Willy.

Ehmke   Who put the leak in their roof and the hole in
their shoe?

Guillaume   Willy. Willy, Willy, Willy.

Ehmke   He's dropped ten points in the polls. Even the
left-wing press have turned against him.

Kretschmann   – Get him out of there, Günter. Get him
on the train again. More upturned faces. More smiling lips
and shining eyes. Make him happy again, Günter!

Guillaume (*with* **Brandt** *and* **Bauhaus**)   Frimmersdorf
. . . Koblenz . . . Darmstadt . . . Suit pressed, clean shirt . . .
Who's who in Frimmersdorf, what's what in Darmstadt . . .
Uli – another bottle . . . ! Sign hanging in the cloakroom of
the Bundestag: Members Only. Scrawled across the bottom:

Also hats and coats . . . Neumarkt . . . Regensburg . . .
Straubing . . . A listener writes to Radio Yerevan: 'Is there
life on Mars?' Radio Yerevan replies: 'No, there is no life on
Mars, either . . .' Look at them out there, Chief! All those
faces gazing up from the darkness! Two words from you –
that's all they want! 'Dear friends . . . dear friends . . .!' No?
Look at *her*, then! The way her eyes are fixed on you! The
softness of her cheeks as she smiles! And those two women
further back. And more women, further back still, that you
can't quite see. And more again at the next station. So many
of them, Chief! So many different roads you could take!

Brandt   What have I done with my life, Günter? Moved
on, moved on. Adapted, adapted. Turned my back on
anyone who ever loved me. Forgotten anyone who ever
helped me on my way. Shed my skins, one after another,
like a snake . . . On and on the stations come. Plattling,
Vilshofen, Passau . . . Willy Flamme, Karl Martin, Felix
Franke . . . One face after another. One defeat after
another. And where do I end up? On a train, travelling
from nowhere to nowhere, to no point or purpose, making
my confession to Pastor Nobody.

Guillaume (*with* **Kretschmann**)   It doesn't work any
more, Arno. Not even the train. Then we're back in Bonn . . .
and there's another problem. They're tailing Christel.

Kretschmann   She's certain?

Guillaume   Certain.

Kretschmann   You want us to withdraw you?

Guillaume   Too late, now they're on to us. Everyone will
know it's true. A spy in Willy's own office! That really will
finish him. And anyway . . .

Kretschmann   *He'll* know.

Guillaume   Stupid, isn't it? He's going to know sooner or
later. And half of me longs to tell him!

Kretschmann   But face to face.

Guillaume   Not just run away, like a naughty little boy.

Kretschmann   You want to see the look in his eyes as he feels the knife go in.

Guillaume   I want him to see it was hard for me, as well as for him. Anyway, it may be a false alarm. Christel's up for a job in the Ministry of Defence. Routine check of some sort.

Kretschmann   Lie low for a bit. Take a holiday. Somewhere in the sun. Some place where the skies are blue all day. Wait and see.

Genscher (*with* **Brandt** *and* **Nollau**)   I understand that Herr Guillaume is out of the office today.

Brandt   Taking a well-deserved holiday.

Genscher   The best part of a year has gone by since you authorised Herr Nollau to place him under observation. I have been pressing Herr Nollau to tell me whether we now feel able to present the case for prosecution.

Brandt   Dear God, I assumed all that was long forgotten. Not that I ever saw the slightest sign of any activity. Your people are very skilled, Herr Nollau.

Nollau   Thank you, Herr Chancellor.

Brandt   You have actually found some evidence?

Nollau   We think so. We believe so. We feel we may have. On the other hand . . .

Genscher   Yes or no?

Nollau   Some difficulties and inconsistencies remain. One can imagine defence counsel making much of the second man, for example.

Genscher   The second man? What second man?

Nollau   In the original clandestine message on which the case would still largely depend. It referred, if you recall, to a second son.

Brandt   A second son? Or a second man?

Nollau   Let me see . . .

Genscher   Oh, no! Oh, for heaven's sake!

Nollau   'Congratulations on the second man.'

Genscher   The second *man* in the family is the son!

Nollau   I see. Of course. So the first man is . . . ?

Brandt   Resting from his labours.

Guillaume (*with* **Kretschmann**)   I set off before dawn for the long drive south. I glance in my mirror as I turn out of the petrol station, and there, in the first grey light, is a car waiting on the hard shoulder about three hundred metres behind me. I move off. He moves off. I turn onto the autobahn. He turns onto the autobahn. I hit a steady 120. He stays sitting in my mirror. Across the frontier into Belgium and he's still there. On into France, and he holds 160 with me all the way to Paris. My own personal assistant! As faithful to me as I am to Willy. Then at Fontainebleau the French police take over . . .

Kretschmann   They let you have your holiday?

Guillaume   My last holiday. In the south. In the sun.

Kretschmann   You thought of staying there? Of never coming back?

Guillaume   Every sunlit hour of every sunlit day. The simple life. A glass of wine on a shaded terrace. The scent of rosemary and thyme. All thought jammed out by the cicadas . . .

Kretschmann   Your life's work done.

Guillaume   At peace with the world around me. My own simple self at last. Not even my own self. No one.

Kretschmann   You could have gone home. Now you knew you were blown. You could have crossed back to the East.

Guillaume   They gave me the chance. They followed me north as far as Fontainebleau. Then this afternoon – nothing. All the way to the border – no one. Petrol in the tank. Money in my pocket.

Kretschmann   Why didn't you? Pierre?

Guillaume   Also Christel.

Kretschmann   And your current lady-friend.

Guillaume   You. Mischa.

Kretschmann   Willy, of course.

Guillaume   Such an ignominious exit. I don't want him to remember me like that.

Kretschmann   Our last meeting, then?

Guillaume   Looks like it.

Kretschmann   Four years, though!

Guillaume   Not bad.

Kretschmann   One for the history books, Günter. In the chapter on Willy Brandt you'll always have your paragraph.

Knocking. Darkness. Doorbell. A crack of light.

Voice   Herr Günter Guillaume?

Guillaume   Yes?

Voice   We have a warrant for your arrest.

The crack of light opens to the width of a door.

Nollau (*with* **Brandt** *and* **Guillaume**)   Half-past six this morning, Herr Chancellor. At his flat. His wife was also arrested.

Brandt   And Pierre. Their son. Was he present? Did he see it happen?

Nollau   I believe he came out of his bedroom while the arrest was being made. I'm pleased to say Guillaume confessed at once.

Guillaume   I am a citizen of East Germany, and one of its officers. I must ask you to respect that.

Brandt   A citizen of East Germany. One of its officers . . . He gave you the case. You wouldn't have had one otherwise. He sentenced himself.

Nollau   I realise that a number of mistakes have been made in the course of this investigation, Herr Chancellor. I hope you feel it has now been pursued to a satisfactory conclusion.

Brandt   He did it for Pierre. He betrayed me – and then he betrayed his other master as well. To explain to Pierre.

Nollau   Perhaps also to explain to you, Herr Chancellor.

Guillaume (*alone, sits*)   Sorry, Arno. The only time I dropped my guard in all the eighteen years I've spent here. The only mistake I made . . . I wonder where *you* are now? Vanished into the mist, I hope . . . Strange – *you* can see *me*. Gazing out at you from every newspaper and television screen in West Germany. You can guess what I'm doing, too. Reporting to you still! Inside my head. Telling you everything! Telling you sorry. Telling you I know I let Mischa down.

Brandt (*with* **Ehmke**)   Trust no one. That's the miserable lesson of these last four years.

Ehmke   Not even me. I hired him. I vetted him. Not even you. For a whole year you've known he was under surveillance. And not a word of warning to me.

Brandt   What kind of man must he be, though? What kind of people are they who sent him? You're robbed by the beggar you befriend, and you feel ashamed for him. Ashamed for yourself, too, for trusting him.

Guillaume   – And Willy. I let Willy down. I saw him on the news. He looked sick at heart. His first trip without me to watch over him. Wearing half of one suit and half of another! And no upturned faces! Who wrote his schedule? Who sent him on a walkabout when everyone was at home watching the football?

Wilke (*with* **Ehmke**)   All the journalists are complaining. One of them said: 'It was never like this when Günter was organising it.' Meanwhile there's Willy, standing on a clifftop above the North Sea, gazing into the depths below.

Brandt   – If you're going to fall, where's the better place to land? In the soft swamp of disgrace, to flounder helplessly on? Or on the hard ground, with all your struggles over? One long moment of terror, and then such . . . such simplicity.

Ehmke (*with* **Wilke** *and* **Brandt**)   Come on, Willy. We can soon fix this. All it needs is for me to go on television and say that at every stage in Guillaume's career the proper vetting and security procedures were followed.

Wilke   They weren't.

Ehmke   You're not the one who's going to say it.

Brandt   If only I hadn't given up smoking.

Ehmke   So, Willy, your great reshuffle. What are you going to do with Helmut? He wants the Foreign Ministry, and so does Genscher.

Brandt   Such a shabby way to go. Such an ignominious exit.

Ehmke   Leave it all to me, Willy. I'll fix it. We'll have you chancelling again in no time.

Nollau (*with* **Bauhaus**)   The women? What women?

Bauhaus   On the train. On his travels.

Nollau   Oh, I see. I don't think this is in any way relevant to our inquiries, Herr Bauhaus.

Bauhaus   I'm sorry. I thought I should mention it.

Nollau   There's no secret about Herr Brandt's weakness in this direction.

Bauhaus   Anyway, I've given your people the list if you need it . . .

Nollau   You made a list?

Bauhaus   Part of my job – check his visitors. I couldn't always get their names. Time in and time out, though. And some kind of rough indication of the different categories. Journalists, party workers, and so on. Local supporters, prostitutes . . .

Nollau   I don't think we need to pursue this any further, Herr Bauhaus.

Bauhaus   No, only I just thought, if Herr Guillaume was keeping a list as well . . .

Nollau   Guillaume? *Guillaume* knew about Herr Brandt's proclivities?

Bauhaus   When we were on the train. Herr Guillaume had to help me . . . well . . .

Nollau   Help you what?

Bauhaus   Control the queue. And I just thought, if he'd given the list to his people in East Berlin . . .

Nollau   So . . . Journalists, you say? Party workers? What kind of numbers are we talking about . . . ?

Guillaume   – The women! Suddenly it's the only thing my interrogators are interested in! But everyone knew! Everyone's always known! Why have people suddenly started to talk about it?

Genscher (*with* **Brandt**)   I hardly need say that I find this an intensely distasteful task. I knew as soon as Nollau put it in my hands, though, that I had no choice but to show it to you.

Guillaume   – It wasn't me, Arno! Not a word have I said! Not me, Chief! Not me!

Genscher   Every single time we sit down to negotiate with them, whatever it's about – trade, refugees, border controls – we'll know they're holding this behind their backs.

Brandt   Pure nonsense, of course. For the most part. Sadly. Rather flattering, though, for a man of my age.

Wehner (*with* **Schmidt**)   We've put a knife in their hands.

Schmidt   One in *your* hands as well, of course . . .

Wehner   Not a weapon I should have chosen.

Schmidt   This list. It's in your handwriting.

Wehner   Nollau read it aloud to me.

Schmidt   And you took it down? At dictation? All ten pages?

Wehner   Old journalist – I write shorthand. I'm sorry it should have happened like this, Helmut. I know how distasteful you find it.

Schmidt   Every encounter. Every category of woman at every stop along the line. In shorthand.

Wehner   Helmut, we both always knew he'd have to go in the end. It was only a question of when he became more of a liability than an asset to the party.

Bauhaus (*with* **Brandt**)   I'm sorry, Chief. I know you feel I've let you down.

Brandt   *I'm* sorry. I seem to have given you an inordinate amount of labour.

Bauhaus   They kept on and on at me! I got confused! I'm an ordinary family man. I was out of my depth. Chief, I've served you faithfully for four years! Day in, day out! Fetched and carried for you! And always ready, at the slightest sudden movement in the corner of my eye, to step between you and the gun!

Brandt   And all the time there was another Uli there, waiting to emerge from the shadows when the moment came.

Schmidt (*with* **Wehner**)   We'll all have to give him our support, of course.

Wehner   Of course. Our full support.

Schmidt   You'll make that clear to him?

Wehner   Don't worry, Helmut. Your hands will be clean. Just as Number One's always were.

Guillaume   – The Chief knows he can rely on me! He knows we'd never try to undermine him! That's not what we meant at all!

Wehner (*with* **Brandt**)   The choice is obviously yours. You could resign the chancellorship, but stay on as party chairman – or you could give up the party as well.

Brandt   You've seen Nollau's list?

Wehner   I didn't note the details.

Brandt   Pity. They would have amused you.

Wehner   Or you could try to struggle on. Whatever you decide, you know I'll stand behind you.

Brandt   Where you have always stood.

Wehner   Precisely where I have always stood.

Brandt   With Helmut beside you.

Wehner   And if you do decide to hang on then you can count on us both to support you in exactly the same way as we always have.

Brandt   It's helpful to know that one has some friends one can rely upon not to change.

Wehner   Shall I ask Helmut to join us?

Brandt   So many people, with so many different views and so many different voices. And inside each of us so many more people still, all struggling to be heard. For a moment one voice rises above the others, and everyone picks up the tune. And then the cacophony resumes. Until sooner or later another voice is raised . . .

Wehner   Helmut! (*With* **Brandt** *and* **Schmidt**.) I think Number One has reached a decision.

Schmidt   I felt I should wait until you'd made up your own mind. I shouldn't like anyone to think I'd attempted to influence you. Let me merely say that, whatever your decision is . . .

Brandt   I have your support.

Schmidt   My unswerving support.

Brandt   Thank you. I think I can see a way of doing it that would enable me to offer you the Foreign Ministry.

Schmidt   Offer me the . . .?

Brandt   Foreign Ministry. Isn't that what you want? When I reshuffle? Keep Genscher out of it, at any rate. I'm

going to make a completely fresh start. Get rid of Grabert.
Bring in someone else to run the Chancellor's office.

Schmidt   I see. You're not . . . ?

Brandt   Not what?

Schmidt   I thought . . . Herbert thought . . .

Wehner   I think even Number One thought.

Brandt   Thought, yes. Thought and thought. Decided
even. But what voice will speak when you open your mouth
you never know for certain until it does.

Schmidt   So . . . Well . . . Of course . . .

Brandt   Not even *you.*

Schmidt   No . . . Only . . . Well . . .

Brandt   Will you fight or will you run? Who knows until
the moment comes? And since I have your support. Your
unswerving support . . .

Bauhaus (*with* **Nollau**)   One other possibility I should
mention. Guillaume may also have had well . . . photos.

Nollau   More photos?

Bauhaus   He was a professional photographer.

Nollau   So?

Bauhaus   When we were on the train he had the
compartment adjoining the Chief's . . .

Wilke (*with* **Wehner** *and* **Schmidt**)   No more than one
might expect from the gutter press, of course. I thought
you'd better see it, though.

Wehner   'Did Brandt Spy Take Sex Photos?'

Schmidt   Where did this one come from?

Wehner   No idea.

Wilke   Have you seen him today? He looks just about at the end of his tether.

Wehner   Been up all night, I gather. Drinking. Wavering. Muttering about pistols and high cliffs . . .

Brandt *joins them.* **Wilke** *gives him the newspaper.*

Wilke   I'm sorry to be the messenger . . .

Brandt   So many people eager to lend a helping hand.

Schmidt   But where did they get the story?

Guillaume   – Not from me, Chief! No story – no photographs! You know that!

Brandt (*to* **Wehner**)   I never asked how your meeting went. With your friends in East Berlin on Friday.

Wehner   Fruitful, I think.

Brandt   Prisoners and families?

Wehner   Not this time.

Brandt   No?

Wehner   Economic co-operation. Long-planned. As you know.

Brandt   So much support . . . You open your mouth to surrender, and you hear a voice saying: 'I'm damned if I will!' You open it again, and this time it's another voice altogether. Saying: 'Done for. Finished. Sunk.' Well . . . Various people I shall have to inform first, of course. My family. The party. Our coalition partners. My official letter of resignation Grabert can take to the President this evening. (*To* **Schmidt**.) I know that Herbert will give you exactly the same kind of support as he has always given me.

Schmidt   Willy, stop. Stop, stop, stop. Let's all just pause and think for a moment. Let's not get ourselves rushed into a decision we might all regret. Willy . . .!

Wehner (*with* **Schmidt** *and* **Wilke**)   I shouldn't get too excited. He'll change his mind a few more times yet.

Schmidt   One of us must go after him, stop him, reason with him!

Wehner   Don't worry. It's me they'll point the finger at, not you.

Schmidt   We can't survive without Willy! I'll never carry the party! They love him!

Wehner   They'll love you, too. In time. If you feed them and keep them warm. If I'm there to be hated. If love is what you want.

Schmidt   I can't do it, Herbert! Not like this!

Wehner   He was right about one thing. Fight or run? Pull the trigger or drop the gun? Not one of us who knows which it will be until it's happened.

Ehmke (*with* **Schmidt**, **Wehner** *and* **Wilke**)   Where's Willy? I think I may have swung it! Went on television and really did my stuff. Said we'd done all the security checks in the world. Done them ten times over. Lied and lied until I believed it myself . . . Where is he?

Wehner   Resigning.

Ehmke   I knew it.

Wehner   Or not resigning.

Wilke *gives* **Ehmke** *the newspaper.*

Wehner   In two minds about it. Making up both of them.

Ehmke   Someone should go and make sure he's all right.

Schmidt   You, presumably.

Ehmke   Strange, isn't it. Everybody loves him – and nobody does he have to turn to. Nobody in the whole wide world.

Schmidt   He has you.

Ehmke   Not even me.

Guillaume (*alone*)   The nobody he turned to once was me. An upturned face like all the others that he spoke to from his heart. The upturned face for ever at his side. The smiling face with nothing behind it. No secret ambitions, no concealed disagreements, no hidden resentments. He didn't like me much. He told Horst Ehmke to get rid of me.

The expectant murmur of an audience.

Told him to, but never made him do it.

Handbell. Silence.

Woman's voice   Ladies and gentlemen, I declare the result of the vote to be as follows. Those in favour: 267. Those against: 225.

Applause. Lights up on Schmidt.

I therefore declare, according to article 63 paragraph 2 of the Basic Law, that the proposed Member has received the votes of the majority of Members of the Bundestag. Herr Schmidt, I must ask you if you accept election as Chancellor of the Federal Republic of Germany.

Guillaume   – His faithful nobody. And just when he needed me most I wasn't there.

Schmidt   Frau President, I accept the election.

Guillaume   I think about it all over the years as I serve my long sentence, and I see just how the pieces in the puzzle fall into place. The distrust, the jealousy. The economics, the illness. Schmidt and Wehner. Nollau and Genscher and Bauhaus. Herbert Frahm and Herbert Möller. And finally me. I've let myself be used! Not just by Mischa. Not just by you, Arno. By Herbert Wehner. That's what burns. I've been picked up by Wehner, like a handy lump of wood by a murderer, and used to club Willy down. Not for one moment do I let anyone see my shame. But ashamed I am, Arno! Ashamed at last . . .

Kretschmann – Nothing I can do for you now but count the days of your sentence off with you one by one, while we wait for Mischa to get you exchanged. Six years it takes us before we manage to bring you home.

Guillaume Home, yes. Only I've got cancer by this time. I've lost all contact with Pierre.

Kretschmann (*with* **Guillaume**) Thirty prisoners we paid for you, Günter! You always wanted to know if it was true about the prisoners. And the price has gone up. They're worth almost a hundred thousand marks a head now. Three million marks we valued you at!

Guillaume Home. Is it? I see it with very different eyes now. And how thin that single voice sounds once your ears have got attuned to the complexity of counterpoint! In any case you were right. Now Willy had made peace with the Russians they didn't need to keep their wretched little ally on its feet any longer.

The faint thudding of a pickaxe.

(*with everyone.*) That knocking in the timbers grows louder and louder as the months and years go by – and it turns out that this is where the noise was coming from all the time. Not that house. The house next door. Our house.

Brandt The journalists rang me in the middle of the night to get my reaction. The event we'd waited so long for has actually begun to happen. The state whose existence I recognised is passing out of existence before our eyes. The point of all that suffering and struggle and deception is crumbling into dust.

The single pickaxe is joined by more. The sound grows louder. Everyone rises and gazes out into the house. The thudding of the pickaxes culminates in the rumble of collapsing masonry. Light.

And at last what belongs together is coming together. Our divided self has become one self.

Guillaume   The old peacemaker sets out on his travels once again. So many new lands to wander! So many more upturned faces!

Brandt   Eisenach and Dresden . . . Leipzig and Rostock . . .

Guillaume   All wanting to see the man who first began to make this happen. Does he ever miss me organising the timetables and laying out his suit? Does he ever consider that I played my own small part in all this? The little man who looked at the great man, and saw that he could be trusted.

Brandt   I sometimes wonder about him, of course. His son's turned his back on him, his homeland's vanished. We're both mortally ill.

Guillaume   I watch him as he passes. He's changed. So have I. So has everyone and everything. Herbert Wehner . . .

Wehner   Dead and with the angels.

Guillaume   Helmut Schmidt . . .

Schmidt   Long since out of office.

Ehmke   And our great party with him.

Guillaume   Hans-Dietrich Genscher, who could never be Foreign Minister . . .

Genscher   Foreign Minister for the last fifteen years.

Guillaume   And where are you, Arno? Vanished again before they arrest you. Melted into the crowd, like so many others.

Kretschmann   – I stand among them and cheer with all the rest as Willy passes. Cheer with all my heart. A great man!

Brandt   We're healed and whole. For a little while, at any rate. And for a little while everyone's glad.

Guillaume   And wherever he goes, my shadow goes with him. Together still.

Darkness.

Postscript

Nineteen seventy-two marked the high summer of Willy Brandt's brief but remarkable career as German Chancellor. It was also, as it happened, the year in which I made my first serious visit to Germany, and first became fascinated by it – particularly by its evolution since the Second World War. Perhaps this is why the complex and painful story of Brandt's downfall two years later captured my imagination at the time, and has been lurking at the back of my mind ever since.

Brandt was one of the most attractive public figures of the twentieth century, who won people's trust and love not only in Germany but all over the world. He first became a national and international celebrity in the 1950s, when he was Governing Mayor of West Berlin, and led the city's resistance to the efforts of the Soviet Union to undermine and intimidate it so that it could be absorbed into the East German state surrounding it. After his resignation from the Federal Chancellorship in 1974 he won himself a completely new reputation with yet another career as an internationalist and champion of the Third World. His greatest achievements, though, were in Federal politics. The first of them was to help reform his party, the SPD (the Social Democrats), so as to make it electable by the cautiously conservative German voters. The second was single-handedly to seize the chance, when it was at last offered by a modest improvement in the party's share of the vote in 1969, of forming an SPD-led coalition – the first left-of-centre coalition in Germany, with the first left-of-centre Chancellor, since Hitler had crushed parliamentary democracy in the early thirties. His real triumph, though, was the use to which he put the power he had gained: to secure what had hitherto seemed a politically impossible goal – a reconciliation with Germany's former enemies in Eastern Europe.

The difficulty was that this could be done only by at last recognising the painful realities created by the outcome of the war. One of these was the loss of nearly a quarter of Germany's territory in the East. The other was the existence

within the remaining German lands of the second state that
had grown out of the Soviet zone of occupation – the
German Democratic Republic, alien in its political
character, bound hand and foot to the Soviet instead of the
Western power bloc, and sealed off behind closed frontiers
that sundered all natural family and social connections.
There was entrenched and embittered opposition to
accepting either fact, particularly from those most directly
involved – the 8 million Germans who had been expelled
from the former German territories east of the Oder and
Neisse rivers, which had now been divided up between the
Soviet Union and Poland, plus the 4 million who had fled
from East Germany, and the millions more who had
relatives still trapped there. But Brandt succeeded in doing
it, and succeeded totally. The consequences of this
reconciliation reached far beyond Germany. They changed
the face of Europe, and of the world, by making possible the
gradual scaling down of the Cold War – and thereby,
eventually, an event that Brandt never foresaw: the end of
the very state whose existence he had recognised, followed
by the collapse of the entire Soviet empire.

In the summer of 1972, when I arrived in Germany,
Brandt's government was in the middle of this great work.
In spite of the severe difficulties it was encountering at home
because of its small and steadily vanishing majority in the
Bundestag, it was already ratifying the treaties it had
negotiated with the Soviet Union and Poland. I can't say
that I paid very much attention to these triumphs at the
time. Federal politics happened in Bonn, and Germany for
me that summer was Berlin, the once-great city I had come
to Germany to write about, now only notionally the capital,
left marvellous but functionless deep inside East Germany,
like a luxury liner that had somehow become beached in the
sandy wastes of the Mark Brandenburg.

The city compelled the imagination in all kinds of ways.
Its greatest fascination, though, was undoubtedly its greatest
monstrosity – the Wall, the hideous concrete barrier,
enforced by armed guards and a complex series of lethal
mantraps, that the East German government had been

forced to erect in 1961 to stop the massive haemorrhage of its citizens to the West. Another much longer wall, from the Baltic to Thuringia, divided the German Democratic Republic from West Germany proper, but the Berlin Wall obtruded more on the consciousness because it closed in the Western half of the city as tightly as the fence round a suburban garden. Wherever you went you came face to face with it barring the street you were in, and defining the geography of Berlin even more sharply than the Hudson river does the geography of New York.

Somewhere out of sight behind it that summer Egon Bahr and Michael Kohl, the representatives of the Federal and Democratic German Republics respectively, were negotiating the terms of the Basic Treaty by which the West was at last to recognise the East, and by which relations between the two states were at last to be given some semblance of normality. Already a new agreement on Berlin itself, signed by the four former allies, was for the first time making it possible for West Berliners to visit the Eastern half of their city. Friends of mine came back to the modern wonderland of West Berlin stunned by the different kind of wonderland that they had found on the other side of the Wall: cobbled streets, unlit villages, pockmarked tenements, snorting steam trains – the long-lost old Germany of the Weimar Republic and the Third Reich, magically preserved in all its nostalgic dullness and shabbiness, as if in some vast grey heritage park, by the conservatism of the Communists and the backwardness of their economy.

The existence of this other Germany, and the endless puzzle of its relations with the Federal Republic, was part of what made modern German politics the most interesting in Europe. How even to refer to it officially without seeming to acknowledge that it was a separate state? The right-wing press stuck with 'the Soviet Zone', or even simply 'the Zone', long after it had acquired a government of its own. The usual official euphemism was 'the other part of Germany'. Kiesinger, Brandt's predecessor as Chancellor, described it not as a state but a 'phenomenon'. Brandt was prepared to concede that it was a state, but refused to see it as a foreign one. As he famously said, in the statement of his new government's policies in 1969: 'Even if two states exist in Germany they are not foreign to each other; their relations to each other can only be of a special sort.'

Whatever West Germans called it, there were endless practical difficulties in coping with a hostile next-door neighbour that was obsessed with spying on every aspect of life, not only internally but externally – particularly since all its 15 million citizens were potential agents because they spoke exactly the same language – and since a further 4 million of them were inside the gates already. What could such close cousins, who found themselves upon such different paths in life, make of each other? How would they behave as their relationship began to change?

The complexities of the situation were made painfully personal in the story of Willy Brandt and Günter Guillaume. Guillaume, who had crossed over from East Berlin thirteen years earlier, joined the Chancellor's office as a junior aide within weeks of Brandt's election in 1969. For the next four years he served Brandt with devotion and efficiency, and rose to become the personal assistant who organised his travels and accompanied him wherever he went. He was also spying on him, it turned out, with equal devotion and efficiency, on behalf of his employers in the East German Ministry of State Security, and his arrest in 1974 precipitated Brandt's resignation.

Exactly why it did, though, is by no means obvious. In his official letter of resignation Brandt said that he assumed political responsibility for negligence in connection with the affair. The security services had indeed committed a catalogue of errors in failing to vet Guillaume properly before his appointment, and in allowing him to continue even after the first serious suspicions had been raised against him. In private some of Brandt's colleagues told him that he was open to blackmail by the East German government, because Guillaume had presumably supplied them with a list of Brandt's extra-marital activities. But historians tend to agree that the unmasking of Guillaume was more the occasion of the Chancellor's downfall than its cause. It took

its place among a complex of factors arising from the
political situation inside the Federal Republic, from the
internal conflicts of the SPD and its leaders, from Brandt's
own character and physical condition – even from the very
success that he had achieved.

Peter Merseburger, Brandt's most recent biographer,
mocks supporters of Brandt who detect treachery and see
his fall as a kind of regicide. 'As if, in the respectable
republican court at Bonn there had been Shakespearean
dramas, opponents are demonised as Brutus-figures who
carried daggers under their robes, even as dark Nibelung
warriors who had nothing in mind but to assassinate the
Chancellor's character.' Politics, as Merseburger says, is
mostly 'terribly banal', and the events of 1974 were no
exception. Among the banalities, nevertheless, were many
strands of powerful personal feeling, of loyalty and jealousy,
of courage and despair. It was really the sheer complexity of
this mixture that finally decided me to write the play.
Complexity is what the play is about: the complexity of
human arrangements and of human beings themselves, and
the difficulties that this creates in both shaping and
understanding our actions.

*

The only part of German history that seems to arouse much
interest in the British is the Nazi period. That brutal holiday
from the moral restraints under which West European
societies normally labour possesses a kind of corrupt
glamour for even the most timid and law-abiding. The half-
century that has followed Germany's awakening from the
sick dream is thought to be a time of dull respectability, with
the Federal Republic characterised by nothing much except
material prosperity, and formed in the image of the peaceful
and provincial Rhineland town which was the seat of its
government for most of the period.

To me, I have to say, that material prosperity, that
peacefulness, even that supposed dullness, represent an
achievement at which I never cease to marvel or to be

moved. It's difficult to think of parallels for such an unlikely political, economic and moral resurgence. What other nation, even Japan, has risen so swiftly from beginnings as abject as the physical ruin, moral degradation and political paralysis in which Germany found itself in 1945? Federal Germany began life as a graveyard in which almost every city had been reduced to rubble, and almost every institution and political resource contaminated by complicity in the crimes of National Socialism; yet from this utter desolation, without recourse to despotism or military means, its citizens constructed one of the most prosperous, stable, and decent states in Europe, the cornerstone of a peace which has endured now, at least in Western Europe, for nearly sixty years.

The process was greatly assisted, it's true, by some of the consequences of defeat itself. It was in the first place the presence of the occupying armies that probably saved Germany from the revolutions and counter-revolutions by which it was ravaged after the First World War. Then there were the refugees from the East. By 1950 nearly 8 million of the 12 forced out of the lost provinces of East Prussia and the Sudetenland flooded into the Western zones of occupation. How the shattered country ever absorbed them beggars the imagination. A further 3 million arrived over the years, plus another 4 million from East Germany. This flood of immigrants, though, provided the Federal Republic with the labour it needed to rebuild. Recovery was also helped by Marshall Aid, provided to the Western zones of occupation by America even while the Russians were still pillaging their own zone (though the net value of it, when offset against reparations and occupation costs, has been queried by some historians; and in any case Germany received less of it than Britain and other European countries).

Even the famous currency reform of 1948, which gave birth to the mighty Deutschmark, and which first kicked the moribund economy into life again, was sprung upon Germans not by Ludwig Erhard, their economics minister, as is generally supposed, but by the Americans (and hijacked by Erhard in a spectacular double-double-cross which would provide the material for another play). The currency reform also precipitated the splitting of the nation, because the Soviet Union refused to accept the Deutschmark in its zone of occupation. But this, too, had its positive effects for West Germany, because it marked a further step in the division of the entire world into two competing empires, whose confrontation in the ensuing cold war swiftly transformed America's defeated enemy into its crucial front-line ally.

German politicians were reluctant to endorse the dismemberment of their nation, and the concept of West Germany as a separate political entity seems to have originated once again with the Americans (according to Dean Acheson, it was first proposed by the US Military Governor, General Lucius Clay). The new state even acquired the constitution that has served it so well ever since (more properly called the Basic Law, so as not to imply any constitutional acceptance of the country's division) only because it was instructed by the occupying powers to compose one.

In the end, though, the success of the new state was created by the efforts of its own citizens – by the sheer hard labour of its workers, by the crafts that were lying dormant in people's fingertips and the professional and entrepreneurial skills in their brains, by the readiness of so many people to put the public good at least as high as their own personal profit – and by the political skills of the leaders it found. The Basic Law was signed into effect, and the first Federal election held, in 1949, but there was already a complex political landscape in place: the *Länder*, the patchwork of provinces that make up the German nation (eleven of them at the time), together with their governments. Their heterogeneity reflects the very different characters and histories of the various German states that were assembled to compose Imperial Germany in 1871, and the combination of their individual politics with their participation in the Federal politics of Bonn created the characteristic complexity of modern German politics.

Since that first election in 1949, which brought the wily Konrad Adenauer to power, the Federal government has gone through many crises and scandals. It has survived many revelations that its members or officers had been implicated in the crimes of the past, or were working for East German intelligence, and many alarms when the nationalistic right seemed to be resurgent, or when the electorate seemed to be still nostalgic for past glories. In the last decade the longed-for reunification with the Eastern *Länder* has plunged the nation into its most severe and prolonged difficulties yet. But the Federal Republic has worked. It has proved stable and moderate. It has even survived its dependence upon coalition as a way of life – something which appears unworkable to British and American eyes, which has caused endemic weakness in France and Italy, and which indeed destroyed the Weimar Republic and opened the door to Hitler. Every West German government since the Federal Republic was founded has been a coalition, usually between the CDU/CSU (the conservative alliance formed by the Christian Democratic Union of the northern *Länder* and the Christian Social Union of Bavaria) on the one hand and the tiny FDP, the Free Democratic Party (aka the Liberals) on the other.

In 1966, though, coalition politics reached its bizarre apotheosis in the so-called Grand Coalition, when the junior partner of the CDU/CSU became not the FDP but the SPD, their principal antagonist, hitherto apparently doomed to serve as the permanent Opposition. Willy Brandt was bounced into the arrangement against his wishes by his colleagues Herbert Wehner and Helmut Schmidt, because the plane bringing him from Berlin to the crucial meeting was delayed by fog. But, once again, the arrangement worked. Brandt himself, with his charm, his fluency in other languages, and his impeccable political past, made a natural Foreign Minister. And although he loathed Georg Kiesinger, the CDU Chancellor and a former member of the Nazi Party, to the point where he claimed to feel physically ill in his presence, the coalition lasted for three years, and is regarded by some commentators as one of the most successful governments in the history of the Federal Republic.

The elections in the autumn of 1969 transformed the politics of coalition once again. Although it still trailed the Christian Democrats, the SPD picked up enough seats to raise the possibility of securing a slim majority in the Bundestag by going into coalition with the FDP. Wehner and Schmidt were against it; they wanted to continue with the existing arrangement. With entirely uncharacteristic decisiveness, Brandt seized his chance. Wehner and Schmidt had bounced him into the Grand Coalition; now he bounced them out of it. Without a word to either of them he went on television on election night and announced that he would seek to form a new government with the FDP. He succeeded, and three weeks later the new Bundestag elected him Chancellor.

Which is where my play begins.

*

Two mutually contradictory developments had conspired to bring the SPD and the electorate somewhat closer together. The first was the change in the nature of the party that had begun at its conference in Bad Godesberg ten years earlier, when Brandt, Wehner and Schmidt had persuaded it to dump its residual Marxism in favour of the so-called social market economy. The second was the change in the nature of the electorate brought about by the events on the streets of Germany in the previous year.

The 'student movement' of 1968 swept all the way across Europe and the USA. But it had begun the year before in Berlin. The trigger was a demonstration against a visit by the Shah of Persia, and its heavy-handed suppression by the police, during which they shot and killed a student called Benno Ohnesorg. The wave of demonstrations, strikes and sit-ins that ensued all over the world was like the long-stored energy released in an earthquake. It came from a huge idealism that had found little outlet in the cautious compromises of parliamentary democracy. In Germany there were two additional causes of frustration. One was the new generation's realisation that the apparently solid fabric of German society rested upon foundations built out of the rubble of its National Socialist past, and which were by unspoken common consent not to be inspected too closely. The second was the extreme expression of the consensuality of post-war German politics in the Grand Coalition, which left all the functions of an Opposition to the tiny, impotent and far from radical FDP.

So the radical left had constituted itself as an informal 'extra-parliamentary Opposition'. This chaotic grouping was, needless to say, far more disparate than any official coalition could ever be, and it was the spectacular array of its fission products that caught my eye when I arrived in Berlin in 1972. Some of its factions were rigidly subservient to the SED (the 'Socialist Unity Party' that ruled East Germany), some of them were Maoist, some of them nostalgic throwbacks to the KPD, the old Communist Party of the Weimar years, some of them engaged in increasingly brutal terrorism. A wide range of idealistic lifestyles and business enterprises had sprung up in the city, a kaleidoscope of 'left-oriented' communes, of pubs and cafés selling drinks and hot cakes at 'comrades' prices'.

The movement produced a sympathetic shift to the left among many voters who were never part of it. A number of its most active and effective adherents, in any case, decided to pursue their battle within the framework of practical politics. They proclaimed 'the long march through the institutions', including the unions and the SPD, with the intention of bringing them under their control by constitutional means. All this helped to earn the party the small increase in its vote in 1969 (3.4 per cent) that put it within reach of real power. The pressures it produced inside the party, though, and the expectations that the party's success aroused in its new adherents, created great difficulties for Brandt. It also produced a backlash among voters, particularly since left extremists in the Baader-Meinhof group, now reconstituted as the Red Army Fraction, had taken to robbing banks and murdering judges. Brandt's proposal to encourage yet another manifestion of the left by offering concessions to Soviet Communism and by recognising its client regime in East Germany became even more alarming than it had been before. He had to find ways of reassuring people. One attempt was the proclamation of the so-called 'Radicals Edict' of January 1972, more usually known abroad as the *Berufsverbot* (bar to the professions), designed to exclude radicals from teaching and other public services. If Brandt's greatest achievement was the Ostpolitik (and the Deutschlandpolitik, as the part of it relating to *deutsch-deutsche* relations was more properly called), then his greatest mistake – or so he said himself – was this reactionary domestic counterpoise to it.

All politics is necessarily complex, since its essence is the practical resolution of differences of interest and outlook which are in principle irreconcilable. All human beings, too, are complex – but Brandt (like German politics) was perhaps more complex than most. He was certainly more complex than he seemed. In public there was something engagingly open and straightforward about him, even when he was at his most devious – something recognisably decent and human, to which many people in many different parts of the world responded. Even the new leftists were charmed by him. Even the personal assistant who was spying on him. His associates, though, often complained about the weaknesses he showed in private: his indecisiveness, his avoidance of confrontation, his uncommunicativeness, his proneness to depression, and his vanity. He made many conquests, but had few real friends. He extended a personal intimacy to a hall full of people, but not to many individuals taken on their own.

He *did* it, though; he achieved his great goal. This is the most difficult thing of all to understand about him. He performed that one single act that makes its mark upon the world, that defines and validates a life, and that eludes almost everybody.

*

With this play as with an earlier one of mine, *Copenhagen*, the question arises as to how much of it is fact and how much of it fiction. The division there, it seemed to me, was

reasonably clear, since the characters were all shades
returning from beyond the grave – and in any case almost
every aspect of the real event that they were discussing was
open to dispute. Even so I found myself being solemnly
asked by probing interviewers if audiences might not be
misled into thinking they were watching 'the truth'.

This play is open to more reasonable objections. The
characters are all shown as being alive, the events in which
they are participating as unfolding in the present tense.
Very few of the words that these characters speak, however,
were ever actually spoken by their real counterparts. What
the feelings and ideas of those counterparts were, and
whether the feelings and ideas expressed by my characters
have anything in common with them, is a matter of
interpretation and conjecture. The events themselves, and
the world in which they take place, are hugely over-
simplified. Any librarian should unhesitatingly file the play
under fiction.

But, for anyone who is interested, this fiction does takes
its rise from the historical record. All the political events
referred to are real ones: the trips to Erfurt and Warsaw, the
vanishing majority and the no-confidence vote, the triumph
in the 1972 election and the gathering difficulties that
followed it. The personalities of the protagonists are very
much those attributed to their real counterparts by
observers and historians. Brandt's drinking and womanising
are not in dispute, nor are his 'feverish colds' and his taste
for jokes. (Almost all the jokes that Brandt makes in the play
are taken from a written collection he assembled.)[1] All the
circumstances of his childhood that Brandt recalls, and all
his adventures when he was operating underground in the
1930s for the Socialist Workers' Party, are taken from his
memoirs and the standard biographies. The picture of life in
the Palais Schaumburg, where the Federal Chancellor's
office was housed, comes from various recorded accounts.
So does that of life aboard the special train (which was

[1] For the reference to this and all other books mentiond in the Postscript,
see the list of sources on page 129.

indeed built for Reichsmarschall Göring, and which you can
see now preserved in the historical museum in Bonn).

Two of the murkier topics touched upon in the play are
factual. The first is the bribery that perhaps saved Brandt in
the no-confidence vote. The truth about this began to come
to light a year later, in the summer of 1973, when a CDU
deputy called Julius Steiner confessed to having received
50,000 marks for withholding his vote against Brandt. He
claimed that the money had come from Karl Wienand, the
business manager of the Parliamentary SPD, who notoriously
assisted Herbert Wehner in many of the shadier dealings on
behalf of the Party for which Wehner enjoyed taking the
credit. The money came from the Stasi, the East German
Ministry of State Security.[1] Or so it is claimed in his memoirs
by Markus Wolf, the legendary head of the Stasi's foreign
intelligence service ('Mischa' to his colleagues, and said to
be the model for John le Carré's Karla), and the allegation
was accepted by the court that tried him in 1994, though
Wienand, for what it's worth, denied it. The name of a
second Christian Democrat deputy has since come to light
in the Stasi files.

The other topic is the Federal Republic's secret ransoming
of the Democratic Republic's political prisoners, and the
equally secret payments it made to have people allowed out
of East Germany to rejoin their families in the West. The
DDR[2] carried on this cynical extortion at arm's length,
through an East German lawyer called Wolfgang Vogel.
When I stumbled across the trade in 1972 I was begged by
officials of Amnesty International not to refer to it in the
articles I was writing, for fear of jeopardising it. The income
was so vast that it covered something like 20 per cent of the
DDR's chronic balance-of-payments deficit in 'inter-
German' trade. According to Vogel's own records, between

[1] More properly the MfS, the Ministerium für Staatssicherheit, which was
responsible for both internal surveillance and for the foreign intelligence
service. The latter, the HVA, the Hauptverwaltung Aufklärung (Chief
Reconnaissance Directive), was the arm controlling Guillaume.
[2] Often known in English as the GDR, but this seems as awkward to me
as it would be if in German the USA became the VSA.

1964, when the trade started, and 1989, when the Wall came down, the Federal Republic bought out 33,755 prisoners and 215,019 people to be reunited with their families, at a total cost of 3,436 million Deutschmarks.

*

The most fictitious-looking aspect of the play is the role played by Günter Guillaume. Once again, though, I have followed the outline of the story fairly closely. His career in the Chancellor's office did begin almost simultaneously with Brandt's own. The doubts that were raised about his background were dismissed much as described in the play. Brandt did repeatedly ask his chief-of-staff Horst Ehmke (and later Günter Grabert, Ehmke's successor) to replace him; but somehow instead he did indeed get promoted from one position to another until, at the start of the 1972 election campaign, he took over as Brandt's personal assistant, with access to his files and in charge of organising the Chancellor's special train. On the train journeys he also accompanied Brandt as his valet, among other things, and was in charge of all his communications with Bonn and the rest of the world.

There are plenty of photographs of him, because he's in a lot of the pictures that were taken of Brandt. He's at the side of the room, or in the background, or walking a few paces behind the Chancellor, his hands folded respectfully behind his back, a dull, cosy, chubby figure in horn-rimmed spectacles and polite smile. He was known for his endless capacity for work and his equally endless good humour. He was always described as *kumpelhaft* (matey), a characteristic that was thought to be typically *berlinisch*. According to *Die Zeit*, he 'never lost the fried food smell of the Berlin *Hinterhof*'. A lot of the journalists around the Chancellor's office seem to have appreciated his easy-going chumminess. Brandt didn't; he found him servile. In some ways he was a kind of dim reflection of Brandt himself, with the same taste for the good life, and the same eye for women. Wibke Bruhns, a brilliant journalist on *Der Stern*, and one of the women with whom Brandt was said to have been involved, wrote memorably of Guillaume that he was 'nothing . . . a servant – not a person but a part of the place. You'd find him there just as you'd find a chair in the room.' Marianne Wichert-Quoirin, a local journalist who had known Guillaume at the time, described him to me as quite visibly the type of man that the DDR sent over – slightly old-fashioned and formal, given to wearing suits and buying flowers for ladies and helping them on with their coats.

His job as Brandt's assistant was a demanding one. The working day ended only when he laid out the last batch of papers on Brandt's night-table, and began again when he collected them first thing next morning, marked up with Brandt's annotations in green pencil. His few hours off each day must have been largely taken up with copying or photographing documents for his other employer. His home life was bleak. Wibke Bruhns caught the anonymity of the apartment where he and his wife Christel lived with her observation that it was furnished with the kind of potted plants that people give as presents; 'no one likes them, but no one throws them away.' Christel (somewhat too loud, sharp-tongued and rather charmless, according to Bruhns) was also a spy, and had been seen by their employers as the star until Günter had been so unexpectedly catapulted into the Chancellor's office. Their marriage was on the rocks. His only consolations were good lunches and dinners with his controller, an undetermined number of extra-marital liaisons, his teenage son Pierre, and the great secret that he nursed.

Apart from a conviction for drunk driving in 1972, there seems to be only one moment recorded when he showed any sign of the strain that he must have been living under. This was on a trip he made with Brandt in the following year to the South of France. Brandt was informed later, according to his memoirs, that Guillaume had fallen asleep after he had been drinking, and a notebook dropped out of his pocket. When the security men accompanying the Chancellor thoughtfully tried to put it back, Guillaume awoke and mumbled: 'You swine! You won't catch me, though!'

There were evidently more Günter Guillaumes than the two who played out their simultaneous parts in the Palais

Schaumburg. When he finally appeared in court, the summer after his arrest, a number of journalists noted the change in his manner and appearance. *Der Spiegel* decided that he had been underestimated. The new Guillaume, said the magazine, was visibly endowed with 'judgement, vitality and willpower'. He radiated, said the magazine, an extraordinarily direct and intense warmth that made his successes with women understandable. And in a long television interview he gave much later, after he had been released from prison and returned to the DDR, he has changed once again. It's difficult to make any connection between the pudgy little man in Bonn and the slim, bearded figure on the television screen, whose alert dryness and sharp tongue suggest the retired senior administrator rather than the willing dogsbody.

All the aspects of the surveillance on Guillaume which seem hardest to credit come from the record. Brandt was indeed informed of the suspicions against his assistant and sworn to silence. He was indeed encouraged to take Guillaume off to Norway with him as his only assistant, because Wilke and his deputy Schilling had holiday arrangements of their own, and Guillaume was indeed allowed to handle all the teleprinter traffic between Norway and Bonn, unchecked and unobserved. Guillaume and his wife did indeed throw a party for all the security staff. Also taken from the record is the even more farcical confusion between 'the second son' and 'the second man', and the belatedness of its resolution.

*

About other details I have to sound a note of caution. The ticking of an unseen insect in the rafters of the Palais Schaumburg[1] and various other colourful touches are certainly taken from a published source. But the source in

---

[1] Guillaume calls it a woodworm, but I'm informed by experts on infestation that if it knocked or ticked it must have been a death-watch beetle.

this case is Guillaume's own memoirs – and these have to be treated with a great deal of reserve.

They were ghosted, and first published in 1988 in the DDR – not for sale to the public but 'for official use only' (by the East German security services) – then reissued in the Federal Republic two years later. Markus Wolf, in *his* memoirs (also, of course, to be treated with circumspection), says that Guillaume's book was 'written in part to rub in the embarrassment of the affair to Bonn (after careful combing and adaptation by my service as disinformation – to protect other sources – and as positive PR for our work and its necessity)'.

Guillaume's book is curiously engaging, in spite of (or perhaps because of) its dubious provenance. But, some time between the collapse of the DDR in 1989 and his death in 1995, he gave a long interview to the journalist Guido Knopp, who was preparing a television programme about him, in which he cast even further doubt on it as a source. The ghost, he says, was 'a very nice journalist' supplied by the Stasi, who encouraged him to improve his stories somewhat. One of them, which had always puzzled me, about a meeting Guillaume claimed to have had in the Picasso Museum in Vallauris with 'a high-ranking man' in the intelligence service – presumably Wolf himself – he now disavowed completely. He also confessed to having built up the story of persuading Bauhaus to take the wrong dispatch-box back to Bonn at the end of the holiday in Norway. There were a whole series of boxes, he admitted, not just two, and he hadn't intended any deceit in getting Bauhaus to take one full of left-over souvenirs. I confess in my turn to having kept to Guillaume's first version of the story, for the same reasons as he first told it.

Wolf in his memoirs is rather disparaging about Guillaume and his vanity, and he confesses frankly that he sees the downfall of Brandt through his agent's actitivities as 'the greatest defeat we suffered up to that time . . . equivalent to kicking a football into our own goal'. This may go some way to accounting for another discrepancy between Guillaume's book and the later interview. In the book Guillaume speaks about Wolf with the greatest warmth and respect. In the interview his tone has grown much sharper. 'Herr Wolf,' he says, 'shouldn't say things today that were not so. Just because it doesn't suit him in retrospect to accept responsibility. He was very quick to excuse himself before God and the world.'

Guillaume's attitude to his other employer, too, has become a little more critical. In the book he speaks of him with nothing but admiration (and his attitude was remarked upon at the time by Bruhns and others). Now he says that Brandt was not always easy to work with. He would much rather have been personal assistant to Helmut Schmidt, whom he regards as the Federal Republic's greatest Chancellor.

*

I have in any case exercised a good deal of licence in other directions, though I think this is in most cases fairly obvious. The continuous contact that my Guillaume has with his controller is plainly a dramatisation of their discrete monthly meetings. The conversations that Guillaume has with Brandt on the train go much further in this direction. In his memoirs Guillaume says that Brandt became another man on his travels: 'Other cities, other faces, other thoughts, other problems – he discovered a new impetus towards them. Suddenly he seemed free and relaxed . . . He became talkative, excited by every good joke . . . En route he tanked up, and I made it my business to give him as much chance as possible to do it.' When there were no election trips in prospect, Guillaume invented the excuse of 'information journeys' instead. He alleges that on their travels together Brandt sometimes called him '*du*', and he felt obliged to return the compliment. Nowhere, though, does he claim that Brandt ever carried this intimacy as far as conversations about his childhood or his personal feelings.

I have extended my licence even further in the case of the holiday in Norway. The two families *were* together, and they did have a certain amount of social contact. The story of the relaxed mushrooming with Bauhaus, and of the games that Matthias and Pierre played together in the woods, come from Guillaume's memoirs. He says he was convinced that Brandt had long since suppressed the memory of the allegations against him – probably because he simply didn't want to spoil the holiday. In the interview with Knopp, however, a rather different picture emerges. Guillaume says that Brandt was unusually silent with him in Norway, partly because they both felt constrained by the presence of their families. (Christel seems to have done most of the talking when they were all together.) It is in any case unlikely that Brandt had forgotten the allegations. Klaus Harpprecht, Brandt's speechwriter, told Knopp that Brandt had made an effort of his own before they left Bonn to get evidence against Guillaume. He had 'touchingly' left threads on his desk overnight, and carefully arranged files and pencils; 'he'd probably read about this in novels when he was a boy.' His attempts in the play to sound Guillaume out while they are in Norway by telling him about his own involvement in underground activities before the war are my purely invented equivalent to the threads and pencils (though what Brandt recalls from those years is based very closely on what he says himself in his memoirs).

I can only say that fact has subsequently outstripped any fiction of mine in sheer implausibility. Brandt's son Matthias, who is said to have played so happily in the Norwegian woods with Guillaume's son Pierre, is now an actor. A German television company has recently produced a dramatised reconstruction of the case, and Matthias has entered the story once again. Playing the part of Günter Guillaume.

*

Further licence with the narrative: I have made the emergence of the Ostpolitik seem rather more clear-cut than it was. Brandt had already been pursuing a policy of *rapprochement* with the East as Foreign Minister in the Grand Coalition. The desirability of improving relations with the Soviet Union and its allies was a matter of general agreement; the stumbling-block was the precondition for this – acceptance of the Oder–Neisse frontier and recognition of the DDR. What Brandt says on the subject in the early stages of Act One is based closely upon various speeches he made, but I'm not aware of any occasion where he articulated it as completely as he does here, or where he laid quite as much emphasis on it in a general context. In later years he saw the Ostpolitik as his life's work, and historians agree that it was the core programme and real achievement of his government. But he knew only too well how sensitive the subject was with a large proportion of the voters, and in his declaration of the new government's policy that followed the 1969 election he gave more prominence to security, continuity and internal reform ('daring more democracy' – a famous phrase said to have been contributed by Günter Grass). There are certain parallels, one might think today, with the British government's handling of entry into the European single currency.

No one knows exactly what Brandt, Wehner and Schmidt said to each other the night before the Chancellor's decision to resign, and it notoriously happened not in Bonn but at a party conference in the resort of Münstereifel; the name has become part of SPD mythology, like Erfurt (where in 1891 the party adopted Marxism), and Bad Godesberg (where in 1959 it abandoned it). I have also shifted some actions from offstage characters to onstage ones. According to Guillaume's memoirs it was not Ehmke who gave Guillaume his promotion to be Peter Reuschenbach's replacement but Reuschenbach himself. Then again, Bauhaus didn't volunteer his information about Guillaume's knowledge of Brandt's womanising to Nollau personally but to his interrogators. The general absence of police and security men from the play is symptomatic of the staff shortages imposed by the economics of drama (both literal and metaphorical). Real politics is a labour-intensive business, and the Bundestag should have been teeming with deputies, the Palais Schaumburg with Ministers, advisers and civil servants – not to mention Germany as a whole with Germans.

For similar reasons I have sacked even a number of the principal protagonists in the story. The dismissal I regret most is that of Egon Bahr. Bahr was Brandt's closest confidant, a former radio journalist who had become his press representative back in the Berlin days. He was Brandt's trusted representative in the gruelling process of negotiating all the Eastern treaties (fifty meetings with the Russians alone). Brandt joked that Bahr didn't even know where France was, but he had a fascination with power politics and a natural bent for secret negotiation. Guillaume called him 'the sly fox', others 'Tricky Egon' (in English, presumably by analogy with the Tricky Dicky who was forced out of the White House three months after Brandt was out of the Palais Schaumburg).

He was an engaging and somewhat eccentric figure, who began his career as a pianist, but who was unable to pursue it in the Nazi period because one of his grandmothers was Jewish. In his retirement he took up one of the oddest hobbies I've ever heard of – travelling around the world with his wife as the only passengers aboard container ships, from one grim depot to another. When Wehner stood up in front of the party leadership after Brandt's resignation and talked about his love for Brandt's person and politics, Bahr put his hands over his face and wept. (Though it has to be said that this was on camera, and Karl Wienand remarked coldly that he'd seen Bahr weep before.) The dramatic problem is that, while he was away negotiating, his role in Bonn was more or less duplicated by Brandt's other confidant, Horst Ehmke, who coaxed Brandt out of his depressions (and got sidelined for his pains), and who as Brandt's chief of staff was much more closely involved in the events surrounding Guillaume.

Also missing is another confidant of Brandt's, the publisher Klaus Harpprecht, whom Brandt brought into his second government as a speechwriter, and whose diary supplies a lot of the atmosphere in the Palais Schaumburg during those last eighteen months. I also wish I could have found a way of introducing a most remarkable man who made a marginal appearance earlier in *Copenhagen* – Georg Duckwitz. In the 1940s, as the shipping specialist in the German Embassy in Copenhagen, he had warned the Danes exactly when the SS were to begin their round-up of the Jews, which enabled almost all of them to be saved. After the war he went back to Copenhagen as German Ambassador, and was greatly honoured by the Danes, before finishing his career as head of the Eastern Department in the Foreign Office. Brandt was a personal friend, and when he was still Foreign Minister in the Grand Coalition brought him back from retirement, then as Chancellor moved him to his personal staff to work on the Ostpolitik.

The oddest economy of all, one may think, is the exclusion of the entire female sex – particularly since it was Brandt's relations with women that undid him. German parliamentary politics at the time, though, was a man's world; the story of Brandt's government might have been rather different if it hadn't been so closed off from normal demographic reality. There were a few women in the Bundestag (and by the time Helmut Schmidt took office one of them was President of it), but only one in the Cabinet. In general, though, as was often noted, the only women whom German politicians saw during the course of the working week in Bonn were wives, secretaries and journalists, and there are no women at all who are recorded as playing any significant role in the arguments and struggles that form the background to the play.

Two remarkable women stand on the fringes of it, though, and there are other plays to be written about both of them. One of them is Brandt's wife, Rut. He had been married before during his time in Norway, and he married for a third time in his late sixties. But for almost the whole of his career his partner was Rut. She was a Norwegian who had been involved in distributing material for the Resistance during the German occupation, and he met her in Stockholm in 1943. She was as attractive and charming as her husband, the kind of wife that every traditional male politician must dream of having at his side, and she behaved with great dignity, generosity and humour throughout their trials in 1974, and in their later divorce. The account she gives in her memoirs of her escape as a girl from occupied Norway, through the mountains into Sweden, is compelling; so is her description of the devastation and misery that she found in Berlin when she arrived with Willy at the end of the war. By 1974 their marriage seems to have been reduced more or less to a social arrangement, and during the crisis she says that when Brandt was at home he went around 'like a stranger in the house'. He subsequently blamed her (along with Wehner) for his resignation, because she had agreed with him that he should take responsibility for the situation, and had made no attempt to dissuade him.

The other remarkable woman is Guillaume's wife, Christel. She might have been created as Rut's antithesis – cold, charmless and unapproachable. She was thought by the journalists who met her to be much more intelligent than her husband, and for a long time it was she who had the starring role as a spy, because she had managed to get a job in the Chancellery of Hesse, in Wiesbaden. She must have had to make a painful readjustment when Guillaume leapfrogged over her into the Federal Chancellery and she was ordered to act as his courier – though by the time they were both unmasked she seemed to be about to recover some of the lost ground by getting a job in the Ministry of Defence.

At no point, though, did she have much control over her own destiny. She was not consulted about the Stasi's plan to send her with her husband to the West – merely informed about it and told to keep quiet and co-operate – while her mother, who had Dutch nationality, was used as the lever for getting permission for the three of them to settle in the Federal Republic. She put on a great performance of marital solidarity at their trial, because, she said much later, she didn't want to appear weak. But the marriage had long been dead, and kept in being only because the Stasi required them to be a married couple. Many years later, after the collapse of the DDR, she gave a long and desolating television interview. Her life, she said, had been a series of uprootings. She had been taken out of her own country and dumped in the West to live a life of fiction. Then dumped in prison, where she served over five years of the eight to which she was sentenced, during which time she lost contact with her son Pierre (another victim who could step forward to claim a play about his own story). Then she was dumped back in the DDR, and, as soon as her husband was also exchanged and arrived to join her six months later, dumped by him. Then dumped again, by the collapse of the DDR, in

yet another new and alien society. At the end of the interview
she sat in silence for some moments, thinking back over it all.
'*Ein verpfuschtes Leben*,' she said eventually – 'a botched life'.

*

There is a third, more shadowy, woman missing from the
play: Nora Kretschmann, the wife of Guillaume's controller.
But then my Arno Kretschmann himself is a simplification
of reality. At the beginning of his career in the Federal
Chancellery, Guillaume had other controllers whom he does
not name. In his interview with Guido Knopp, Guillaume
says that Kretschmann took over at the time of the election
campaign in the autumn of 1972. In his memoirs, though,
Guillaume dates his arrival a year earlier, and gives so many
circumstantial details that I suspect this version is more
likely to be the correct one. Although Kretschmann was
younger than him they seem to have hit it off immediately.
They had lunch together at their first meeting and found
themselves enjoying 'a conversation about God and the
world as completely unconstrained as any two men who
wanted to spend a stimulating afternoon with beer foam
under their noses'. After this he remained controller until
the Guillaumes were arrested.

It was proposed for a start that their meetings should take
place in a secluded boat-house, but this meant that
Guillaume would have to take up sailing, which he thought
would be found to sort oddly with his known aversion to
sporting activities, and in the end they agreed to meet quite
openly in and around Bonn. So openly, in fact, that
Kretschmann would occasionally come to the Chancellery
and have Guillaume summoned on the house phone. But
usually they met in restaurants and bars, often for convivial
evenings with their wives present. Guillaume says that
Christel and Nora got on well together, and if this is true
then these occasions must have been one of the brighter
spots in his wife's bleak life.

The Kretschmanns had been fictionalised long before I
got near them. They were a married couple, names

unknown, who had been sent separately to the West, as 'Franz Tondera' and 'Sieglinde Fichte', and they had begun by establishing separate and very different cover stories. According to Guillaume in his memoirs, Franz travelled for a well-known firm in the motor industry (he doesn't say which), while Sieglinde, having given up her training as a vet in the DDR, worked on a factory production line with Turkish and Greek women guest-workers. They were then directed to make each other's acquaintance by chance on a ski-ing course, fall in love, conduct a bashful courtship and get married all over again. So now Sieglinde Fichte of Ulm, otherwise Ursula Behr of Stuttgart, was Sieglinde Tondera of Cologne. Except that the Tonderas for some reason became Arno and Nora Kretschmann (their given names were extracted, according to the *Spiegel*, from a rearrangement of letters in 'Tondera'.) When the Guillaumes were arrested, the Kretschmanns, in all their shifting avatars, vanished, and even the most diligent searches since the collapse of the DDR in the files of the Stasi, the source of so many revelations about so many people, have so far uncovered no trace of them.

*

A number of other questions about the case remain unanswered. Exactly what information, for a start, did Guillaume pass on? He preferred to report to his controller orally, and his information – certainly before the election campaign of 1972, when he first had access to documents – came by his own account chiefly from office gossip. Files and notes, Brandt is reported to have said when he gave evidence at the Guillaumes' trial,[1] were much less important than the insights he could have got from informal functions. Various journalists covering the case filled in the likely circumstances.

[1] Any account of the case has to rely heavily upon press reports (often remarkably divergent) because in German law there is no such thing as an official transcript of the proceedings, only a summary of the evidence made by the court as part of its judgement.

Lunch with a Minister President, coffee with a city mayor – on such occasions not every word is carefully weighed. What relations do leading politicians have to one another . . . ? When, for example, after a session at a Party conference, Schmidt, Wehner, and Brandt visited a *Weinstube* and went on talking – Guillaume would be at the next table . . . In the car after long sessions of the Party Executive, when Brandt gave vent to 'expressions of displeasure', or 'characterised' somebody . . . When the SPD chiefs talked over a cup of coffee or – at the end of the day – over something stronger, about who was going to be renominated or not and where . . . He could catch the nuances of what was said, and hear confidential briefings to journalists on matters that might later make the headlines. He knew much more than any state secret – he knew about the moods, connections, and developments that could lead to the decisions taken later.

As Bahr said in evidence: 'He was always there, but people weren't aware of him.' Wilke recalled him as always wanting to be in on everything, whether it concerned him or not. Guillaume himself said in his interview with Knopp that he couldn't remember what he'd passed on, but agreed that it included everything he could lay his hands on about the negotiations with Moscow and East Berlin. Stephan Konopatzky, a researcher working on the Stasi files now held in a massive archive in Berlin, can find relatively little information credited to XV/19142/60 and XV/11694/60, aka Hansen and Heinze, aka Günter and Christel Guillaume, and less still that was regarded as of any great value. He concedes that Guillaume's reports may, because of their importance and sensitivity, have been handled by some special channel as yet unexplored in the archive, but thinks it more likely that he was being used very cautiously to protect his unique position. When one thinks of all those monthly debriefings by Arno aka Franz, though . . . What happened to everything that was said? Was it the supportive Arno who thought it wasn't worth passing on?

If Wolf is telling the truth in his memoirs he must have received much more material than the files reveal. He says that before Brandt's visit to Erfurt in March 1970 – i.e., even at the very beginning of Guillaume's employment in the Chancellor's office, when he was still concerned with nothing more than trade union liaison – he 'gained access to some of the West German plans, which, combined with information from other sources, gave us a clearer idea of Brandt's intentions and fears'. He also says that Guillaume's 'real importance for us in East Berlin lay in his political instincts. Through Guillaume's judgements we were able to conclude sooner rather than later that Brandt's new Ostpolitik, while still riven with contradictions, marked a genuine change of course in West German foreign policy. As such, his work actually aided détente by giving us the confidence to place our trust in the intentions of Brandt and his allies.'

There is a further striking discrepancy between the files and Wolf's account. The files contain nothing about Brandt's extra-marital affairs. In his memoirs, though, Wolf claims to know that 'Guillaume soon realised that Brandt's adultery was frequent and varied'. Then again, after Guillaume was unmasked, and the head of the Federal Criminal Police wrote his report on Brandt's private life, cataloguing what Wolf calls 'his affairs with journalists, casual acquaintances, and prostitutes', he claims that 'Guillaume had of course been telling us about this kind of behavior all along'. So perhaps the surviving files don't record the whole story.

The range of material on which the court case was based was narrow. The charge brought against the Guillaumes was the most serious possible: *schwerer Landesverrat* – high treason. It would have been impossible to secure a conviction on this merely for passing on gossip and unspecified overheard remarks – or even documents, if no one knew what the documents were. So the case depended largely upon Guillaume's spontaneous admission at the moment of his arrest to being an 'officer' of the DDR, and also upon the only specific documents that he was known for certain to have handled – the teleprinter traffic on the Norwegian holiday.

There remains some doubt, however, as to whether any of this material ever reached East Berlin. In his memoirs Guillaume says that he didn't attempt to contact his controller during the holiday, but gives a very graphic and circumstantial account of how he arranged for the copies of all the documents in his possession to be photographed by a courier while he was making an overnight stop at a hotel in Sweden on the way back to Bonn. In the interview with Knopp, as we have seen, he withdraws his claim to have deliberately fooled Bauhaus into thinking that he was carrying the documents himself, but doesn't modify any other part of the story. All this is cast into doubt by Markus Wolf's memoirs, however. Wolf says that the copies were handed over by Christel to a courier called Anita at the Casselsruhe restaurant in Bonn, and that Anita, realising she was being followed, threw them into the Rhine. So he never received them, though he kept this fact from Guillaume so as not to hurt his pride. Konopatzky agrees that there is no trace of any of the Norwegian messages in the files.

Oddly, though, Wolf makes no reference at all to Guillaume's version of the handover, by way of the courier in the Swedish hotel. Even more oddly, perhaps, he recounts in some detail the contents of the three most important messages that Guillaume copied, but doesn't explain where the information came from; not from the Guillaumes' trial, plainly, where the evidence relating to this was given in camera. More oddly still, in a television interview with Guido Knopp for his programme on Guillaume, he says that the documents in the dispatch-box *did* reach East Berlin, though he refuses to say what happened to them.

The story of Christel's meeting at the Casselsruhe restaurant, incidentally, is recounted in Guillaume's book. As in Wolf's version, her lunch companion realised she was being kept under observation, and found herself being tailed when she left the restaurant. Guillaume, who calls the

woman not Anita but Thomin, purports to be much amused
by his interrogators' suspicion later that she had been a
courier. She thought, he says, that the watchers were private
detectives employed by her husband because she was having
an affair.

*

There are a number of other points of dispute in the record,
where I have had to choose one version or another.
According to Brandt's notes on the case (see the list of
Brandt's writings on page 130), his bodyguard Ulrich
Bauhaus came to him 'with tears in his eyes' and assured
him that he had given his interrogators information about
Brandt's women only under pressure; he was astonished at
how much had already been collected. In a television
interview much later, however, Karl Wienand says that
Bauhaus went voluntarily to offer his evidence, because he
and the other security people, as ordinary citizens in
bowler hats and umbrellas, were genuinely shocked by the
Chancellor's behaviour. Neither Wienand's record nor his
appearance incline one to place much confidence in
anything he says, but *someone* must have first brought up
the question of the women, and of Guillaume's awarenesss
of them, and I have followed Wienand's version.

I have also given expression to some of the many
conspiracy theories that have been aired. Most of them have
centred on the role played by Herbert Wehner, the
Chairman of the Parliamentary Party of the SPD and its
éminence grise. There is general agreement that Wehner was a
Machiavellian figure, and relations between him and Brandt
had always been difficult; even during the Grand Coalition
they had been reduced to communicating through an
intermediary. Brandt's single-handed 'cavalry charge' to the
Chancellorship in 1969 was perhaps, among other things, a
declaration of independence fromWehner, and in no way
improved Wehner's low assessment of Brandt's suitability
for the job. He thought Brandt a lightweight. The publisher
Rudolf Augstein once overheard him saying that Brandt

and Walter Scheel (the Foreign Minister and leader of the FDP, therefore Brandt's coalition partner – another central character missing from the play) were both gigolos – '*Sie können nicht regieren, sondern erigieren*' ('Their forte is not so much government as erection'). Wehner went to quite extraordinary lengths to undermine Brandt during his second term, and to prepare the way for Helmut Schmidt to succeed him. But, only a few weeks before Brandt's resignation, when Schmidt at last made an open bid for the Chancellorship, Wehner seems to have had a sudden belated realisation of how much he needed Brandt's appeal to both voters and party members, and the two men had a bizarre *rapprochement* (which I reluctantly cut out of the play as one complication too many) – a long meeting at Brandt's home, with many pauses for thoughtful silence and the consumption of red wine, conspiring together against Schmidt.

This odd turn of events, however, did nothing to allay the suspicions of both Brandt and the press later that Wehner had played some kind of underhand role in the Chancellor's resignation. The version in the press was that Wehner had conspired in one way or another with his protégé, Günther Nollau, the President of the Federal Office for the Protection of the Constitution (the counter-espionage service). It was suggested that in 1973 Nollau had informed Wehner of the suspicions against Guillaume before he told Hans-Dietrich Genscher, the Minister of the Interior, to whom he was formally responsible. Nollau always vehemently denied this. He insisted that he had told Genscher on 29 May, and Wehner not until 4 June. He remembered the latter date very clearly, he said, because it was his own birthday. Genscher, however, seems a little sceptical of this in his memoirs. 'What did worry me,' he says, 'was that Nollau kept Wehner informed of the investigation. What would Wehner do with this knowledge, since as everyone knew, he was increasingly critical of Willy Brandt's chancellorship?' Arnulf Baring, the standard historian of the period, is inclined to agree. Nollau's forewarning of Wehner, which might have been on 23 May, the very day that the file landed on Nollau's desk, he finds 'exceedingly likely'.

Genscher didn't like Nollau, and blamed him afterwards for telling untruths about the amount of information he had passed on about the case. His behaviour, he said, 'confirmed many of the prejudices raised against him previously'. Brandt didn't like him, either, and refers to him sarcastically in his memoirs as 'supposedly able'. Nollau certainly pursued the case with remarkable ineptitude and desuetude, if nothing worse. His appearance in subsequent television interviews inclines one to share all the prejudices and suspicions that were expressed against him; just as well, you feel, as with Wienand, that he was not in the second-hand car trade, or he might not have got as far as he did.

Guillaume also came to believe that there was a conspiracy – but in his version Wehner, Nollau and Genscher were all in it together. Nollau, he is reported to have said in the evidence he gave when his old employer Markus Wolf was in his turn tried for treason in 1933,[1] was the confidant of Genscher as well as of Wehner, and both of them wanted to force Brandt out. 'Nollau held out the knife, and Genscher gave Brandt the necessary push to make him run on to it.' He himself, he said, in a slightly different version of the metaphor, had been used as the club with which Brandt had been struck.

Brandt himself was obsessed with suspicions of a rather different conspiracy against him – between Herbert Wehner and the East German leadership. He recorded them in a series of cryptic notes, written at some point after his retirement but not published until 1994, and held to them for the rest of his life. They centred on Wehner's known

---

[1] Wolf was convicted, but two years later the judgement was overturned by the Federal Constitutional Court, which ruled that former officers of the DDR intelligence service could not be prosecuted for treason and espionage. Whether he was at all grateful for this expression of the rule of law, or even amused by the irony of it, in the Federal Germany of which he now found himself a citizen, and which he had worked so hard and so skilfully to undermine, he does not say in his memoirs. Brandt, incidentally, was one of the people who had spoken out against his prosecution in the first place.

contacts in East Berlin. Wehner reported to Brandt two
meetings there. The first was with Erich Honecker, the East
German party leader, and its purpose, according to
Wehner, was to relaunch the secret trade in political
prisoners and family reunions, which had ironically been
brought to an end by the regularisation of relations between
the two states in the newly signed Basic Treaty. The second
was with Wolfgang Vogel, the middleman in this trade,
though the subject in this case was said by Wehner to be
economic collaboration in general. The timing of both
meetings was unsettling – the first on the evening of 29 May
1973, the day that Nollau told Genscher, and Genscher told
Brandt, about the suspicions against Guillaume, and the
second on 3 May 1974, the day that Nollau told Wehner
about the list of Brandt's women. In any case Brandt
believed that Wehner had had additional contacts with East
Berlin which had gone unreported. In the course of them,
he suspected, Wehner had been told that Guillaume was a
spy, and had also been primed to launch his extraordinary
attack on him from Moscow in the autumn of 1973.

Brandt's information was provided by Egon Bahr, who
had obtained it from the Russians. It had come by way of
the secret system of communication that Bahr had
established with the Soviet leader Leonid Brezhnev, in
imitation of the 'back-channels' used by Henry Kissinger to
negotiate with the Soviet Union. The historian August H.
Leugers-Scherzberg has recently cast more light on this dark
corridor, and the allegations against Wehner that it was
used to convey. What neither Bahr nor Brandt realised, says
Dr Scherzberg, is that the chain of communication led
through Yuri Andropov, later Brezhnev's successor, but at
that time head of the KGB. Andropov had reasons to want
Wehner discredited in Brandt's eyes, because Wehner
distrusted the 'back-channel', and wanted to replace it with
a more direct link, while Andropov himself naturally wished
to preserve it as an instrument for his own influence.
Wehner also dissented from Brandt's belief that an
understanding with the Soviet Union was the key that would
unlock relations with East Germany, and wanted to

distribute the Federal Republic's efforts at reconciliation more broadly around Eastern Europe.

Whatever Wehner did or didn't do behind the scenes, however, his assurance of support for Brandt at the crucial moment in Münsteifel seems to have been less than whole-hearted, and Brandt always held him responsible (together with Rut) for failing to dissuade him from a decision that he never ceased to regret.

*

I've had much help with this project. First of all (once again) from Sarah Haffner, who got me off on the right foot as soon as I told her what I had in mind, by recommending me to read Arnulf Baring's *Machtwechsel*, and who subsequently supplied me with further parcels of books and help in translating a number of particularly awkward phrases. Peter Merseburger, the political journalist, who was working in Bonn during the Brandt Chancellorship and whose own biography of Brandt has since appeared, gave me a great deal of patient advice. He also introduced me to Klaus Harpprecht, Brandt's speechwriter, and asked his old colleague Fritz Pleitgen to open the film archives of Westdeutscher Rundfunk in Cologne for me.

Eva Giesel, a colleague of my German play agent Ursula Pegler, spent much time, energy and ingenuity making contacts and inquiries on my behalf. I originally expected the play to lay more emphasis on the Guillaumes' trial, and Frau Giesel worked particularly hard at putting me in touch with officials of the court where it took place, the Oberlandesgericht in Düsseldorf. My thanks, too, to Herr Bundesanswalt Lampe, in the office of the Generalbundesanwalt in Karlsruhe, who explained some of the basics of German law to me, and to Professor Peter Brandt, Willy Brandt's eldest son, who most kindly offered to see me, though in the end I decided it might inhibit me; to Frau Gertrud Lenz in the Friedrich-Ebert-Stiftung in Bad Godesberg, where the Brandt papers are lodged; to Fritz Pleitgen at WDR; to ZDF for the text of Guido Knopp's interview with Guillaume; to Frau Marianne Wichert-Quoirin, who covered Federal politics in Bonn and the Guillaume trial in Düsseldorf for the *Kölner Stadt-Anzeiger*; and to Finn Aaserud for the Norwegian.

The amount of material available turned out to be oceanic, and for the first time in my life, when I finally had to recognise that I was drowning, I got the help of a research assistant. My choice – Stefan Kroner, the dramaturg who had worked on one of the German productions of *Copenhagen* – turned out to be inspired. He was not only unbelievably quick and industrious, but had an uncanny ability to guess what I should find useful. He plunged into the archive of the Friedrich-Ebert-Stiftung, and of WDR in Cologne, and reduced the tons of press-cuttings and weeks of newsreel to proportions I could just about manage. He found books long out of print, and trawled information from the huge deposits of old Stasi files in Berlin (still not fully explored, and a rich potential source of fossil fuel). We also had a delightful trip around the Rhineland together, to see where it all happened and to visit the various archives.

*

For anyone interested in finding out more about the case itself, or the personalities and politics of the period, the following is a short list of the more easily available material:

General

Baring, Arnulf: *Machtwechsel, die Ära Brandt-Scheel* (1983, 1998). The standard history of the period. Long (nearly a thousand pages), but boldly and incisively written. The chapters on the Guillaume affair and Brandt's resignation are relatively brief and particularly fine.

Harpprecht, Klaus: *Im Kanzleramt: Tagebuch der Jahre mit Willy Brandt* (2000). Harpprecht is a well-known publisher who joined Brandt's office at the beginning of 1973 as a speech-writer and adviser. He was also a personal friend of Brandt's, and provided him with a holiday house in the

South of France which gave him some respite from the political storms of that difficult year. His diary of life in the Palais Schaumburg is sharp, worldly and observant – and a salutary corrective to the schematic oversimplification of my picture.

Rehlinger, Ludwig A.: *Freikauf* (1991). For the rate of ransom per prisoner charged by the DDR.

Whitney, Craig R.: *Advocatus Diaboli: Wolfgang Vogel – Anwalt zwischen Ost und West* (1993). For the complete figures of the trade in prisoners and family reunions, as given in Vogel's own files.

Brandt's own writings

Brandt, Willy: *Erinnerungen* (1989). The 1994 edition also contains the *Notizen zum Fall G*, the notes about the Guillaume affair that he made around the time of his resignation. There is an English edition, *My Life in Politics* (1992), but it doesn't include the *Notizen*.

A complete collection of Brandt's works is in the course of publication (the *Berliner Ausgabe*). The volume relating to the domestic and social policy of his government is Volume 7, *Mehr Demokratie wagen: Innen- und Gesellschaftspolitik 1966–1974* (2001). The volume relating to his government's foreign policy (including relations with East Germany) is Volume 6, *Ein Volk der guten Nachbarn, Außen- und Deutschlandpolitik 1966–1974.* This has not yet appeared, however, and for his speeches and other statements on foreign policy I have used:

Brandt, Willy: *Reden und Interviews 1968–1969* (German government publication, undated), and *Bundeskanzler Brandt: Reden und Interviews* (1971).

Brandt, Willy: *Lachen hilft – Politische Witze* (2001). A collection of jokes, mostly but not exclusively political, assembled by Brandt over the course of the years. It was completed and published after his death by his widow, Brigitte Seebacher-Brandt. This is the source of most of Brandt's jokes in the play.

Biographies of Brandt

Merseburger, Peter: *Willy Brandt 1913–1992, Visionär und Realist* (2002). The most recent. Well-written and comprehensive, unashamedly partisan, with a foreword that gives a particularly brilliant overview of Brandt's achievements.

Koch, Peter: *Willy Brandt* (1998). Colourful, journalistic, gossipy, and highly readable.

Marshall, Barbara: *Willy Brandt, a Political Biography*. In English. Short but to the point.

Schöllgen, Gregor: *Willy Brandt – die Biographie* (2001). Compact and serviceable.

Guillaume

Guillaume, Günter: *Die Aussage*. The original edition, described as '*protokolliert von Günter Karau*', was published by the East German military publishing-house in 1988 for the benefit of the security organs and the National People's Army, marked 'for official use only'. In 1990 it was reissued in West Germany in a revised form, as *Die Aussage – wie es wirklich war* ('The Testimony – how it really was'; the implication is presumably that the book is a substitute for the testimony which Guillaume refused to give at his trial). For the reserve with which this source should be treated see above. It should really be read in conjunction with:

Knopp, Guido: *Top Spione* (1997), and the TV programme that this was published in association with (ZDF 1994); or, better still, the transcript of the interview conducted with Guillaume by Knopp and Steinhauser that was obtained for me from ZDF (TV2) by Stefan Kroner, though this seems not to have been published. It appears to be the full text of a conversation from which only excerpts have been used in the programme itself, though it has no date or other indication of its provenance.

The assessment of Guillaume's reports as it appears in the files of the Stasi comes from a contribution by Stephan Konopatzky to a conference on the role of the Stasi in the West, in November 2001, organised under the auspices of the organisation that now holds the archive, the office of *Die Bundesbeauftragte für die Unterlagen des Staatssicherheitsdienstes der ehemaligen DDR* (the Federal Commissioners for the Documents of the State Security Service of the Former DDR).

Other characters in the story

Wolf, Markus: *Man Without a Face* (1997). His memoirs, in English. Very lively and absorbing, and apparently frank about many things, though reserving the right to silence on others.

Genscher, Hans-Dietrich: *Erinnerungen* (1995). Memoirs. In English as *Rebuilding a House Divided* (1995).

Brandt, Rut: *Freundesland* (1992). Her memoirs, and as engaging as Frau Brandt herself.

Schmidt, Helmut: *Weggefährten* (1996). Memoirs.

Leugers-Scherzberg, August H.: *Die Wandlungen des Herbert Wehner, von der Volksfront zur Großen Koalition* (2002). This is the standard biography of Herbert Wehner, but it takes him only as far as the Grand Coalition. Until the next volume appears:

Leugers-Scherzberg, August H.: *Herbert Wehner und der Rücktritt Willy Brandts am 7. Mai 1974* (in the *Vierteljahreshefte für Zeitgeschichte*, Part 2, April 2002).

Nollau, Günther: *Das Amt* (1982) Memoirs. Relevant extracts in *Der Stern* (11 September 1975).

Ehmke, Horst: *Mittendrin* (1994). Memoirs.

Bahr, Egon: *Zu meiner Zeit* (1996). Memoirs.

Afterlife

Afterlife was first presented in the Lyttelton auditorium of the National Theatre, London, on 11 June 2008. The cast was as follows:

Max Reinhardt	Roger Allam
Helene Thimig	Abigail Cruttenden
Gusti Adler	Selina Griffiths
Rudolf 'Katie' Kommer	Peter Forbes
Franz	Glyn Grain
The Prince Archbishop of Salzburg	David Burke
Friedrich Müller	David Schofield
Players	Nicholas Lumley
	David Baron
	Colin Haigh
	Sarah Head
	Elizabeth Marsh
	Charlotte Melia
	Hugh Osborne
	Peter Prentice
	Claire Winsper
	Rupert Young

Director Michael Blakemore
Set Designer Peter Davison
Costume Designer Sue Willmington
Lighting Designer Neil Austin
Music and Sound Designer Paul Charlier

Characters

Max Reinhardt
Helene Thimig, *his companion and then second wife*
Gusti Adler, *his personal assistant*
Rudolf ('Katie') Kommer, *his man of business*
Franz, *his valet*
The Prince Archbishop of Salzburg
Friedrich Müller, *a citizen of Salzburg*
Thomas, Josef, Liesl, Gretl, *and* **Others**

Act One

Stairs, levels, galleries.

Enter all: the **Prince Archbishop, Thimig, Adler, Kommer, Müller, Thomas, Josef, Liesl, Gretl** *and* **Franz.**

Reinhardt
> Draw near, good people all, I pray!
> Give heed while we perform our play,
> Wherein we show, as best we can,
> The Summoning of Everyman.

And we stage it very simply. Here, if Your Grace should give us permission. On the square in front of the cathedral. Under the open sky. The way the old morality plays were done five centuries ago. Your Grace . . .

He indicates a chair for the **Prince Archbishop.**

Reinhardt All of you . . .

Thomas, Josef, Liesl, Gretl *and* **Franz** *help* **Thimig, Adler, Kommer,** *and* **Müller** *to find places to sit, but themselves remain discreetly standing.*

Reinhardt A few boards thrown across trestles for the actors to stand on. Boards and benches round the square for the audience. Nothing else. And we start in the afternoon. In the plain light of day. The doors of the cathedral are thrown open, the cast enters . . . The audience quietens and settles . . . The Prologue speaks . . .

> Here all shall learn, with eyes to see,
> How short our days on earth do be,
> How sorrowful must be our end,
> Should we our ways neglect to mend.
> Plain be the matter, plain our speech,
> And plain the lesson here that each
> May haply in our story find,
> And henceforth ever bear in mind . . .

Whereupon the play proper commences . . .

Prince Archbishop   Perhaps we might pause for one moment first, Herr Reinhardt.

Reinhardt   Your Grace.

Prince Archbishop   Let me make sure I understand exactly what I am to be presented with. I am of course very conscious of your reputation, and, I may say, impressed by your command of the text . . .

Adler   Herr Reinhardt always knows the whole play by heart before he begins.

Reinhardt   My personal assistant, Fräulein Adler.

Adler   He has the whole production in his head. All written down in his prompt-book. (*She shows him.*) Every inflexion, every gesture. Every pause, every breath.

Thimig   The sort of thing that actors usually hate. But Herr Reinhardt is an exception to all the rules.

Reinhardt   Fräulein Thimig, who is one of our cast.

Prince Archbishop   I have had the pleasure of seeing you perform in Vienna. Ophelia – yes? Most touching.

Thimig   Your Grace is very kind.

Prince Archbishop   So, Herr Reinhardt, let me be quite clear. This is a morality play? A play of a religious nature?

Reinhardt   A traditional English morality play. But freely adapted by Herr von Hofmannsthal.

Prince Archbishop   Herr von Hofmannsthal is a Jew?

Reinhardt   A Catholic, Your Grace.

Kommer   His grandfather was a Jew!

Reinhardt   Herr Kommer, my irrepressible man of business.

Prince Archbishop   Herr Kommer . . .

Kommer   Call me Katie, Your Grace. Everyone else does.

Prince Archbishop   Katie. Very well. Herr Katie? Or Frau Katie?

Kommer   Now, now, Your Grace!

Prince Archbishop   And you, Herr Reinhardt? A Jew?

Reinhardt   A Jew, Your Grace.

Prince Archbishop   A Jew. And you have chosen a work of Catholic piety to open your new festival?

Kommer   You want Jewish piety? In Salzburg? What else? Ice skating in hell?

Reinhardt   Thank you, Katie.

Prince Archbishop   And yet I believe your choice has so far found little favour in the city.

Kommer   You're our last hope!

Prince Archbishop (*to* **Reinhardt**)   Yes?

Reinhardt   Yes, Your Grace.

Prince Archbishop   As long as we know where we stand. So, let us hear the play, then, Herr Reinhardt.

Reinhardt   Your Grace. Suddenly . . . a voice comes down from heaven:

> Should I, who rule as God on high,
> Stand patiently for ever by
> While men on earth below ignore
> My dread command, and mock My law?
> While they on evil gorge and feast,
> More vile than e'en the lowliest beast?

Prince Archbishop   The Almighty?

Reinhardt   Indeed, Your Grace.

Prince Archbishop   And you have every gesture of the Almighty written down in your book?

He holds out his hand for the prompt-book. **Adler** *glances at* **Reinhardt**, *who nods. She hands the* **Prince Archbishop** *the book. He leafs slowly through it.*

Reinhardt   Indeed, Your Grace.

Prince Archbishop   Every inflexion? Every breath? Of the Lord God Himself?

Reinhardt   Your Grace, we find ourselves living in the year 1920, in an age when faith has been questioned, and it is difficult to speak of God without self-consciousness. But for a few short hours we shall relive the simple-hearted innocence of the fifteenth century, when God was as real and familiar as the local weaver and the local tinker and the local bellows-maker. When a weaver or a tinker or a bellows-maker could offer himself to his fellows in all humility as a representation of God, no less than of God's creatures. This is how the theatre allows us to explore God's creation. We all have possibilities in us that ordinary life won't let us realise. We all have only one birth and one death. We are all different, but in the narrow stream-bed of everyday life we are rolled together like pebbles until we all look alike. Or until we shake ourselves free and begin to act out the other parts that life denies us. And here, on the cathedral square in Salzburg, we shall do it as simply and naturally as children do in their games. No sound effects. Only the cathedral bells.

Sound effects of bells.

Only the distant sound of traffic in the streets.

Sound effects of traffic.

Only the whirr of the pigeons' wings, as they swirl up and away like a sudden eddy of smoke from a bonfire.

The sound of pigeons. Everyone turns to follow them.

Only the voice of God.

Reinhardt *as God.*

> Sunk deep in sin they know me not;
> That I am God they have forgot.
> And scant the care of aught they show
> Save worldly weal and worldly woe.

No lighting effects. Only the afternoon sunlight coming and going . . .

The sunlight comes and goes.

Only the words. Words, words, words. The old resource. The words and the weather. Chill flurries of wind off the mountains behind us . . . Rain at times, of course. This is a rainy town! Heavy rain and we run for cover . . .

The **Prince Archbishop** *studies the prompt-book.* **Adler** *and* **Thimig** *look at each other apprehensively.*

Prince Archbishop (*reads thoughtfully*)

> They little mark what coin I paid,
> What sacrifice for them I made.
> To spare their feet from hidden thorn
> I let instead my brow be torn.
> All care I could of man I took –
> Yet now by man am I forsook . . .

He stops and considers. **Kommer** *makes a thumbs-down to the others.*

Prince Archbishop (*stands, authoritatively*)

> Therefore have I with sudden speed
> A day of reckoning decreed,
> When Everyman shall give at last
> Account of all things, now and past.
> Where art thou, Death, my strong right hand?
> Come forth, approach. Before me stand.

Reinhardt (*as* **Death**)

> Thy will, Almighty God, convey;
> Most punctually shall I obey.

Prince Archbishop

> To Everyman I charge thee go.

In My name shalt thou make him know
He stands required to engage
Upon a solemn pilgrimage –
And that right soon, this very day.
Hear no excuse, brook no delay.
And let him bring his reckoning book
That I may open it and look
To see what rightful balance should
Be struck 'twixt evil deed and good.

Reinhardt
Like bolt from thundercloud I go
To seek out Everyman below.
Thy dread command will I make known,
And speed him hence before Thy throne.

Prince Archbishop (*hands the prompt-book back to* **Adler**)
Thank you.

Thimig   Bravo, Your Grace!

Kommer   Give him a contract!

Prince Archbishop   You were telling us, I believe, that we all have more possibilities in us than our everyday selves can encompass. Even as Archbishop of Salzburg –

Kommer   Prince Archbishop of Salzburg!

Prince Archbishop   Even as Prince Archbishop of Salzburg one has less opportunity than might be supposed to play God. No opportunity at all, really, to preside over the Day of Judgment.

Kommer   You're presiding over it now!

Reinhardt   Katie, Katie . . .

Prince Archbishop   So I am. Then let us continue. My good friend Death, I believe, is out scouring the streets of Salzburg for Everyman.

Reinhardt   There he goes. Up the Franziskanergasse, down the Judengasse . . . Past the Collegiate Church and the

University . . . He looks into the beer-gardens and the coffee-houses, the hospitals and the night shelters . . . There . . . ! There . . . ! But you can't see him. He's just a passing breath of cold air, like the wind off the mountains. The only man who will ever see him is the one he is looking for. Everyman. And who is Everyman? It could be anyone. Someone with no suspicion of what's about to happen to him. Someone in the prime of life, perhaps, who's enjoying everything that the world can offer, and proud of it. Me. Your Grace. Death will know him when he sees him! Now, the scene changes. We are in front of a great house somewhere on the outskirts of the city.

Prince Archbishop   How will you manage that, Herr Reinhardt?

Reinhardt   We shall listen to the words. Yes? And use our imagination.

Prince Archbishop   Of course, of course.

Reinhardt   The doors open. We enter the lofty hall. And there in front of the great hearth stands . . .

Prince Archbishop   Everyman.

Reinhardt   Everyman.

> A lordly house I own and fair,
> Magnificent beyond compare.
> Full many a chamber call I mine
> With costly furnishings and fine . . .

Liesl *and* **Gretl** *set a few costly furnishings.*

Reinhardt
> Full many a chest with riches laden . . .

Thomas *and* **Josef** *carry in a large trunk.*

Reinhardt
> Full many a serving man and maiden.
> With precious plate my cupboards gleam,
> With good fat kine my pastures teem.

And sweet the heavy harvest yield
Of golden rent from every field.
So I, untouched by care or sorrow,
May smile today, and laugh tomorrow.

Prince Archbishop   This house you have conjured up,
Herr Reinhardt . . . It looks remarkably like your own house!

Kommer   It *is* his own house!

Reinhardt   Welcome, Your Grace.

Kommer
Draw near, good people all, I pray!
Max Reinhardt is at home today!

Thomas, **Josef**, **Liesl** *and* **Gretl** *serve champagne and canapés.*

Prince Archbishop   And a famous house it is. One of our
great baroque palaces!

Reinhardt   Built by one of our great baroque princes. Your
illustrious predecessor. There he is.

Prince Archbishop   Twice life size. Hanging in the place
of honour.

Kommer   He built this house – good! Chucked all the
Protestants out of Salzburg – not so good!

Reinhardt   It was one of Your Grace's predecesssors,
though, who helped to give Mozart his start in life.

Kommer   And another one had him kicked out on his
behind. Great chuckers-out, you Prince Archbishops!

Reinhardt   This house. The music of Mozart. They were
the legacy of your predecessors to future generations. Our play
could be Your Grace's.

Kommer   Does everyone have a glass? Ladies and
gentlemen – His Grace and Highness the Prince Archbishop
of Salzburg!

Everyone   His Grace and Highness!

Prince Archbishop   Come, come. Simply 'His Grace'.

Kommer   So, Your Grace, what's the answer going to be? Yes or no?

Prince Archbishop   My word, though! Look at it! The great hall! The ceremonial staircase! The galleries!

Reinhardt   Most of it in a woefully dilapidated state. It will be my life's work to restore it to what it once was.

Kommer   If there's one thing Herr Reinhardt loves it's a lordly house! A wing of the Crown Prince's palace in Berlin. An apartment in the Emperor's palace in Vienna.

Reinhardt   Merely *pieds-à-terre*. Now I have found Leopoldskron I intend to make this my home. I have a passion for the baroque, Your Grace. The baroque is the extension of the theatre into the everyday world. And that is what I have devoted my career to – breaking down the barriers between the actual and the imagined. Between art and life, between theatre and audience. And doing it as simply and naturally as children do in their games. A few props – pictures, footmen . . . and at once we're in the eighteenth century – in a play – in an opera – in a dream . . . I want to do it not just for the wealthy and the privileged few, sitting in some small room sealed off from the world, but out in the world itself, where popular drama began. So that all of us, princes and footmen alike, ladies and ladies' maids, can escape for a few brief hours from the life sentences we are serving inside our own selves.

Prince Archbishop   Some of the local residents have not so far been as appreciative as you might have wished.

Kommer   Everyman has the same trouble! Where's the book . . . ? Poor Neighbour. As soon as Everyman sets foot outside his house, up comes Poor Neighbour, hand out, pester pester . . .

Reinhardt   Poor Neighbour. Will someone read Poor Neighbour . . . ?

Müller   Poor Neighbour? I'll read Poor Neighbour!

He takes the prompt-book from **Adler**.

Kommer   Who are *you*?

Müller   No one. I live in Salzburg.

Kommer   So what are you doing here?

Müller   Nothing. Out of work, like everyone else. Passing the time. Playing Poor Neighbour for you.

> I dwelt once in a house as fine
> Until my fortune's late decline . . .
> Now must I kneel to thee and plead
> For help in this my hour of need.

Reinhardt   Excellent. Most convincing. Thank you.

> To hear thy woes I cannot stay.
> Here – take this coin and go thy way.

He fumbles in his pockets.

Adler   Coin, someone? Cash?

Kommer   Herr Reinhardt's like royalty. Never soils his fingers with money.

He gives **Reinhardt** *a coin.*

Reinhardt (*passes the coin to* **Müller**)
> Here – take this coin and go thy way.

Müller
> Hath God such meagre comfort sent me?

Reinhardt
> Meagre? Odd's teeth! I do repent me!

He takes the coin back again, and gives it to **Kommer**.

Kommer   Anything to do with money – me.

Reinhardt
> Thou – to my counting-house repair
> And fetch the bag of money there.

Kommer   You see?

> I run thy orders to obey –
> Already I am on my way.

Reinhardt (*to* **Thomas**, **Josef**, **Liesl**, *and* **Gretl**)
> And you – go tell my cooks: 'Tonight
> I shall a hundred guests invite.'
> A banquet let them conjure up
> On which an emperor might sup:
> The best of wine, the best of meat –
> And more than any man can eat.

Kommer *returns and hands* **Reinhardt** *a bag.*

Müller
> The gold thou hast in this one sack
> Would more than furnish all I lack.
> Some part of it I beg thee share –
> Thou hast enough and more to spare.

Reinhardt
> No groat of it that ever could
> Become thine, even if I would.

Takes the prompt-book back from **Müller** *and hands it to* **Adler**.

Reinhardt
> A pleasure garden have I bought
> Whereto my mistress may resort.
> This day am I obliged to go
> And pay the balance that I owe.
> The wealth thy envious eyes here see
> In truth belongs no more to me.

Kommer   Nor to Herr Reinhardt! The gardens are soaking up as much as the house!

Prince Archbishop   The palace gardens – yes! You are restoring *them* to their former glory?

Reinhardt   More than restoring them. I am making plans beyond even what your great predecessor ever imagined.

Shows him the view.

Kommer   Lakeside terraces and walks – fountains – a menagerie – an open-air theatre . . .

Prince Archbishop   And such serenity . . . The last of the day's light reflected in the lake . . . The profound blue stillness of the mountains beyond . . .

Reinhardt   I love this time of day, Your Grace. Twilight . . . It's where I have spent my life. In the border lands between the hard light of day and the ghosts of night. Smuggling whatever I could across the uncertain frontier between reality and dream.

Prince Archbishop   What about the frontier we're looking at up there in the mountains, Herr Reinhardt? Your greatest triumphs were on the other side of it, were they not?

Reinhardt   The frontier between Austria and Germany is the frontier between past and present, Your Grace. Germany is behind me. I have come back to Austria. To my native land.

Prince Archbishop   You don't feel a little wistful, when you see the bright lights of Germany twinkling away up there?

Reinhardt   I have come home, Your Grace! In every sense . . .

Thimig   And Herr Reinhardt intends to make this house a home not just for himself, but for all the actors and artists who come to perform here.

Adler   Somewhere they can share a simple communal life together.

Thimig   A kind of artistic cloister.

Kommer   With Max Reinhardt as its abbot!

Reinhardt   I am restoring the old chapel. Perhaps it could be reconsecrated? I should welcome your advice.

Prince Archbishop   You Austrian Jews! If only all our Catholics took as much interest in the faith!

Kommer   We love it! Of course we love it! Baroque curlicues! Fugues and kyries! Wine and blood! Smoke, music, gorgeous dresses! Confessions! Curses! Murders! Deathbed repentances! – Pure theatre! We're all in the same line of business!

Reinhardt   Easier, perhaps, to be what one isn't than what one is. May I show you my plans, Your Grace . . . ?

Exit **Prince Archbishop** *and* **Adler**.

Reinhardt (*to* **Thomas**, **Josef**, **Liesl** *and* **Gretl**)   Lanterns, candles!

They exit. **Thimig** *detains* **Reinhardt**.

Thimig (*to* **Reinhardt**, *aside*)   He knows! About you and me! When you said about a pleasure garden for your mistress! He gave me a look!

Kommer   Everyone knows, my darling! Everyone knows!

Thimig   Not in Salzburg!

Kommer   No, or we'd be in even more trouble than we are.

Exit **Reinhardt**, **Thimig** *and* **Kommer**.

Müller (*takes a canapé*)   So what's your name?

Franz   Franz, if you please, sir.

Müller   Franz . . . Franz what?

Franz   Just Franz, thank you, sir.

Müller   Herr Reinhardt's footman?

Franz   Herr Reinhardt's valet.

Müller   Oh yes. His famous valet. Sit down, Franz. Put your feet up. Have a canapé. You don't have to bother about me. I'm nobody.

Franz (*declines*)   Thank you, sir.

Müller   No? Well, as you please. (*Sits.*) Franz, yes. You were in service with the late Emperor's brother.

Franz   Sir.

Müller   Nothing but the best for Herr Reinhardt! Even his valet belonged to an Archduke. The lovely Luziwuzi. An Archduke and an Archduchess combined. Did you have to dress him on the days he was an Archduchess? Skirts, petticoats? Or did he have a lady's maid for his more feminine side?

Franz   More champagne, sir?

Müller   What a life we lead in Austria today, Franz! First you have to dress a gentleman up as a lady. Then you have to dress a bankrupt corsetmaker's son up as a gentleman. Herr Goldmann, from the Vienna slums, now acting the part of Herr Reinhardt, proprietor of a baroque palace. Luziwuzi may have been a lady, but at least he was a gentleman.

Franz   Sir.

Müller   And now Herr Goldmann is offering us a play addressing the problem of excessive wealth. I hadn't realised that it was quite so pressing. We've just lost the Great War. The currency has collapsed. So we have various problems. Unemployment. Hunger. Disease. People seeing their entire life savings wiped out. But *wealth*? Do you feel that wealth is putting *your* immortal soul in jeopardy?

Franz   Not in my place to say, sir.

Müller   'Not in my place to say, sir.' Forty rooms! When people are living on the streets! So, he's descended from the metropolitan heights of Berlin to come and save our souls in poor little provincial Salzburg. Or was he on the way down in the world anyway? Going out of fashion with the critics and the public in Berlin? And did he pick Salzburg because of our particular spiritual need? Or because there happened to be a baroque palace here that my desperate fellow-countrymen were selling for next to nothing? 'Not in my place to say, sir.'

Enter **Kommer**.

Müller   But perhaps the day will come when it will be. When we all pluck up our courage and say what we think about such things.

Kommer (*to* **Müller**)   You're still with us? What are you *doing* here?

Müller   The same as the rest of you. Drinking Herr Goldmann's champagne. Eating his *foie gras*.

Kommer   And who invited you?

Müller   I did.

Kommer   Franz, show this gentleman out. The odd coin – yes. But not champagne and *foie gras*.

Franz   This way, if you please, sir.

Müller (*takes the plate of canapés*)   The children in town might like something to eat . . .

Exit **Müller**. *Enter* **Reinhardt**, **Prince Archbishop**, **Thimig**, *and* **Adler**.

Reinhardt   God created the world. But man, whom He created in His image, has created a second world in His turn. The world of art.

Prince Archbishop   This house.

Reinhardt   Certain ways of living.

Prince Archbishop   Your play.

Reinhardt   Indeed, our play.

Prince Archbishop   A banquet has been ordained, has it not? Guests are expected. But Death is on his way! How will Death respond when he finds Everyman living in such style? Will he allow himself to be seduced? Will he forget the summons he is bearing? We are all in suspense.

Reinhardt

> Day's toil is done. Soft darkness falls.
> Sweet sounds of music fill my halls.

Lights down. Music.

Adler (*reads*)　Enter Guests with lanterns.

Enter **Thomas**, **Josef**, **Liesl** *and* **Gretl** *with lanterns. Party noise.*

Adler　A table appears, richly laid and set with lights.

A table appears, richly laid and set with lights.

Enter Everyman's Mistress.

She looks at **Thimig**, *who glances at* **Reinhardt** *and hesitates. He nods.*

Thimig

> Thy guests all wait impatiently
> Their good and gen'rous host to see.
> To fetch him thither am I come
> With pipe and timbrel, shawm and drum.

Reinhardt

> Oh, mistress mine! At once I feel
> The hot blood through my body steal!

Adler (*reads*)　She kisses him –

Thimig *kisses* **Reinhardt**.

Adler (*reads*)　– And sets a wreath of brightly coloured flowers on his head.

Thimig *produces a rose and fixes it in* **Reinhardt**'s *buttonhole.*

Reinhardt

> Thy beauty doth the lamps outshine,
> Thy voice is sweeter than sweet wine –
> A balsam to my weary heart
> That easeth every ache and smart.

(*To everyone.*)
> New love, old friends – what more need we
> To make all care and sorrow flee?
> A glass of wine, a snatch of song –
> Can mortal man for aught else long?
> Most dear you are to me, my friends!
> Enjoy the pleasures that life sends!
> So raise the cup! Drink deep, drink long!
> Lift up the voice! Sing sweet, sing strong!

Thomas, **Josef**, **Liesl**, **Gretl** (*sing in harmony*)
> Oh, here's to you, our merry host,
> May all your troubles fly!
> To you we drink this cheerful toast –
> Live, live until you die!
>
> God send you luck, God send you wealth,
> And praises to the sky!
> God send you love, God send you health –
> Live, live until you die!

All (*join in*)
> As long as life and breath shall last
> We'll sing it low and high!
> We'll sing it slow, we'll sing it fast –
> Live, live until you die!

Death (*off, huge and terrible, from different quarters, drowning the song, but heard only by* **Reinhardt**)
> Everyman! Everyman!

Reinhardt
> Who called?

The singing dies away.

> My name! Who called my name?
> A voice that from the darkness came,
> And through my heart like quickfire ran.
> Who rudely so called 'Everyman'?

Thimig

'Twas but the echo of our song
That in thy hearing lingered on.

Reinhardt

No, no – the voice that I heard call
Came not with soft and dying fall
But like high thunder through the land.
So: 'Everyman!' And 'Everyman!'
I knew that voice! Yet knew it not!
Or knew it once, and had forgot!
A voice that echoed down the years,
And now will ever haunt my ears.
From nowhere, everywhere it came . . .

Death (*off, whispers*)

Everyman! Everyman!

Reinhardt

And comes again, and comes again!

Death

Everyman! Everyman!

Thimig

No voice hear I, nor any sound.
All silent stand thy guests around.
Thy cheek is pale, thy hand is chill –
Thou hast mayhap some sudden ill.

The darkness deepens.

Reinhardt

Now darker grows the gath'ring night . . .
Unsure the candles' flickering light . . .

The masked and cloaked figure of **Death** *becomes visible in the shadows.*

Reinhardt

Methinks I see a strange face there
With eyes that coldly at me stare!

Death *steps forward, and becomes visible to the others. They utter a gasp or horror and freeze.*

Death

In merry mood do I thee find.
Of Him who made thee hast thou mind?

Reinhardt

Why come'st thou here to question me?
What have these things to do with thee?

Death

On God's high mission am I bent.
To seek thee out He hath me sent
And fetch thee thence with urgent speed.

Reinhardt

How so? Of me what hath He need?

Death

While yet of Him thou thinkest not,
He hath not thee likewise forgot.

Reinhardt

Of me in what wise thinketh He?

Death

That soon and plainly shalt thou see.
To thee He bade me straightly say:
A reckoning will He have! Today!

Reinhardt

And who art thou, who art so bold
The Almighty's purpose to unfold?

Death

My name is Death. I favour none,
Nor any fear. To all I come.

The others shrink away from him.

Quick now, make haste, no more delay!
A long road must thou walk today.
Thou trav'lest to that far-off land
Where thou before God's throne shalt stand,

And there, for thy day's work, shalt draw
Thy wages – neither less nor more.
What – hast thou like a fool believed
That this thy life, from God received,
And these thy earthly goods, were *thine*?

Reinhardt

I did believe that they were mine.

Death

Not so. They were but held in trust.
Inherit them another must.
Until on him I shall attend –
And his lease, too, be at an end.

Reinhardt

Yet grant me, I do thee implore,
One day on earth, one short day, more!
I fain would seek some company
To walk this fearful road with me,
That when I stand before God's throne
I stand not nakedly alone.

Pause.

Death

Thy prayer I grant. Go! One more day!
Make thou wise use of this brief stay!

Death *vanishes. Lights up. Everyone laughs and relaxes.*

Reinhardt

So Death gives Everyman a space,
To mend and then present his case.
Grant us the same, Your Grace – a day
To mend and then present our play.

Prince Archbishop

No less than Death himself am I
A servant of great God on high.
How can it then be meet for me
To be less generous than He?
Besides, I'm all on fire to know

How things for Everyman will go.
So childish of me! Even worse,
I do believe I'm speaking verse.

The **Prince Archbishop** *blesses them and exits.*

Thimig
You saw? He raised his hand to bless!

Reinhardt
I think that means . . .

Kommer
                                    . . . the answer's yes!

Cheers. Raised glasses.

But . . . who played Death, then? Death was who?

Thomas
Not me.

Kommer
                So you?

Josef
                        Nor me.

Kommer (*to* **Franz**)
                                Nor you?

Reinhardt
Some stranger, doing good by stealth!

Exit all except **Franz**.

Franz   I saw his eyes. 'Twas Death himself.

Darkness.

Thomas (*as Prologue*)
Draw near, good people all, I pray!
Give heed while we perform our play –

Daylight. On a lower level downstage **Thomas** *is rehearsing. Above him, upstage,* **Reinhardt**, *immaculate as ever, watches, with* **Adler**,

Liesl *and* **Gretl**, *who quietly set a rehearsal table and supply him with pencils, coffee, the prompt-book, etc.*

Thomas
　　– Wherein we show, as best we can,
　　The Summoning of Everyman.
　　Here all shall learn, with eyes to see,
　　How short our days on earth do be,
　　How sorrowful must be our end,
　　Should we our ways neglect to mend . . .

Reinhardt　Thank you. From the beginning again, please. 'Draw near, good people all, I pray . . . '

Thomas
　　Draw near, good people all, I pray . . .

Reinhardt *(demonstrates)*
　　Draw near, good people all, I pray . . .

Thomas *(attempts to imitate)*
　　Draw near, good people all, I pray . . .

Reinhardt
　　Draw near, good people all, I pray . . .

Thomas
　　Draw near, good people all, I pray . . .

Reinhardt *(always calm, collected, and patient)*　What we are trying to achieve is very simple. It is perfection. Simple perfection. Life is not perfect. It is confused and elusive and shabby. We have six weeks in which to make one small piece of it, approximately four hundred metres square by two hours long, into something that we can lay before our benefactor, the Prince Archbishop of Salzburg, and all the other citizens of this town. Something of which we can say, Look, this is how life really is!

He picks up the prompt-book and demonstrates it.

This is life, this is death, when all the confusion and shabbiness have been stripped away, when we really look at them and get hold of them. They are part of each other. Everything is inextricably part of everything. And yet, for these two short hours, it is also very simple and very elegant. That is what we are trying to achieve together. Yes? Once again, then, if you please . . .

Adler   Herr Reinhardt . . .

Reinhardt

Draw near, good people all, I pray . . . !

Adler   I'm sorry. You wanted me to remind you about your cable to New York . . .

Reinhardt   Draft something for me, will you, Gusti?

Adler   And your mother's birthday. I'll get another silk scarf . . . Oh, and there is a problem with the whores. For the banquet scene this afternoon. We will only have six whores.

Reinhardt   Six? I asked for twenty.

Adler   Two of them are off sick, Herr Reinhardt. One's got choir practice. One's taking her school-leaving exam . . .

Reinhardt   That still leaves sixteen.

Adler   No, because Katie said . . .

Reinhardt   *Katie* said?

Enter **Kommer**.

Kommer   Ten. Katie said ten whores.

Reinhardt (*patiently*)   I want twenty.

Kommer   You won't have noticed this, but we have a production budget.

Reinhardt   Twenty whores.

Kommer   We have exceeded the production budget. The production is in deficit. There is also a world economic crisis. The country is going smash. We have no costumes for any more whores. There are no more whores in Salzburg.

Reinhardt   I want twenty whores.

Kommer   You want two hundred whores! But you can't have them!

Reinhardt   I don't want two hundred whores. I am trying to purge the theatre of excess. I am trying to produce this play in the simplest imaginable way with the simplest imaginable means. But it is physically impossible to stage this particular scene with less than twenty whores.

Adler   When Herr Reinhardt was doing *The Miracle* in Vienna . . .

Kommer   He had a thousand extras.

Adler   He had fifteen hundred extras.

Kommer   And everyone thought it was completely ridiculous! The notices were terrible! There were more extras than audience!

Adler   Excuse me – there were nine thousand in the audience.

Reinhardt   My brother made no difficulties about finding me fifteen hundred extras.

Kommer   Your brother, your brother!

Reinhardt   Be careful what you say about my brother, please.

Kommer   Your other self – I know, I know! The only soul in the world you actually love. And he understands money. Which you don't. And I don't, and no one does, only your beloved brother. So ask *him* for whores!

Adler   His brother has more important things to think about than a few extras! He has Herr Reinhardt's entire business empire to manage! He has two huge theatres to run!

Reinhardt   So, more whores by this afternoon.

Kommer   By this afternoon you will have my resignation in your hands.

Adler   We still have it from last week.

Kommer   Excellent. Then I can leave at once.

Reinhardt   The whores first, though, please. Now if we can possibly get on with the rehearsal . . .

Enter **Franz** *with documents.*

Reinhardt   Bills? Anything to do with money – give it to Katie.

Kommer   No money. No Katie.

Franz (*to* **Reinhardt**)   It's the dwarfs, Herr Reinhardt.

Reinhardt   Dwarfs?

Franz   Two of them have come without their heads. For the garden, Herr Reinhardt.

Reinhardt   Katie will deal with it.

Kommer   Katie *won't* deal with it. Katie has resigned.

Reinhardt   From the beginning of the scene, please.

Draw near, good people all, I pray . . .

Death . . . Where is Death?

Adler   He had a costume-fitting this morning, Herr Reinhardt. Shall I run and see how long he's going to be?

Reinhardt   Katie can do it on his way to deal with the dwarfs. Katie!

Kommer   He never takes the slightest notice of anything I say! I resign, and he doesn't even hear it!

He begins to leave.

Also it's going to pour with rain. You want me to get the rain stopped?

Reinhardt   If you would be so kind. And, Katie . . . more whores!

Exit **Kommer** *and* **Franz**. **Reinhardt** *waits patiently. Enter* **Thimig**.

Thimig   Time, Gusti! Time, time, time! He never has enough time! Every night he sits up half the night rewriting that prompt-book . . . What time did you get to bed last night, Reinhardt?

Reinhardt   Last night? I had an early night for once.

Thimig (*to* **Adler**)   An early night. That's two or three o'clock. Then of course he's exhausted, and he gets up late. But he will never hurry! Twenty minutes every morning to clean his teeth!

Enter **Franz** *holding a selection of ties.*

Thimig   Then it's the suit . . . And the tie . . .

Adler   He wants everything to be just right, Helene! The play. The house. His appearance.

Franz   Or perhaps the blue, Herr Reinhardt.

Reinhardt (*examines himself in the looking glass*)   Perhaps the blue . . .

He unhurriedly takes off the tie he is wearing and tries **Franz***'s selection.*

Thimig   Reinhardt! You will be late for rehearsal! You're always late for rehearsal! You keep everyone waiting!

Reinhardt   I *am* rehearsing, Leni. I am rehearsing myself.

Thimig   Always late! Always exhausted! Never any time!

Adler   He doesn't want to have any time left over, does he, Helene, with nothing to fill it? Nothing in front of him. Nothing in his head. Nothing to do.

Reinhardt   I think the blue is a little adventurous.

He unhurriedly changes back to his original tie.

Adler   And don't worry, Helene. He always gets everything done. It's all down here in the diary . . . Auditions at eleven, Herr Reinhardt. Costume-designer at twelve . . . And the rehearsal schedule, Herr Reinhardt. Prologue . . .

Enter **Thomas**, *as Prologue in everyday clothes.*

Thomas

Draw near, good people all, I pray . . .

Continues the speech in the background, repeating if necessary.

Adler   House . . .

Enter **Josef**, *as Everyman, likewise.*

Josef

A lordly house I own and fair . . .

Adler   Poor Neighbour . . .

Enter **Franz**.

Franz

I dwelt once in a house as fine . . .

Adler   Banquet . . .

Enter **Liesl**.

Liesl

Thy guests all wait impatiently . . .

Adler   Prologue again . . .

Thomas

Draw near, good people all, I pray . . .

Adler   First dress rehearsal! First dress rehearsal, please!
Dress rehearsal, everyone . . . !

The Actors *hurry offstage.*

Reinhardt   Second dress rehearsal . . . And then . . .

He finishes tying his tie.

There we are. Once again. Ready to face the world. Ready to
go before the judgment seat.

Adler   Beginners, please . . . ! Quiet, everyone . . . Quiet
backstage . . . !

Everyone scatters. The expectant murmur of an audience.

Reinhardt   Listen, listen!

Adler   An audience!

Thimig   The sound they make! That terrifying sound!

Reinhardt   I know what Everyman felt as he took his stand in the courtroom. Already dead. And intensely conscious of being alive. Why do we do it, Leni? Why do we put ourselves through it?

Adler   Toi toi toi, Herr Reinhardt! Toi toi toi, Helene!

Kommer, **Müller**, *the* **Prince Archbishop**, **Josef,** **Thomas**, **Gretl** *and* **Liesl** *appear in various places, looking out into the auditorium, together with* **Franz**, *waiting.*

Reinhardt   Full house?

Kommer   Full square.

Adler   Two minutes, everyone . . . !

Reinhardt   Who have we got out there?

Kommer   Everyman, by the look of it.

Müller   Every man in Salzburg who is able to afford the luxury of being told by Herr Goldmann that he shouldn't be.

Reinhardt   Yap, yap! What *is* it that they all find to talk about . . . ?

Kommer   It's going to rain, it's going to rain, it's going to rain . . .

Franz   What happens when they all open their umbrellas . . . ?

Adler   One minute . . . Good luck, everyone . . .

Thimig *blows* **Reinhardt** *a kiss.* **Kommer** *bobs his head, praying.* **Reinhardt** *looks at him. He stops.* **Adler** *puts down the diary and takes up the prompt-book. She watches* **Reinhardt**, *waiting for the order to start. He nods. She signals to someone off.*

Adler   Cue music . . . Cue cathedral doors . . . Cue cast . . .

The offstage audience quietens.

Thomas (*as Prologue, off, distant, echoing round the square*)
Draw near, good people all, I pray!
Give heed while we perform our play,
Wherein we show, as best we can,
The Summoning of Everyman . . .

Adler   Cue God . . .

*Cathedral bells, and the faint echoing murmur of voices from the stage
continuing off.*

Cue Everyman . . .

Reinhardt (*to himself*)   Settle down! Don't rush it! Wait for
them to come to you . . .

Adler   Cue Banquet . . .

Music, odd half-heard snatches of dialogue, audience reaction.

Cue Death . . .

Thimig
Words, words. Words and weather.

Adler
Chill flurries of wind off the mountains.

The light begins to fade. Only **Adler**, **Reinhardt** *and* **Thimig**
remain lit.

Thimig
The shadows in the square gradually lengthening.

Adler
The summer twilight creeping in.

Thimig
Night falling.

Adler
And already Everyman is chastened and repentant.

Thimig

Already his last day on earth is coming to its end . .

Josef (off)

Eternal God! Eternal light!
Eternal way of truth and right!
In my last moment, as I die,
Hear Thou my cry, Lord, hear my cry!

Reinhardt *begins to mouth Everyman's words along with* **Josef**, *and act out his moves.*

Now down into the grave I go,
Down, down into the dark below.

Thimig *mouths Faith's words along with* **Liesl**.

Liesl (*off*)

Thy Faith by thee will faithful stand.

Adler *does the same with Works's words along with* **Gretl**.

Gretl (*off*)

And I, thy Works, at thy right hand.

Liesl (*off*)

I hear the angels' heavenly song.
Their voices ring out sweet and strong
Poor weary souls to welcome in.
For him it is, methinks, they sing.

The angels sing. Music. The last light on **Reinhardt** *fades to darkness. Applause, off.*

Lights up. **Reinhardt**, **Thimig**, **Adler**, **Kommer** *and* **Franz** *listen to the applause, trying to judge it.*

Reinhardt   Yes? No? Yes . . . ?

Kommer   Possibly.

Reinhardt   And His Grace?

Adler *indicates him. He is still sitting, forgotten, dabbing a handkerchief to his eyes.*

Thimig   Your Grace . . . ?

Prince Archbishop (*smiles through his tears*)   Happy ending!

They are all relieved. Laughter. Embraces.

Adler   Now all we have to do is . . .

Thimig   Do it again!

Adler   And again!

Thimig   And again!

Prince Archbishop   But, my son, my son, one day he will come for *you*, that fearful messenger!

Reinhardt   He will come for all of us, Your Grace.

Prince Archbishop   For all of us, for all of us. But, my dear boy – *you* will not hear the angels sing! You will go down into the pit, and you will be gone for all eternity! You don't understand the images you have conjured up . . . And yet something in you longs to. Isn't that why you have produced this play?

Kommer   Never mind that.

> Herr Reinhardt says, it being a first night,
> He doth everyone back to his house invite.
> His cooks have a light supper conjured up
> On which His Grace and other dignitaries might care to
> sup!

Exit all noisily, except **Thimig**. *Sudden quiet.*

Thimig   Listen!

Enter **Adler**, *holding mail.*

Adler   What? What . . . ?

Thimig   Nothing! Silence. Everything – vanished like a dream!

Adler   The season's over. They've broken up the stage.

Thimig   Just you and me, creeping about an empty house.

Adler   The leaves are falling.

Thimig   Autumn . . . Winter . . .

Adler   Snow on the mountains . . . Snow hiding the garden . . .

Thimig   The house is full of pale light. Great empty staring rooms where nothing ever happens. Where's it all gone, Gusti? All the rush, all the long days and late nights? All the exhaustion?

Adler   It's moving around the world with Reinhardt.

She sorts mail and hands some to **Thimig**.

Vienna, Berlin . . . Paris, London . . . New York, Los Angeles . . . Plays, operas . . . All over the world they want him!

Thimig   I miss him so much, Gusti! 'Triumph . . .' 'Disaster . . .' 'Encouraged . . . ' 'Exhausted . . . ' That's all he is – telegrams! Our lives are going by, and he's never here!

Adler   Money, Helene! He has to earn money! For the house! For next season! And every day he writes to you

Thimig   Plans, plans. Nothing but plans. Plans for the house . . . Oh, the roof!

Adler   I've got the quotations.

Thimig   The herons for the lake!

Adler   The herons are on their way.

Thimig   The house. The garden. Next season. Always the future. Never the present. Always things that don't exist.

Adler   They will, though, Helene, they will!

Thimig   And the commission for the play! The life of Christ!

Adler   I have written to Bernard Shaw.

Thimig   Meanwhile we're stuck here, in these great empty rooms . . .

Adler   You've got your Schiller to do in Vienna! Your Shakespeare in Innsbruck!

Thimig   Where is he now, Gusti? At this very minute? What's he doing?

Adler   Missing you. Thinking about you. Wishing he was here.

Thimig   I miss him, Gusti! I miss him, I miss him!

Adler   *I* miss him, Helene.

Thimig   That's different.

Adler   Yes, that's different . . .

Thimig   And then suddenly . . . Sunlight

Thomas   (*off*) Draw near good people all, I pray . . . !

Thimig   It's summer again.

Adler   It's Everyman again.

Thimig   It's long days and late nights. It's problems, lines, costumes,   fallings out . . .

Enter **Reinhardt**.

Reinhardt   My money hath much work to do . . .

Adler   Money scene, Herr Reinhardt ? Money scene, please! Money scene, everyone!

Enter **Josef***, as Everyman, and* **Thomas***,* **Liesl***, and* **Gretl** *with rehearsal table and boxes of props.*

Reinhardt   Everyman!

   My money hath much work to do . . .

Josef

> My money hath much work to do –
> Must dig and sow and build and hew . . .

Reinhardt   Simply, simply! A man telling us as innocently as a child about the problems of good fortune. No irony! No hint of what's to come . . . !

> My money hath much work to do –
> Must dig and sow and build and hew,
> Nor ever pause nor ever sleep,
> If I my just reward will reap . . .

Josef, **Thomas**, **Liesl**, *and* **Gretl** *carry in Old Masters, antique furniture, statues, etc.*

> Yes, great may be my wealth – but great
> The cost of running my estate.
> My servants must have coats and bread,
> My dogs and horses must be fed,
> My parks and pleasure gardens made,
> My gamekeepers and bailiffs paid.
> My hunting grounds must be secured,
> My private fishing rights ensured.
> And constantly must things be mended,
> Renewed, replaced, improved, extended.
> The more one hath, the more immense
> Becomes the burden of expense . . .

Enter **Kommer**, *holding documents.*

Kommer

> The more one hath, the more one fills
> Th' entire house with unpaid bills!

And tax. More tax. You already owe so much back tax that it's being discussed by the government at ministerial level.

Reinhardt   Money, money! I have other things to think about!

Kommer   What I can never decide, Herr Reinhardt, is whether you are feeble-minded, or whether you are an

imposter. Everyone in the world is one or the other!
Professionally you are an imposter, and I honour you for it,
because you are able to put on a performance that convinces
actors, audiences, and archbishops alike. But when it comes to
money . . .

Reinhardt   When it comes to money – I leave all that to my
brother.

Kommer   Your brother, thank God, is an imposter through
and through, like me, and without him your great empire
would collapse like a rotten mushroom. But where is even
your brother going to find the kind of money you now owe?

Adler   He can raise another loan!

Kommer   Another loan? Excellent idea! On the security of
what?

Adler   Of this house! He's done it before!

Kommer   He certainly has. We have six mortgages on the
security of this house. Not to mention the furniture. Or the
pictures and statues. This house, which is supporting the
weight of not only enough artwork and statuary to satisfy
Lorenzo the Magnificent but also the greater part of all serious
theatre in German-speaking Europe, is entirely constructed
out of debt. It is a monument not so much of baroque
architecture as of baroque pawnbroking.

Enter **Thimig**, *holding a telegram.*

Kommer   And, if I may quote from the wisdom of
Everyman in the play:

   It followeth, as B from A,
   And always hath, since Adam's day:
   Who buildeth house, and needs must borrow,
   Will build a house of pain and sorrow . . .

(*To* **Thimig**.) Not another bill?

Adler   A telegram . . . ? Helene! What is it?

Thimig (*to* **Reinhardt**)   I'm so sorry . . .

She hands him the telegram.

You loved him. We all loved him.

Reinhardt *reads the telegram.*

Death (*off, distant*)   Everyman! Everyman!

Adler   His brother?

Reinhardt *goes out.*

Adler   Oh, no! Oh, Helene! Whatever are we going to do without him?

Thimig   What everyone always does. Miss him. And wonder how we'll ever manage. And manage. And remember him. And then forget him.

Exit **Thimig** *after* **Reinhardt**.

Adler   Poor Edmund!

Kommer   Poor us.

Adler   Katie! We can't think about the money now!

Kommer   Someone will have to. Another imposter.

Enter **Reinhardt**.

Kommer   And who is the only other real imposter we know . . . ?

He indicates himslef. Exit **Kommer**.

Reinhardt   And on we go.

Draw near, good people all, I pray . . . !

Adler *settles to the prompt-book.*

Adler   Which scenes are we doing, Herr Reinhardt?

Reinhardt   The same as last year and the year before.
The same as next year and the year after. Prologue, Banquet,
Death . . . House, Money . . . Money, Money . . .

My money hath much work to do −
Must dig and sow and build and hew . . .

Poor Neighbour:

No mortal ill can do worse harm
Than money, with its cursed charm . . .

Enter **Kommer**. *He silently holds out a document and a pen to*
Reinhardt.

Reinhardt
In glitt'ring spiderwebs of gold
Doth Satan seek us to enfold.
Whoso succumbeth to that spell
Embarketh on the path to hell.

He takes the document and pen as he continues.

Everyman . . .

Thou fool, this benison to despise!
Learn this from me: the man was wise
Who first the great discov'ry made . . .

(*To* **Kommer**.) Something to do with money?

Kommer   I read, you sign.

Reinhardt (*signs as he speaks*)
                        The man was wise
Who first the great discov'ry made,
And elevated thus our trade
From petty barter and exchange
To nobler aims and wider range.

He hands the document back but keeps the pen. **Kommer** *waits, hand
out.*

Reinhardt
Once money shows her smiling face

Our world becomes a better place,
For each man in his chosen field
A godlike power doth learn to wield.

He pats his pockets as he speaks.

He can command the seeds to grow
And make the living waters flow,
Send this man here and that man there,
Make square the round and round the square,
For naught there is on low or high
That money cannot sell or buy.

He finds a handful of banknotes.

Admire this rare and wond'rous thing!
That serves as slave and rules as king,
That answers every beck and call,
Yet holds all men within its thrall!

He hands the banknotes to **Kommer**, *who looks at them.*

Reinhardt   What?

Kommer   This? It appears to be *money*. You appear to be giving me *money*. Is this a *tip*?

Reinhardt   I'm sorry. You had your hand out.

He takes them back. **Kommer** *takes them off him again.*

Kommer   You're not carrying cash around? You're not giving tips?

Reinhardt   I am trying to take control of my financial affairs.

Kommer   Of about four times the average monthly wage?

Reinhardt   But I cannot count out money and direct at the same time.

Kommer   *I* look after the money! *Franz* looks after the money! *I* hand out the tips! *Franz* hands out the tips! Fräulein Thimig, Fräulein Adler – the second under-gardener and the third under-footman – anyone. But not you, if you please, Herr Reinhardt!

Reinhardt   I accept that I don't understand money . . .

Kommer   'I don't understand money!' Do you think *I* understand money? Do you think *Rothschild* understands money? *Nobody* understands money!

Reinhardt   My brother actually did understand money.

Kommer   What your sainted brother understood, God rest him, was how to pay the lowest wages in Europe. And persuade people to accept them because it was such an honour to work for you. What he understood was how to make you hear what he said when he said no. Of me you take no notice whatsoever, and we are all going smash! The house, the city, the festival! The whole country! So, my revered Herr Reinhardt, any waiters with their hands out, any beggars, anyone collecting for charity – refer them to me. I know I can never replace your brother. But somehow I have got myself in the position where I *am* replacing your brother! So I have to *act the part* of a man who understands money! *Someone* has to, otherwise nothing would happen! No house, no cathedral to perform your simple morality play in front of! No simple morality play! No simplicity! No morality!

Reinhardt *retreats.* **Kommer** *pursues him.*

Kommer   'Admire this rare and wond'rous thing!' Yes? And since I have many columns of figures to add up and balance out, perhaps you would be kind enough to return my *pen* . . . ?

Exit **Reinhardt** *and* **Kommer**. *Enter* **Thimig**, *holding telegrams and letters.*

Thimig   Autumn again . . . Winter . . . It's always autumn! It's always winter! He's nothing but letters and telegrams!

Adler   'Cable producers Philadephia . . . ' 'Check bookings Rome . . . '

Thimig 'Cast contracts *Everyman* . . . ' 'Three hundred rose-bushes . . . ' It's never even autumn, it's never even winter! It's not *now*! It's never *now*! It's always next season!

Adler Next season on tour.

Thimig Next season in the garden.

Adler Next season in Salzburg.

Thimig He's with that woman.

Adler No, he's not, Helene! What woman? Which woman?

Thimig You know which woman.

Adler That drug addict woman? Of course he's not.

Thimig Of course he is. As soon as I'm not there, she is. And there's someone else in America.

Adler There's no one in America, Helene.

Thimig There's always someone. Always someone somewhere.

Adler There's only you, Helene! Only you!

Thimig Once it was me. Once I was the someone he was running off to meet.

Adler It's still you, Helene! Still you! Look! Telegrams! Letters!

Thimig That's all I ever see of him! You, taking his part! You,waving his ridiculous telegrams about and covering up for him . . . !

Sunshine.

Until . . . suddenly it happens all over again . . .

Adler The snow has gone from the mountains.

Adler The snow has gone from the mountains.

Thimig The garden is green.

Adler   Next season is this season.

Thimig   Now is now.

Enter **Reinhardt***. He and* **Thimig** *look at each other, smiling.*

Adler   Oh, Herr Reinhardt! Welcome home! Did you have a good crossing, Herr Reinhardt? Was New York impossible? The advance on *Everyman* is twelve per cent up on last year. Oh, and the new altarpiece has arrived. And Graz is up in arms because they say you're going to do the Pirandello in Linz first, and New York must have the final dates for the tour of the *Dream*. Also one of the monkeys has bitten the kitchenmaid, and the new flamingos are not the same pink as the old ones. Also . . .

Thimig   Gusti! Go and help Franz unpack!

Adler   Oh . . . yes, of course. I'm sorry, Helene. I'm sorry, Herr Reinhardt.

Exit **Adler***.*

Reinhardt   My wonderful house! The only production of mine that will endure. Everything else is written on the wind.

Thimig   The house . . . and the garden . . .

Reinhardt
> Let me, I pray thee, take thy hand
> And lead thee into thine own land.
> For thy delight, my fairest fair,
> Do I this pleasure park prepare –
> Our Eden, where we may enjoy
> The happy hours without annoy.
> Here nature doth conspire with art
> To please the eye and glad the heart.
> In this dear place thou mayest see
> A token of my love for thee.

Thimig
> Here hast thou planted many a flower
> To deck with jewels each golden hour!
> The lily here – and here the rose –

And here sweet honeysuckle grows
To freight with heavy-swooning musk
The dewy morn, the lang'rous dusk.
Here woodland walks and many a glade
Extend a soft and verdant shade
Whereto we haply may retreat
To scape the drowsy noonday heat,
And by cool springs and winding streams
Long wander lost in summer dreams.

Reinhardt
If thou find'st here, in this green place,
Some cloudy mirror for thy grace,
Some passing moment of delight,
It will thy gard'ner's pains requite.

Peace, quiet. **Reinhardt** *sits and closes his eyes. Enter* **Adler**.

Adler   I'm sorry, Herr Reinhardt. I'm sorry, Helene . . .

Thimig   Gusti, I am trying to give Reinhardt a few precious
moments of peace!

Adler   Yes, but his wife has telephoned.

Thimig   Oh, *no*! Reinhardt! (*To* **Reinhardt**.) I thought you
had told her *not* to telephone? I thought she had *promised*!
What did she want?

Adler   She wanted to talk to Herr Reinhardt.

Thimig   Of course! Reinhardt, don't pretend you're asleep.
That woman is poisoning our lives! I have tried to make our
home a refuge for you. But how can I, when she keeps
pursuing us? You and I both want to live quietly and
peacefully together like any other couple. But we can't until
we've got you divorced! I know how difficult that is. It's the
same as with this house. Or the play. Making something
simple and natural is very complex. I know you can't get a
divorce in Austria . . .

Adler   Or anywhere else. She won't give him one! His brother tried and tried to find a way round it! But not even *he* could do it!

Thimig   Maybe because his brother could read his mind, and he knew he doesn't really want one.

Adler   Doesn't really want one? Helene, what do you mean? Of course he wants one! He's been all over Europe trying to get one!

Thimig   The present arrangement is rather convenient for him, isn't it? Isn't it, Reinhardt? It means you don't have to marry *me*! I'm just part of the house! I'm just one of the artworks!

Adler   Helene! I really don't think that is quite fair to Herr Reinhardt. He loves you. He wants to marry you.

Thimig   Gusti, the fact that you and I were at school together doesn't give you the right to tell me whether people love me and want to marry me! That's not why I asked you to come and work for Herr Reinhardt!

Adler   You asked me to come and work for him because you wanted to make his life a little easier.

Reinhardt   Ladies . . .

Adler   And also, no doubt, because you thought that whoever he runs off with next at least it won't be *me*!

Thimig   Gusti, control yourself! I know you worship the ground he walks upon. There's nothing very special about that, Gusti! *Everyone* worships the ground he walks upon! Even Katie! Even his wife! But you make a fool of him, Gusti! You don't stand up to him! You always let him have his way! And how can we ever discuss anything between us if you immediately take his side?

Adler   Helene!

Thimig   His wife telephones – you take *her* side!

Adler   You know that's not true!

Thimig   I can't think why Reinhardt *needs* a personal assistant. Everything you do for him I could perfectly well do myself.

Adler   You have your own work to do! You're an actress, not a secretary! You're away in Vienna, you're off on tour!

Thimig   And if it's like this when I'm here, heaven knows what it's like when I'm not!

Pause.

Reinhardt   Do you think we should try to find another figure to go at the end of the avenue there? Something very still and very calm?

Thimig   I'm sorry to get upset. But this is our home. We made it together. When we have guests, when the Prince Archbishop comes, I want to stand in the great hall and receive him, like any other wife in the world. I want to say goodbye to him at the end of the evening.

Adler   Helene, you *do* say goodbye to him at the end of the evening!

Thimig   As *I* leave! I want to say goodbye to him as *he* leaves!

Adler   Our relations with the local citizens are bad enough as it is.

Thimig   Anyway, Katie says you can get one in Latvia.

Adler   A divorce? In Latvia?

Thimig   It's just a matter of six months' residence.

Adler   He has to go to Paris, Helene. Then Stockholm. Then he's got the American tour.

Thimig   After the American tour.

Adler   He has to take his sons on holiday.

Thimig   His sons can come here.

Adler   Helene, if the boys come here *she* has to come, too!
She has a court order!

Thimig   And there you go, taking his side again! Why don't
you invite his *daughter's* mother as well? And that female drug
fiend who always descends as soon as my back is turned? And
that other trollop in London? – Yes, I *do* know about her!

Enter **Kommer**.

Thimig   And Katie! You can all fight over him together . . .
!

Kommer   I hate to interrupt this idyll . . .

He shows documents.

Adler   *Another* tax demand?

Kommer   A German one this time.

Reinhardt   Money. I am to leave all questions of money to
you, I believe.

Exit **Reinhardt**.

Adler (*reads the tax demand*)   Oh, my God!

Kommer   Exactly. Herr Hitler is obviously taking a
personal interest in ruining him.

Thimig   What do you want him to do about it? Chop down
the trees and build holiday homes? Go off on tour again? He's
only just come back! You will kill that man!

Enter **Reinhardt**.

Reinhardt   And Gusti – the zoo place in Hamburg. We
need a few pelicans. About a dozen. Also nightingales.
Chinese nightingales.

Exit **Reinhardt**.

Thimig   Reinhardt! Wait! The new altarpiece! We must get
another altar to put it over . . . !

Exit **Thimig**.

Adler   So what are you suggesting?

Kommer   This house, Gusti. Our one asset, while it lasts.
We must make use of it. Get some money into the house.

Adler   Oh, not one of your terrible parties!

Kommer   One of *his* terrible parties. Money walking round
the house and some of it will stick!

Adler   We're already entertaining half Salzburg every night
of the season!

Kommer   Not that Herr Reinhardt often deigns to put in
an appearance.

Adler   He never knows what to say to people.

Kommer   He knows what to say to people when he wants
something out of them.

Adler   This house was supposed to be a retreat for actors
and artists, not a feeding trough for local dignitaries.

Kommer   Never mind local dignitaries. Celebrities, Gusti!
Bankers who want to meet celebrities! Financiers who want to
be celebrities! Money! 'A lordly house and fair' – yes, and this
is what it's *for*! The masterpieces on the walls, the flamingos in
the garden, the footmen, the maids – this is what it's all
leading up to! To say money! To scream it out – money,
money, money! Money attracts money, Gusti! Money talks to
money!

> And so, a fortnight from tonight
> We shall three hundred guests invite,
> And serve the kind of banquet up
> On which financiers might sup.

Adler   He so hates entertaining!

Kommer   But he loves *rehearsing*! Our own banquet scene!
One of his gigantic productions. We've got the décor. Now all
we need are the extras to dress it.

Lights down. Gathering rehearsal noise.

Tables . . . ! Chairs . . . ! Set the sideboard . . . ! Franz! Where are you, Franz . . . ?

Enter **Josef** *and* **Thomas** *as peruked footmen, and* **Franz**.

Kommer   Maids! Extra maids! Extra footmen! Candles! Trays!

Adler   Maids and footmen, please! Candles! Trays!

Enter **Liesl**, **Gretl**, *and as many understudies as possible, bringing candelebra, and carrying trays.*

Adler   Lights up . . . ! Music . . . !

Candelebra light. Quartet tunes up.

And . . . enter God!

Enter **Reinhardt**. *He holds up his hand for silence.*

Adler   Quiet, please! Quiet, everyone!

Reinhardt
>   My aim in life has ever been
>   To break the bounds 'twixt world and dream,
>   To make the whole world our theatre –
>   This house, yes! Nowhere better!
>   So let us by the guiles of art
>   Create a day that stands apart
>   From all the grey and shapeless haze
>   Of unremembered everydays –
>   That gives a form, a shape, a face
>   To timeless time and placeless place –
>   That leaves a sign that we were here
>   Before Death whispers in our ear.

So – pre-supper positions, please.

Adler   Pre-supper positions, everyone!

The **Footmen** *and* **Maids** *take up waiting positions with trays.*

Reinhardt   Doors open. Guests arriving any minute . . .
Trays high . . . Left hand in small of back . . . Here they come,
here they come. Cue Franz.

Demonstrates with **Franz** *announcing the guests.*

Reinhardt   'Their Highnesses the Somebodies of
Somewhere . . . His Honour the Somebody of Somewhere
Else . . . '

He shakes imaginary hands.

Your Highness! Your Honour . . . ! Serve drinks, serve
canapés!

He rushes the **Footmen** *and* **Maids** *into action.*

Reinhardt   More guests, more guests . . . ! Canapés, drinks!
Keep moving, keep moving . . . Trays high . . . ! Drink, drink,
drink . . . Talk, talk, talk . . . God knows what about, who
cares, keep drinking, keep talking, keep moving . . . And on we
go. Into supper! Cue Franz! Bang bang bang!

Franz *and* **Reinhardt** *bang for silence.*

Reinhardt   'Your Royal Somethings and Somebodies,
Your This-ships and That-ships . . . Supper is served . . . !'
Start music!

*He demonstrates playing a violin. Musicians off play a minuet. He counts
the bars. On the beat.*

And one . . . two . . . three . . . turn . . . !

The **Footmen** *and* **Maids** *turn to face us.*

Reinhardt   One . . . two . . . three . . . *move* . . . !

They move to reform as a line across the stage.

One . . . two . . . three – *turn* . . . !

They turn away from us.

Trays down. *Nap*kins . . . *Plates* . . . *Spoons* . . .

On the words of command they put napkins over their left arm, and pick up a pair of spoons in their right hand.

Wait for it, wait for it . . . Dramatic moment . . . And . . . *turn* . . . ! Two . . . three . . . *Move* . . . !

They advance to a line of imaginary tables. **Reinhardt** *moves with them, and joins in the actions.*

And . . . *still*! Motionless. Statues . . . Trays up . . . ! Faces like masks . . . Look at Franz's face. He used to serve the Archduke . . . And eyes front again . . . Thank you. Ready to lean . . . Two . . . three . . . *Lean!*

They all lean deferentially foward.

Two . . . three . . . *Spoons*!

They pick up their pairs of spoons.

And when I say 'show' you show them the first choice on the left of the plate . . . The *left* of the plate . . . Two . . . three . . . *show*!

They indicate the left-hand choice on the plate with their pairs of spoons.

Two . . . three . . . Or *how* about *this* . . . ? Or *that* . . . ? Or *this* . . . ? Or *that* . . . ? And now, in your own time . . . *Serve* . . . Good. Good. Well done, five . . . No looking down your nose, two . . . ! Watch Franz . . . Too obsequious, four! Touch of irony! You are playing a part, you are personifying a certain archaic social order. And so are they. And you both know it. And when I say 'Straighten *up* . . . ' Two . . . three . . . Straighten *up*! Two . . . three . . . and step *back* . . . Two . . . three . . . One *place* to the *left*!

They all take one step sideways to the next imaginary place at table.

And again from the top. Two . . . three . . . *Lean* . . . ! Two . . . three . . . *Show* . . . ! And on you go . . .

They repeat the sequence.

Keep the rhythm going . . . Wonderful . . . Perfect . . . Straighten *up*! Two . . . three . . . and step *back*. Two . . . three . . . And one place to the *left*!

They repeat the sequence at the next imaginary place along the table, and the next. It becomes a full-scale minuet.

Plié, rise . . . Plié, rise . . . Left-hand turn . . . Honour your partners . . .

Kommer *and* **Adler** *join in.* **Thimig**, **Prince Archbishop**, *and* **Death** *enter from the shadows and join in as well.*

Reinhardt *holds up his hand. The music stops.*

Reinhardt (*to audience*)
　Dear guests! Before you join us, take
　A well-earned twenty-minute break!

Adler
　So, twenty minutes! Don't be late!

Reinhardt
　The lady there . . . Your wig's not straight . . .

The minuet resumes, faster and wilder. Lights down.

Act Two

The same.

Enter **Kommer** *and the* **Prince Archbishop**. **Kommer** *gazes down into the auditorium. A murmur of conversation and Mozart.*

Kommer
Draw near, good people all, I pray!
Give heed while we perform our play,
Wherein we show, as best we can,
The Summoning of Absolutely Everyman Who is Anyman.

A princess, a grand duke and grand duchess, three American film stars, four leading investment bankers, two of the richest men in Europe, not to mention your good self – and no Reinhardt!

Prince Archbishop   So much that Herr Reinhardt has done to this house since he first came here. Surely the greatest of all his celebrated stagings! The statues in the garden . . .

Kommer   Carted here complete with a century's growth of moss and lichen on them.

Prince Archbishop   The Venetian room . . .

Kommer   Transported here, mirror by mirror. The great houses have been stripped for miles around.

Prince Archbishop   His wonderful library.

Kommer   Copied gallery by gallery from a Swiss monastery. They wouldn't sell! And now all decorated with a better class of extra than he has ever had on a stage before! Look at them down there! Half of them are feeble-minded millionaires who wish for nothing better than to give their millions to some great artistic imposter! But where is the imposter himself? Vanished! It's like putting on one of his great spectaculars and not bothering to sell the tickets! *Is* he a real imposter? We have to ask ourselves! Or is he as feeble-minded as they are?

Enter **Müller**.

Müller   Look at it all! The corsetmaker's dream of paradise.

Prince Archbishop   Now that you and your friends are so prominent in local politics, Herr Müller, you must be grateful to Herr Reinhardt. So much he has done for Salzburg! The whole world comes to the festival.

Müller   Gawping holidaymakers. All looking for a quick taste of the spiritual nourishment that Herr Goldmann promised us.

Prince Archbishop   Perhaps they find it, Herr Müller.

Müller   They watch the play? And they understand the vanity of worldly possessions? They go out and get rid of their money, like Herr Everyman?

Kommer   They certainly do! They spend it in the new casino!

Müller   And these people. The idle rich of half the world.

Kommer   They're also going to be moved to get rid of their money. We hope. To Herr Reinhardt, if we can find him.

Müller   And you, Herr Archbishop – are you moved by Herr Goldmann's play?

Prince Archbishop   I shed a few tears, I confess, each time I see it.

Müller   Touchingly sentimental, all you people in show business. So you've renounced your stipend? You've given up your palace?

Prince Archbishop   Ah, Herr Mülller, if you and your friends should ever come to power . . .

Müller   We'd have you and Herr Goldmann out on the street as fast as God does Everyman.

Exit the **Prince Archbishop** *and* **Müller**. *Enter* **Thimig**.

Kommer (*to* **Thimig**)   You've searched the garden? You've tried the monkey-house . . . ? I'd better go back and keep them all entertained . . .

Exit **Kommer**. **Reinhardt** *emerges from the shadows.*

Thimig
Thy guests all wait impatiently
Their dear and gen'rous host to see.
To fetch him thither am I come
With pipe and timbrel, shawm and drum.

Reinhardt   They don't need me if they've got Katie. Look at him down there. He's so much better at being me than I am. He's fourteen years younger than me. He's still got the energy. He still believes in it all. The rest of them, though . . . !

Thimig   The footmen and maids are giving wonderful performances.

Reinhardt   The guests! Milling helplessly around! They don't know what they're doing! They haven't been directed! There's no script, no prompt-book! They don't know what to say to each other any more than I do!

Thimig   They're improvising, Reinhardt.

Reinhardt   Improvising! You know what I feel about actors improvising!

Thimig   They're not actors.

Reinhardt   No!

Thimig   Come on, Reinhardt. You know you've got to go down there and play your part.

Reinhardt   I *am* playing my part. I am watching. I am being the audience. There is no theatre without an audience. This is my natural place in life, Leni. In the audience. Looking down on the world from the gallery. Where I spent my boyhood in Vienna. Up in the gods at the Burgtheater, wedged in shoulder to shoulder, looking down on the kings and princes on the stage. Way, way below. In another world. In a better world.

Thimig   For the last thirty years, though, Reinhardt, you've been down there on the stage, rubbing shoulders with the real kings and princess.

Reinhardt   And not one of them with the nobility of the kings and princes I saw every night at the Burg. Not one with the ease and assurance of the heroes and heroines I watched when I didn't have the price of a tram to get home. Oh, the great actors of the Burg! They were angels come down on earth! Just the way Lewinsky laid his hat on a chair was worth the walk! Just the way Schratt turned her head! The way your grandfather drank his chocolate!

Thimig   They were good at putting their hats down and drinking their chocolate because they were all so old they couldn't remember their lines.

Reinhardt   Yes! So the prompter said them first! You heard everything twice!

Thimig   You couldn't even see the expressions on their faces from where you were.

Reinhardt   So you imagined them for yourself! You played the whole thing out for them inside your head! I breathed with those heroes down there, Leni! I wept with them! I laughed with them! Loved and hated with them! Killed and died with them!

Thimig   And then the curtain fell. You came down the stairs from heaven and you started to walk home.

Enter **Thomas**, *as the young* **Reinhardt**.

Reinhardt   There I go. Back to the Fifteenth District. Or the Eighth, or the Nineteenth, or wherever we are living by this time.

Thimig   And gradually . . .

Reinhardt   Gradually the air becomes sour with the sour smell of poverty . . .

Street noise. Trams. Horses. Hurdy-gurdies.

Street after street. Each one meaner than the last. Tenement after tenement . . . And up I go. Up the dim, bleak stairs to the fourth floor, or the third, or the fifth . . . No need for a prompter here, no need for imagination – you can hear everything through the walls . . .

He goes up the stairs. The sounds of children crying, off, and their mothers screaming at them, the words indistinct; drunken men shouting; the smashing of crockery; scraps of music being practised over and over again.

And when I get to our door . . .

Enter **Liesl**, *in coat and hat, holding bags and bales.*

Liesl   Here – you take the silk. Papa and I will bring the machine. We've got to be out of here tonight . . .

Exit **Liesl** *and* **Thomas**.

Reinhardt   So where do I live? Down there, or the Palace of Elsinore? With a bankrupt corsetmaker and five hungry brothers and sisters in Vienna 15? Or with Agamemnon in Argos, with Tamburlaine in Persepolis? Never be homeless, Leni. Never be poor. Never be an exile. Never play Poor Neighbour. Never have nothing.

Enter **Kommer**.

Kommer   And here you are. Of course. In the Burgtheater again. In the back streets of Vienna. Take him in to supper, if you please, Fräulein Thimig. You'll find I have seated him next to Monsieur de Rothschild.

Reinhardt   You have invited Rothschild?

Kommer   Of course not! *You* have invited Rothschild! You are the host! I am merely the master of your revels. Since you don't deign to do the job yourself. And you will not, of course, play Poor Neighbour . . .

> Now must I kneel to you and plead
> For help in this my hour of need.

If you do you will end up like Poor Neighbour, getting a handful of small change. It's *Rothschild* who is Poor Neighbour. His hand out, hoping for a few scraps of charity from the great house of art that you have built. You will be Everyman, gracefully condescending to take him seriously. Only of course you won't show it. Money talking to money. Artist to fellow artist.

Thimig   Are you *directing* Herr Reinhardt?

Kommer   I *am* directing Herr Reinhardt.

Thimig   He *has* talked to money before!

Reinhardt   An advisory committee, yes?

Kommer   An advisory committee. Could he be persuaded to chair it?

Reinhardt   His reputation and his wide range of acquaintance would be invaluable in finding other patrons of the right sort.

Enter **Franz**.

Franz   Your Royal Highnesses, Your Highnesses, Your Lordships and Ladyships, ladies and gentlemen . . . Supper is served.

Kommer   Your entrance, Herr Reinhardt!

> Once Rothchild shows his smiling face
> Our world becomes a better place . . .

Exit **Thimig, Reinhardt** *and* **Franz**. *Enter* **Müller**.

Müller   Look at them all, guzzling the free eats like paupers in a soup kitchen! But Herr Goldmann is right about one thing. A day of reckoning will come. God is not the only one with plans to cleanse the world of its filth. Look at those lights shining up there in the darkness. A new world is being born on that side of the frontier.

Kommer   There's still a frontier!

Müller   Still a frontier, yes. Between Germans and Austrians. Between Germans and their fellow Germans. Still a frontier.

> So! One more day!
> Make he wise use of this brief stay!

Kommer   The soup kitchen, Herr Müller!

Exit **Müller**. *Enter* **Adler** *with the prompt-book.*

Kommer   And on we stagger, bailed out for another season.

Adler   House, banquet . . .

Kommer   Money . . .

Adler   Rehearse, play . . . Summer, winter . . .

Kommer   Money, money . . .

Exit **Kommer**.

Adler   Journey . . .

Enter **Reinhardt**.

Adler   Journey again, Herr Reinhardt?

Reinhardt   Journey again.

Adler   Journey, please, everyone!

Exit **Adler**.

Reinhardt   So Death summons Everyman . . .

He puts on the mask of **Death**.

> Quick now, make haste, no more delay,
> A long road must thou walk today.
> Thou trav'lest to that far-off land
> Where thou before God's throne shalt stand . . .

And off Everyman has to go. Taking all his comforts in life with him.

(*As* **Everyman**.)
> My servants! You! You! – Everyone!
> Out here, and sharp about it! Run!
> I must at once a journey start,
> On foot, with neither coach nor cart.
> The going will be hard indeed,
> And all my people I shall need . . .

Josef! Thomas!

Enter **Josef** *and* **Thomas**.

Reinhardt
> Run back into the house and bring
> The trunk I keep my money in!
> We must have gold to ease our way,
> And tolls and bribes and ransoms pay.

Josef
> The trunk?

Thomas
> What, not the heavy one?

Josef
> That stands this high?

Thomas
> And weighs a ton?

Reinhardt
> Yes! Quickly now! Don't loaf about!
> Just pick it up and fetch it out!

Exit **Josef** *and* **Thomas**. *Enter* **Thimig**.

Thimig   The car's waiting. You've forgotten your lavender water again. And your diamond cufflinks . . .

Enter **Franz** *with clothes.*

Thimig (*to* **Franz**)   You *have* packed a spare dress suit for Herr Reinhardt?

Franz   Also a morning suit, Fräulein Thimig. Just in case. And a small choice of tweeds for the country. One never knows.

Enter **Thomas** *and* **Josef***, carrying with difficulty the trunk we saw earlier.*

Franz *packs more clothes in the trunk.* **Reinhardt** *watches.*

Reinhardt
> Our route lies over unknown ground,
> Unknown the land where we are bound.
> Heretobefore in evil hours
> Some comfort found I in thy powers.
> My trunk! I will not go without thee!
> I must have mine own things about me!

Thimig   You have packed two complete changes of bed linen? The last time Herr Reinhardt was in London he had to spend the night sleeping in hotel sheets.

Franz   In the trunk, Fräulein Thimig.

Thimig   And the feather bed? And the deerskin to go over the mattress?

Franz   All in the trunk, Fräulein Thimig.

Reinhardt   Perhaps I don't need the deerskin . . .

Thimig   Of course you need the deerskin! You won't sleep without the deerskin!

Reinhardt   The first time I came to Salzburg, when I was just beginning as an actor, I lived in one small room. In that one room was everything I needed for my life as a man: a bed, a cupboard, a table, a washstand, a jug, and a bowl. And into that one room I carried one small suitcase. In that one suitcase I had everything I needed for my life as an actor: an evening suit, a pair of evening shoes, a long black coat, and a pair of tights. My whole working life, in one small suitcase.

Josef *and* **Thomas** *pick up the trunk.*

Reinhardt   One last look round . . .

They put the trunk down again.

My wonderful house! Oh God, the baroque is a beautiful period! In architecture, in music . . . You did order me a Linzer Torte from Demel . . . ?

Franz   With the hams and the cheeses, Herr Reinhardt.

Reinhardt   I try to keep things as simple as possible. I travel with almost no servants at all.

Franz   Sir?

Reinhardt   Only a valet. But my entire life has become baroque! How has this happened?

Franz   Life is not simple, Herr Reinhardt.

Reinhardt   Is your life not simple, Franz?

Franz   No, Herr Reinhardt.

Josef *and* **Thomas** *pick up the trunk.*

Reinhardt   Steam iron? Trouser press . . . ?

Thimig   Reinhardt, you're going to miss your train!

Reinhardt (*to* **Franz**)   At least you don't have to pack frocks and petticoats for me.

Franz   No, Herr Reinhardt. Thank you, Herr Reinhardt.

Exit **Josef** *and* **Thomas**, *with trunk, followed by* **Reinhardt** *and* **Franz**. *Enter* **Adler**, *carrying telegrams.*

Adler   Telegrams, telegrams. Every day they come. Paris, New York . . .

She hands a batch of them to **Thimig**.

London, Rome . . . New York, Brussels, New York . . .

Thimig (*reads*)   'Exhausted, depressed . . . ' 'Can't sleep . . . ' 'Superhuman work . . . ' 'Total success . . . ' 'Total despair . . . '

Adler (*reads*)   'Repairs to the roof...' 'Money for daughter...' 'Money for nephews, money for nieces...'

Enter **Kommer**, *with more telegrams.*

Kommer (*reads*)   Money... Money... Money again...

Enter **Reinhardt**, *followed by* **Franz**, *and* **Josef** *and* **Thomas** *with the trunk.*

Reinhardt   And on we go, on we go. Dragging my luggage of cares behind me... Chicago?

Franz   Chicago, Herr Reinhardt. Your usual suite. Specially redecorated for your arrival.

Reinhardt   Time, time! No *time*...! Like struggling for breath...! World so rich, life so short...! And on we go, on we go. Dragging my luggage of cares behind me. If I once lie down I shall never get up again... Every night – despair... Every morning – unpack optimism once again...

Franz *begins to unpack trunk.*

Reinhardt   Wallpaper!

Franz (*baffled*)   Wallpaper?

Reinhardt   Depressing. Find me another room...

Franz (*repacks*)   Another room...

Exit **Reinhardt**, *followed by* **Franz**, *and* **Josef** *and* **Thomas** *with the trunk.*

Adler   'Latvian divorce – '

Thimig   We've got it! We've got it!

Kommer   ' – not recognised in US!'

Thimig   Not divorced?

Kommer   'Reno. Trying Reno.'

Thimig   'Hamburg. First boat New York.'

Kommer   (*looks at telegrams*) The Old Testament. He's staging it in New York. The entire Old Testament.

Adler   Wonderful. And he's divorced!

Kommer   The set's four storeys high!

Adler   They're married!

Kommer   He's rebuilding the theatre!

Adler   'Arriving Salzburg Friday . . . '

Enter **Reinhardt** *and* **Thimig**, *followed by* **Franz**, *and* **Josef** *and* **Thomas** *with the trunk.*

Adler   Welcome home, Herr Reinhardt! Welcome home, *Frau* Reinhardt!

Kommer   Welcome home, welcome home. (*Shows him papers.*) The accounts . . .

Adler   So – tell me about the wedding!

Thimig   Wonderful!

Kommer   For the Old Testament in New York . . .

Thimig   A total triumph!

Reinhardt   Everyman again, please, Gusti! Prologue . . . House . . . Journey . . . Mammon . . .

Adler   Mammon? Mammon, everyone! Mammon emerging from the trunk . . . !

Reinhardt   Where is Mammon? Who's playing Mammon?

Adler   Oh! There's a problem with his contract!

Reinhardt   Katie! Read Mammon . . . !

Kommer   For the Old Testament. The accounts.

Reinhardt   Never mind that. Mammon. Get in the trunk!

Kommer *climbs into the trunk.*

Kommer   I thought you might be interested to know . . .

Reinhardt   Wait for the cue.

Kommer   . . . in very round figures . . .

Reinhardt   Give him the cue.

Adler
'My trunk! I will not go without thee!
I must have mine own things about me!'

Reinhardt   Then out you jump.

'Why, Everyman! What should thee ail?
Thy countenance is deathly pale . . !'

Kommer   . . . how many million dollars you managed to lose.

Reinhardt   Why is it, Katie, that I have to carry on my back not just all the cares of the house, all the cares of my productions, but the dead weight of *you*, forever carping, forever dragging your feet, forever making difficulties?

He slams the trunk shut on **Kommer**.

Reinhardt   And on we go. What is the next scene?

Darkness, and an explosion. Exit **Reinhardt** *and* **Thimig**. *The lights come up on smoke and broken window.* **Liesl** *and* **Gretl** *sweep up shattered glass.*

Franz *ushers in the* **Prince Archbishop**. *Enter* **Thimig** *calmly.*

Prince Archbishop   My dear Frau Reinhardt! I have only just heard! Are you unharmed? And Herr Reinhardt – where is Herr Reinhardt?

Thimig   Choosing a tie. He would not wish to receive Your Grace in his dressing gown.

Prince Archbishop   No one is hurt?

Thimig   No one is hurt. Our friends were not very brave. They seem to have simply opened the front door and thrown the bomb inside. The damage is very slight.

Prince Archbishop   You didn't catch any sight of them?

Thimig   I assume they were the people who did the same to Your Grace's house the other week.

Prince Archbishop   We scarcely need to take their attacks on the Church seriously. In your case, however . . .

Enter **Reinhardt** *calmly.*

Prince Archbishop   My dear boy! My dear boy!

Reinhardt   The house will stink of smoke for weeks.

Prince Archbishop   Your beautiful house! And there will be worse to come.

Thimig   You mustn't worry about us. We have soldiers to escort us to rehearsal each day.

Prince Archbishop   They have already taken your great theatre in Berlin . . .

Reinhardt   Berlin is in Germany. We are in Austria.

Prince Archbishop   Germany is very close.

Thimig   Look at it up there! The sun shining on it as if nothing had changed!

Prince Archbishop   You take no more interest in politics than I do, Herr Reinhardt. But we both know who is up there in Berchtesgaden looking down on us.

Reinhardt   There is still a frontier between us and him.

Prince Archbishop   Frontiers can be crossed. Your own speciality, I believe.

Thimig   The uncertain frontier between reality and dream.

Prince Archbishop   And *that* frontier is one that our neighbour up there has crossed many times. Lines drawn on a map seem to be little hindrance. And when he does come, what will you do? Where will you go?

Reinhardt   We have possibilities all over the world. Unlike most people.

Prince Archbishop   You will lose everything! Your homeland. Your home.

Thimig   We can't even sell it. It's mortgaged, over and over again.

Prince Archbishop   You will exchange your house for a suitcase.

Reinhardt   I think we have little to fear. As long as you are here to stand by us. As you always have.

Prince Archbishop   Yes. As long as I am here. As long as I am here . . .

Death (*calls softly, off*)   Everyman!

The **Prince Archbishop** *listens.*

Death   Everyman!

Thimig   Your Grace . . . ?

Prince Archbishop (*puzzled*)
    Who called? My name! Who called my name?

Reinhardt   I heard nothing.

Thimig   A bird in the garden, perhaps?

Reinhardt   The wind in the trees?

Prince Archbishop
    From nowhere, everywhere it came . . .

Reinhardt *and* **Thimig** *look at each other.*

Prince Archbishop
    And comes again, and comes again!

Thimig   Your Grace! Is Your Grace unwell?

Reinhardt   Sit down, Your Grace, sit down. I will telephone for a doctor.

Prince Archbishop   Just have them fetch my car to the door, if you please, Herr Reinhardt. I have matters to attend to.

Reinhardt *hesitates.*

Prince Archbishop
    I seem to see a strange face there . . .

Thimig   Statues, Your Grace. Only the statues.

Prince Archbishop
                                    He favours none,
    Nor any fears. To all he comes.

Thimig *looks at* **Reinhardt**. *He goes.*

Prince Archbishop   Will you give me your arm, Frau Reinhardt? And escort me to my car? I was always a little saddened to see my hostess leave the house before me, you know. Touched by your thoughtfulness in sparing my blushes. But saddened, saddened.

Thimig   The Jew's whore.

Prince Archbishop   Yes, the Jew's whore. That's what they call you. Even now you're married. Never mind, tonight I shall look back from my car as I leave and I shall see the Jew and his whore standing in the doorway, waving farewell together. And that will be something for me to remember. Something for me to keep in my mind as I lie waiting for sleep.

Enter **Reinhardt**.

Reinhardt   Your car is waiting. I'm so sorry, Your Grace, I'm so sorry!

Prince Archbishop   No need to be sorry for me. I have a home to go to. It's you I worry about.

Reinhardt   The suitcase? I'm used to suitcases.

Prince Archbishop   After the suitcase.

Reinhardt   Another box.

Prince Archbishop   Oh, my dear boy, my dear boy!

He strokes **Reinhardt***'s arm.*

Prince Archbishop   Believe one thing, even though you believe nothing else: if I could take your place I should.

The **Prince Archbishop** *exits on* **Thimig***'s arm. Darkness.*

Müller (*as* **Death***, off*)
      Everyman! Everyman!

Twilight. **Reinhardt** *turns to listen.*

Müller
      Thou fool, the stay that thou hast won
      Its little course hath all but run.

He enters, masked as **Death***.*

      What profit from it hast thou earned
      Now I to find thee am returned?

He discards his mask

It was in the props basket. I thought I should enter into the spirit of things. I am after all here as a messenger from on high. (*He indicates.*)

Reinhardt   Berchtesgaden?

Müller
      While yet of him thou thinkest not,
      He hath not thee likewise forgot.

Reinhardt   You know the play.

Müller   By heart. Difficult not to, if you live in Salzburg.

Reinhardt   And have you come to summon me?

Müller   Sooner or later you will have to go on a journey, Herr Reinhardt. Give up all your money. And all your friends. You won't even have your trunk. Or your princely friend to protect you. My condolences on his death. Much loved in some quarters, I know. Particularly by the Jews. Don't despair,

though, Herr Goldmann! Remember Herr Everyman! How
black things look for him! But he is saved in the end. Escorted
into heaven by his Works and his Faith. You have your Works
to speak for you, Herr Goldmann. In Berlin the greatest
theatre the German people ever had. Another in Vienna. And
here in Salzburg you have created a festival that could become
a beacon of German culture as bright as Bayreuth. With a
little improvement in racial hygiene.

Reinhardt   You're not asking me to convert?

Müller   You *can't* convert! You can change your beliefs, if
you have any. But not your choice of forebears! Not all the
generations of the dead! To cease to be a Jew, Herr
Goldmann, you would have to be born again as an Aryan.

Reinhardt   I don't think I can oblige.

Müller   On the contrary, Herr Goldmann. This is what
I have been sent here to offer you: the same chance that God
offers Everyman. Rebirth!

Reinhardt   As an Aryan?

Müller   As an honorary Aryan. By the grace of the very
highest authority. (*He indicates Berchtesgaden.*) All you will need is
a little help from Faith. Like Everyman. He finds it difficult at
first to believe in God's mercy.

Reinhardt
    God smiteth, smiteth! That I know!

Müller
    Forgiveness also can He show.

Reinhardt
    Great Pharaoh's host He smote and slew!
    Gomorrah smote, and Sodom, too.
    Smote! Smote!

Müller
                Do but believe,
    And thou His mercy shalt receive.

Reinhardt   There is a price to be paid for this miracle?

Müller   Now the real Jew speaks! 'How much does it cost?'
The answer, Herr Goldmann, is – next to nothing. You have a
bargain. You would give up your couple of visits each year to
the synagogue. A few friends and relations. Fräulein Adler and
Herr Kommer, of course. Everything else you can keep. The
house. Your charming new Aryan wife. Congratulations, by
the way! Perfect taste, as in all things. You can go on running
the festival. Go on throwing your parties. Far more generous
terms than Herr Everyman gets! And you have a good chance,
unlike poor Everyman, of being allowed to remain alive.

Reinhardt *rings*.

Müller   Think about it, Herr Goldmann. The offer will not
remain open indefinitely.

Enter **Franz**.

Reinhardt   Franz, will you show Herr Müller out?

Müller   What's the alternative, Herr Goldmann? To
wander, like your parents, like your forefathers. To become
the Wandering Jew once again.

Exit **Reinhardt**.

Müller (*to* **Franz**)   And what will happen to you, my friend?
Your little room in the attics will vanish with all the rest.

Franz   This way, if you please, Herr Müller.

Müller   The Wandering Jew – and his wandering
shoeshine.

Exit **Müller** *and* **Franz**. *Enter* **Thimig**, *carrying a small suitcase,
and* **Adler**.

Adler   The house is for sale? *This* house? What do you
mean?

Thimig   It was in the paper. Reinhardt read it in the paper.

Adler   How *can* it be for sale? *You're* not selling it!

Thimig   The Government is selling it.

Adler   Your house? They can't do that!

Thimig   Apparently they can. Our debts, Gusti, our debts.

Enter **Thomas**, **Josef**, *and* **Franz**, *carrying various items, and* **Reinhardt**.

Reinhardt (*to* **Franz**)   And *two* feather beds, of course. We're both going this time! And both our passports . . .

Adler   But, Herr Reinhardt – the house!

Reinhardt   Money! Only money!

Adler   Katie will find a way round it. He always has.

Thimig   Katie's in New York already.

Adler   I'll cable him to meet you off the boat.

Reinhardt   I'm getting tired of Katie. Money is all he ever thinks about. Money and mockery. I can manage without Katie. (*To* **Thomas** *and* **Josef**.) Fetch the rest of the luggage, will you?

Exit **Thomas** *and* **Josef**.

Reinhardt   Helene – *your* trunk! Where is it?

Thimig (*shows the suitcase*)   We're only going for six months. I'm not like you. As long as I've got a Shakespeare and a change of underwear . . . (*To* **Adler**.) You'll keep an eye on the animals?

Reinhardt   And my family?

Thimig   And the staff?

Reinhardt   And the contracts for next season?

Adler   Oh, I can't bear this moment! Every autumn! And every autumn it get worse!

Reinhardt   We shall be back very soon, Gusti. Like the swallows.

Adler   Perhaps this time you won't be.

Reinhardt   Of course we shall.

Thimig   Shall we?

Adler   You won't, you won't! The Archbishop's dead. The Nazis are just waiting for their chance. And now this business with the house . . . Something even worse will happen . . .

Reinhardt   Nothing will happen.

Adler   Such horrible things everywhere!

Reinhardt   Yes . . . And there he waits, up in the gods. Looking down on us all. Another poor boy who has imposed himself on the world. Aping the kings and princes below. Drunk on the possibilities of life.

Adler   That vile creature he sent!

Reinhardt   Don't worry! By the time we come back all this nonsense will have been forgotten. One last look at our wonderful house . . .

Thimig   We used to laugh in this house once. Do you remember that? When we first came here? Everything so shabby and broken down, everything still to be done, and we stood here one night in the middle of it all, and you took my hand, and we both started to laugh . . .

Exit **Thimig** *and* **Adler**. *The light changes.* **Reinhardt** *touches the trunk.*

Reinhardt
>Our route lies over unknown ground,
>Unknown the land where we are bound.
>Heretobefore in evil hours
>Some comfort found I in thy powers.
>My trunk! I will not go without thee!
>I must have mine own things about me!

The trunk springs open. **Kommer**, *as Mammon, rises from it.*

Kommer

Why, Everyman! What should thee ail?
Thy countenance is deathly pale!

Reinhardt

Who art thou?

Kommer

What, thou dost not know –
And yet with thee wouldst have me go?
Thy wealth am I! Thy worldly all!
Great Mammon, at thy beck and call!
My powers thou knowest. Tell me how
They may be used to serve thee now.

Reinhardt

I know not – but most urgently;
A messenger hath come for me.

Kommer

A messenger? From whence he came?

Reinhardt

Methinks thou knowest, and his name.

Kommer

Thy presence elsewhere is desired?

Reinhardt

And thine likewise by me required.

Kommer

I will not budge from where I stand –
Most happy am I where I am!

Reinhardt

Durst thou defy me, durst repine,
Thou creature, thou mere thing of mine?

Kommer

Thy thing, thy creature, hast thou said?
The truth thou standest on its head!
I giant-like above thee tower,
Thou like a dwarf canst only cower!

Reinhardt
I govern thee and all thou art!

Kommer
I rule as king within thy heart!

Reinhardt
I king – thou subject of my rule!

Kommer
No – I the king and thou my fool!

Reinhardt
Thou wert my lowly serving boy!

Kommer
And thou my jumping jack, my toy!
This trunk doth thy life's work contain –
And in this trunk it will remain.
Thou goest on thy painful way;
I here at my good ease will stay!

Kommer *sinks back into the trunk. The lid falls. Darkness. Exit*
Reinhardt.

Triumphal music. Enter **Müller**, *wearing a Nazi armband, and*
Thomas *and* **Josef**, *also wearing armbands.* **Liesl** *and* **Gretl**
appear at the front of the stage with flowers.

Müller (*formally*)
Heil Hitler!

Liesl, **Gretl** (*and many other voices in the auditorium*)
Heil Hitler!

Thomas *and* **Josef** *remove the trunk, then flank* **Müller**.

Müller
            Now attend to me
While I proclaim my first decree,
Whereby as Gauleiter I ban
All future shows of *Everyman*.
The Jews will now perhaps believe
How short the shrift they will receive,

How firmly we shall use our powers
In this united Reich of ours!

He comes down the stairs, flanked by **Thomas** *and* **Josef**, *and becomes relaxed and welcoming.*

Müller
We shall expropriate the Jew,
And harry his supporters too;
The late Archbishop's grand address
Is now the home of the SS.
While this great palace where we stand –
The lordliest in all the land –
Its owner wisely having fled
Belongs to you and me instead.
Here, as your representative,
I do propose myself to live.
So – make yourself at home! Feel free
To stroll around your property!
Enjoy the gardens, feed the monkeys!
Admire the paintings, tip the flunkeys!
What half so sweet as stolen pleasure?
Or finding someone else's treasure?
The old show ends, the new one starts,
With different management and cast.
One character, though, will remain.
His services we shall retain,
And find him rather more to do.
Our new star, Death, awaits his cue.

He gives the Nazi salute. Applause from the auditorium. Darkness.

Thimig *opens the blinds, and the light reveals* **Reinhardt**, *asleep at his table.*

Reinhardt   Morning? Already?

Thimig   Do you want breakfast?

Reinhardt   Have I had supper?

Thimig   Reinhardt, you will get ill! Then what will become of us? You don't eat! You never go to bed!

Reinhardt   I have always worked hard and late. All day and half the night. Always, always.

Thimig   But not *all* night, Reinhardt! Not *all* night!

Reinhardt   My love, I will never get a movie set up if I don't work! If I don't have a hundred projects to propose! If I don't write outlines and treatments! If I don't draft them and redraft them until I find what the studios want!

Thimig   Oh, Reinhardt, this place, this place! If only I could look out of the window one morning and see rain! Veils of rain sweeping across the lake. The mountains lost in clouds. Water dripping from the plants and statues. The whole world soft and grey.

Reinhardt   Then you would be saying: 'If only the sun would shine!'

Thimig   Yes! 'If only the sun would shine!' If only I could be saying those precious words!

Reinhardt   The Pacific is as beautiful as the lake. In its way.

Thimig   We are never going back. We are going to die in this awful place. We are never going to see our home again!

Reinhardt   Nearly twenty years we lived in that house. Lived in it and lived it! Lived every room.

Thimig   Every table.

Reinhardt   Every chair, every picture.

Thimig   Lived it and gave it life.

Reinhardt   Dreamt of it and dreamt it.

Thimig   Dreamt it and dreamt it until it was real.

Reinhardt   The one production of mine that I thought might endure.

Thimig   And we have lost it. We have lost everything that we carried into it.

Reinhardt   I will not lament it, though, my love. It's gone – it's past. And we are alive. We are free. We have food to eat, we have clothes to our backs. We have beds to sleep in and a table to work at. I have as much as I had when I first went to Salzburg! And I have you. You didn't have to be here. You could have stayed. Poor Everyman never found anyone to accompany him on his journey. I did. We are together.

He kisses her hand. Enter **Adler**, *holding letters.*

Adler   I'm sorry . . .

Reinhardt   My other faithful companion in exile.

Kisses her hand.

The post?

Adler   Nothing you need to see.

Reinhardt   No money?

Adler   No money.

Reinhardt   And nothing from Paramount? Nothing from Metro?

Thimig   Paramount! Metro! You might as well say fairyland, or heaven!

Reinhardt   I am not unknown in this town, my love.

Thimig   You made a movie. Once. Seven years ago. In the past! The past is another world! Reinhardt, our only hope is the theatre!

Adler   Helene, there is no theatre in Los Angeles!

Thimig   There is theatre in New York! At least it sometimes rains in New York! At least New York is halfway home! If I can play Nazis in movies I can play Nazis in plays. In New York.

Adler   Helene, they have Nazis in movies. They don't have Nazis in plays.

Thimig   And still you always take his side!

Adler   No, but Helene, to go to New York –

Thimig   – we need money. Money, money, money! If only Katie were here!

Adler   But he's *not* here!

Thimig   No, because he's in New York already!

Adler   If only Herr Reinhardt hadn't fallen out with him!

Reinhardt   Katie, though . . . (*Rings.*) Katie – yes! (*Rings.*)

Adler   If you could somehow get to New York . . .

Thimig   If you could somehow talk to Katie . . .

Reinhardt   I don't need to talk to Katie! I talked to Katie for twenty years. For twenty years I put up with him. Long enough to know what he would tell me to do! (*Rings.*)

Thimig   What? What would he tell us to do?

Reinhardt   Where *is* that valet of mine?

Thimig   He's mending the Frigidaire.

Adler   He's putting the trash out.

Reinhardt   Yes, but he is supposed to be dressing me. (*Rings.*)

Enter **Franz**.

Reinhardt   Franz, Franz. I must get dressed.

Franz   You *are* dressed, Herr Reinhardt.

Reinhardt   I *am* dressed. Exactly. I know that . . . But, Franz, Franz – we are going to need your expert services! Because as soon as you mentioned Katie it came to me at once. We must do what Katie always told us to do in the past when things were difficult.

Thimig   Spend less? How can we? We don't spend anything!

Reinhardt   Give a party!

Adler   A party?

Reinhardt   Yes! Just the way we used to in the old days! One of our great parties! Invite everyone! All the producers! All the stars! All the big money! 'Mr and Mrs Louis B. Mayer . . . Mr William Randolph Hearst . . . ' This is you, Franz! You remember? 'Miss Betty Grable . . . Mr John Rockefeller Junior . . . '

Thimig   But . . . the *money* . . .

Reinhardt   Exactly. The money. I take it by the elbow. I admit it into my confidence. Just the way Katie taught me to do. 'So do you feel, Mr Rockefeller, that I should turn Faust into a cowboy or into a gangster . . . ?'

Thimig   The money to pay for the party.

Reinhardt   I have a little money put by.

Thimig   Reinhardt! We have no money put by!

Reinhardt   Yes! I know I don't understand money, but I do understand one thing: that everyone must have a last hidden reserve for extreme circumstances.

Adler (*shows letters*)   Herr Reinhardt, look! From the bank! Your account!

Reinhardt   Cash!

Thimig   Cash?

Reinhardt   Dollar bills! Carefully hidden away! Precisely so as to keep it from the bank! Precisely so as to stop the bank eating it up!

Adler   So . . . how much have you got?

Reinhardt   Enough, enough. All I need now is an evening suit! I began with one evening suit and a pair of tights, and with one evening suit, even without the tights, I shall begin all over again. I do still have an evening suit, Franz?

Franz   Where it always was, Herr Reinhardt. At the cleaner's, Herr Reinhardt.

Reinhardt   Collect it, then, Franz!

Franz   A dollar fifty, Herr Reinhardt.

Reinhardt   Take it out of your wages for now, Franz.

Franz   What wages, Herr Reinhardt?

Reinhardt   Never mind, never mind. Wages, cleaning, everything – as soon as I've found the money.

Thimig   Where is it?

Reinhardt   Yes . . . where is it . . . ?

Thimig   You haven't forgotten?

Reinhardt   Of course I haven't forgotten! I hid it. I hid it most carefully. I think – yes – in a book.

Thimig   In a *book*? Which book?

Reinhardt   Which book . . . ? I seem to remember it was a book with a blue jacket . . . Or a red jacket . . .

Thimig   Oh, Reinhardt! Reinhardt, Reinhardt, Reinhardt!

Reinhardt   No! I moved it. It's all coming back to me. It's in my old trunk! Fetch the trunk! We still have the trunk?

Exit **Franz**.

Reinhardt   Pen and paper! I will draw up a guest list. First the party. Show everyone we are alive. Begin to set things up. Then perhaps a season in New York. I will make it up with Katie. Direct one or two shows. Make our mark. Get our finances under control.

Enter **Franz**, *struggling to carry the trunk single-handed. It is now very battered and shabby.*

Reinhardt   Steady, steady! You're not as young as you were! (*He searches in the trunk.*) So, off on my travels again . . . I'm going to need this trunk . . . Deerskin, good . . . Bit moth-eaten . . . The feather bed will have to be aired . . .

Thimig   There *is* no money, is there? There never was. You just imagined it . . .

Reinhardt (*holds up a loose heap of dollar bills*)   I'm going to give it to Gusti to look after.

He hands her the money.

Reinhardt   Gusti – you will be responsible for paying the caterer and hiring the musicians and buying the train tickets and paying Franz . . . Franz, take *everything* in here to the cleaner's. A completely fresh start . . .

Franz *packs everything back into the trunk and takes it off.*

Reinhardt (*to* **Adler**)   You are also responsible for paying the cleaner's. And you will be as careful with the money as you always are – as careful as Katie would be – as careful as my poor brother was – because you will remember that what you are holding in your hands is our lifeline. Our last hope. Now, shave. A good confident suit . . .

Exit **Reinhardt**.

Thimig (*to* **Adler**)   How much is it?

Adler (*counts it*)   Seventeen dollars.

Exit **Thimig** *and* **Adler**. *Enter* **Kommer**, *together with* **Thomas**, **Josef**, **Liesl** *and* **Gretl** *as fellow exiles.*

Kommer   Seventeen dollars! His life savings!

Thomas   So – no party?

Kommer   On seventeen dollars?

Liesl   And no Katie to make it go?

Josef   You know he's here?

Thomas   In New York?

Liesl   Got here from LA?

Thomas   On seventeen dollars?

Josef   Sold the furniture, I gather.

Gretl   Had to leave Helene behind!

Josef   What – minding the shop?

Liesl   Poor Helene!

Enter **Reinhardt**. **Kommer** *and the other exiles watch him, like* **Reinhardt** *and* **Thimig** *watching the party earlier.*

Gretl   Poor Reinhardt!

Thomas   So he's all alone?

Kommer   All alone? Reinhardt?

Enter **Franz** *carrying the trunk.*

Reinhardt (*to* **Franz**)   Careful, careful! No point in saving money on porters if you end up in hospital . . . Is this the only room you could get? Where is the sky? Where are the trees?

Franz   We are in the middle of Manhattan, Herr Reinhardt!

Reinhardt   What was wrong with the hotel we were in before?

Franz   We hadn't paid the bill, Herr Reinhardt.

Kommer (*to* **Thomas** *and the other exiles*)   It's like a play I remember seeing.

Liesl   A man who has everything.

Gretl   Money, friends, a beautiful home.

Josef   And then – pfft!

Thomas   It's all vanished.

Kommer   Forty-fifth Street – coming along the sidewalk – there he was. Eyes down. So aged. So anxious . . . He looked up and saw me. I know he saw me . . .

Reinhardt (*to* **Franz**)   My address book . . . What have you done with my address book . . . ? I must set up some meetings. Producers, agents . . . People I've worked with in the past – they won't have forgotten me . . .

Kommer   For twenty years I put up with that man. For twenty years I kept a warm feather bed of money and friends around him . . . If he'd so much as shaken my hand! So much as nodded and smiled! I could have tried to do something.

Liesl   Poor Reinhardt!

Kommer   Poor us! Poor all of us! None of us knowing where next week's rent is coming from.

Josef   Exiles.

Kommer   The wrong language, the wrong style, the wrong friends. All reduced to playing the same part.

> Now must I kneel to you and plead
> For help in this my hour of need . . .

And who are we kneeling and pleading to? Anyone we can find who understands us. Other exiles. Other Poor Neighbours as desperate as ourself.

Reinhardt (*to* **Franz**)   And yes, they want me, they want me! Broadway again, Franz! A big musical! Contracts almost ready to be signed! The money almost in place!

Kommer   And he's fourteen years older than me. Not long now before he hears the voice whispering from the shadows . . .

Death (*off, whispers*)   Everyman!

Kommer   And there it is!

Death   Everyman!

Kommer   You hear it?

Thomas, **Josef**, **Liesl**, *and* **Gretl** *turn to look at* **Kommer**.

Kommer   Look! Look! There! Standing in the shadows . . . !

The others begin to melt discreetly away.

Kommer   *He* can hear it, though! *He* can see it . . . ! Can't he?

Reinhardt (*to* **Franz**)   I have meetings to go to. The money, of course, the money. As always! Money, money . . .

Darkness begins to close in around **Kommer**.

Kommer   Poor old soul! He must be deaf already, his eyesight must be failing . . . (*Becomes aware that he is alone in the gathering darkness.*)

Death (*off*)   Everyman!

Kommer   Or *me*, then? *My* story all the time? *Me* who's Everyman?

Reinhardt   And get Katie on the phone for me. Never too late to mend a quarrel. Poor devil. I might be able to find him something . . .

Franz *picks up the phone.*

Kommer   Of course! Always a last twist in the plot! Only now I shall never find the answer to my question. Is he feeble-minded, or is he an imposter? Or both? Or is he just possibly something else altogether . . . ?

The darkness swallows **Kommer** *up. Now only* **Reinhardt** *and* **Franz** *are lit.* **Franz** *listens for a moment, then puts down the receiver. He crosses himself.*

Reinhardt   No! Even Katie . . . ? Poor Katie. However did I put up with him for all those years? Never mind. We don't need Katie. I can manage without Katie . . . But this suit, Franz, this suit! I'm an old man in this suit! I cannot meet money looking like this!

Franz   A summer jacket, perhaps, Herr Reinhardt?

Reinhardt   A summer jacket . . . Quickly, then.

Franz *fetches the jacket.*

Reinhardt   I can't play an old man again. I played old men when I was twenty. I was good at it then . . .

He holds out his right arm for **Franz** *to put the summer jacket on, but then cannot get his left arm back for the other sleeve.*

Reinhardt   Help me, then, Franz, help me . . . ! What are you doing . . . ?

Franz   Your arm, Herr Reinhardt . . .

Reinhardt   I can't . . . I can't . . . I can't . . . Help me – I . . . Help me – I . . . Help me . . . !

Franz *drops the jacket and runs to the phone.*

Reinhardt   No! No! Not ill! No! No! Or money won't . . . Money won't . . . Money won't . . . Money . . . Money . . .

Death (*whispers, off*)
Everyman! Everyman!

Darkness. Only **Reinhardt** *remains lit.*

Reinhardt
So . . . my name now! In my own ears
The voice that only one man hears.

Death *emerges from the darkness.*

Death (*whispers*)
Everyman! Everyman!

Reinhardt
For me it comes, the pale face there.
At me those eyes so coldly stare.

Death
God smiteth, smiteth! Smiteth all!
Like grass before the scythe they fall.
Thy brother smote He – smote and slew!
The Prince Archbishop. Katie, too.
Smote! Smote! And smiteth still,
Until the grey cold graveyards fill.

Reinhardt

> Farewell, my shabby trunk, at last!
> My dwindling treasure of things past!
> Now down into the grave I go,
> Down, down into the dark below.

Enter **Thimig**.

Thimig

> Thy Faith by thee will faithful stand.

Enter **Adler**.

Adler

> And I, thy Works, at thy right hand.

Thimig

> Before his Judge he goeth, shorn
> Of all he got since he was born.

Adler

> No riches hath he but the sum
> Of what he hath believed and done.

Reinhardt

> One day of birth, one day of death!
> I tried, as long as I drew breath,
> To melt the frontiers between
> The world we know, the world we dream,
> The things we are, the things we could be –
> And what we would be! – What we should be!
> With art and craft I sought to breach
> The walls dividing each from each.
> My faith? My deeds? I strove to give
> Us mortals other lives to live . . .

A grave opens in front of **Reinhardt***, and he goes down into it.*

Adler

> When man ends his allotted days,
> To God, man's maker, Jews give praise.

Thimig
>   And so to man is tribute paid,
>   For maker is what maker made.

Darkness.

Lights up at once. **Kommer**, **Thimig**, **Adler**, **Prince
Archbishop**, **Thomas**, **Josef**, **Liesl**, **Gretl** *and* **Franz**.
Kommer *has just opened a bottle of champagne.* **Thomas**, **Josef**,
Franz, **Liesl**, *and* **Gretl** *serve drinks and refreshments.*

Kommer
>   Our play is ended, as plays must,
>   And Everyman returned to dust.

Adler
>   At funerals we weep, but after . . .

Thimig
>   We raise a glass and turn to laughter.

Kommer
>   So one last party let us throw,
>   Like all those others, long ago . . .

Prince Archbishop
>   An epilogue to end the show,
>   And homeward cheerful make us go.

Kommer
>   Draw near, good people all, I pray!
>   Max Reinhardt is at home today!

Enter **Reinhardt**.

Thimig
>   To Max, our Everyman!

Adler   And then . . .

Reinhardt
>   To all the other Everymen!

Prince Archbishop
>   The prince who did this house erect . . .

Franz
His bricklayers, his architect . . .

Prince Archbishop
The prince who used his high position
To help a wandering musician . . .

Thomas
Their footmen . . .

Josef
        Gard'ners . . .

Liesl
                Maids . . .

Gretl
                    And cooks . . .

Adler
The inky clerks who kept their books . . .

Kommer
And carefully nurtured all their wealth . . .

Reinhardt
Poor scribbling Amadeus himself . . .

Thimig
And us! And us! Who laboured since
To serve our later, greater prince.

Adler
We too, each in our turn, we all
Have that same secret voice heard call.

Prince Archbishop
We all have that same journey made,
Alone and friendless and afraid.

Enter **Death**.

Death
To all I come, in many guises,
Yet still the sight of me surprises.

And, in my eagerness to please,
Too many sometimes do I seize.
Then even I must turn and see
A shadowed figure watching me.

Reinhardt (*as God, off*)
Where art thou, Death? Thee, too, I call!
Come forth!

Thomas *and* **Josef** *seize* **Death** *and rush him forward.*

Reinhardt
                Unmask!

They rip off **Death**'s *mask and cloak, to reveal* **Müller** *in his Nazi armband.*

Reinhardt
                        Before me fall!

They hang him.

Prince Archbishop
God took us all.

Kommer
                And yet not so!
We live on still with you below!

Reinhardt
Look! Here's the house in all its glory!
High storey still on noble storey!

Thimig
Still flowers the garden every spring,
The fountains play, the blackbirds sing.

Prince Archbishop
And Amadeus?

Thimig
                Every song
He ever sang lives on, lives on.

Kommer
　　And even Death, so I've heard tell . . .

Death *appears in the shadows.*

Death
　　Alive and well, alive and well.

Thimig
　　And us? The partners in the dance?

Adler
　　Helene . . .

Thimig
　　　　　　Gusti . . .

Adler
　　　　　　　　Katie . . .

Kommer
　　　　　　　　　　Franz . . .

Franz
　　Herr Reinhardt . . .

Reinhardt
　　　　　　His High Princely Grace.

Prince Archbishop
　　Well, here we stand, one last faint trace.

Thimig
　　We're only matchstick men, you say . . .

Adler
　　Mere scarecrows stuffed with musty hay . . .

Kommer
　　A grinning turnip for a head . . .

Prince Archbishop
　　Tricked out with words we never said . . .

Franz
　　A tinsel touch of ragged rhyme . . .

Reinhardt
Bare shreds left by the winds of time . . .

Thimig
Mere made-up things, mere Everymen . . .

Adler
Like Everyman himself.

Kommer
But then
Whate'er our faults, whate'er our merit,
We are the world that you inherit.

Thimig
The actors pass, the lines remain.

Prince Archbishop
This year in Salzburg once again . . .

Adler
The summer sunlight comes and goes . . .

Thimig
The pigeons whirr, the cold wind blows . . .

Adler
The old expectant silence falls . . .

Thimig
And once again that same voice calls:

Reinhardt
Draw near, good people all, I pray!
Give heed while we perform our play,
Wherein we show, as best we can,
The Summoning of Everyman . . .

Lights down.

Postscript

The genesis of this play was its setting – Schloss Leopoldskron, the great baroque palace on the outskirts of Salzburg.

It is by any standards what an estate agent would call an imposing residence. It was built in the middle of the eighteenth century by the Prince Archbishop of Salzburg, and its white stucco façades, in the Austrian rococo style, crowned by the Prince Archbishop's coat of arms, give it the appearance of an enormous wedding-cake. It looks northwards towards the Festung, the great fortress that dominates Salzburg, southwards across a lake towards the even vaster backdrop of the Alps.

A huge portrait of its builder, Prince Archbishop Leopold Anton Freiherr von Firmian (one of whose successors, a few years later, was the patron of the young Mozart), hangs in the galleried Marble Hall of the Schloss. It looks down now upon the scholars who come from all over the world to attend the academic conferences organised by the present occupants of the palace, the Salzburg Seminar. I stayed there with my wife, who was speaking at one of them, and I was astonished to discover that for eighteen years, from 1920 until 1938, this princely establishment had been the private home of someone who was in a sense a professional colleague of mine – the great Austrian producer and director Max Reinhardt.

There is a theatricality about all baroque and rococo architecture, and the perfect setting of Leopoldskron almost suggests a painted backcloth. I could see why it might have appealed to a man of the theatre. The sheer scale of it, though, indicated a breathtaking level of social grandeur. There have been many princes (and princesses) of the entertainments industry, from the nineteenth century onwards, who have housed themselves pretty lavishly, but even by the most extravagant standards of show business Leopoldskron seemed remarkable – particularly when I discovered that Reinhardt had owned two other properties at the same time – one, in Berlin, a wing of the Bellevue Palace, the official residence of the former German Crown Prince (and now of the Federal President), and the other, in Vienna, an apartment in the Hofburg, the official residence of the former Austrian Emperor.

The theatre is a notoriously uncertain way of earning a living, and it's always encouraging to find that there are at any rate some people in the business who have managed to keep their heads above water. Reinhardt had been able not only to buy the palace and maintain it in the style to which it was accustomed but to go far beyond. When he acquired it, in 1918, it was in a sadly decayed state, and he devoted himself to restoring it – then went on to raise it to heights of glory that it had never known, even in the days of Firmian. It was his passion. He ransacked the great houses of Austria and south Germany for statuary and pictures – transshipped complete rooms – scoured Europe for antique furniture and books – filled the gardens with exotic plants and creatures – employed the finest craftsmen to carve and gild, to refurbish and replace, to copy the furnishings that could not be bought. Of all his many productions, said Helene Thimig, his companion and eventually his second wife, Leopoldskron was the one he was proudest of. Reinhardt and Thimig had no children together. Leopoldskron was their child, and together they loved it and nurtured it with parental intensity.

And then they lost it.

Reinhardt had made an unwitting early mistake in life that had re-emerged, as in a Greek tragedy, to break him. He had been born a Jew. In 1938, when Hitler absorbed Austria into the German Reich, Leopoldskron was 'aryanised' – expropriated – and Reinhardt was forced into exile.

As my wife and I walked through the gardens that Reinhardt and Thimig had created, she read out to me, from the Seminar's brochure on the history of Leopoldskron, this paragraph in a letter he wrote to Thimig in 1942, the year before he died:

> I have lived in Leopoldskron for eighteen years, truly lived, and I have brought it to life. I have lived every room, every table, every chair, every light, every picture. I have built, designed, decorated, planted and I have dreamt of it when I was not there. I have always loved it in a festive way, not as something ordinary.

> Those were my most beautiful, prolific and mature years . . .
> I have lost it without lamenting. I have lost everything that I
> carried into it. It was the harvest of my life's work.

I was moved by this noble expression of resignation. I walked
straight into the centre of Salzburg and bought all the books
relating to Reinhardt that I could find.

*

Max Reinhardt today is probably not much remembered
outside Germany and Austria. I asked a number of normally
well-informed friends in London if they knew anything about
him. One recalled the British publisher of the same name.
Most of the others confessed ignorance. For the first forty years
of the twentieth century, though, he was a world celebrity.

Outside the German-speaking lands his reputation derived
partly from a legendary *Midsummer Night's Dream* which he
staged in various places, and which eventually became a
Hollywood film (his only one), with the young Mickey
Rooney as Puck. He was probably known mostly, though, for
his spectacular international stagings of a play called *The
Miracle*. This (as even serious theatre historians may now need
to be reminded) was the story of a medieval nun who falls in
love with a knight, and is first abducted from her nunnery
and then abandoned by him. But God takes pity on her and
sends a miracle. A statue of the Virgin comes to life and takes
on the identity of the fallen sister to conceal her absence.

This heart-warming tale was told with a lavishness that
far outdid any modern musical or rock show. The Vienna
production in 1912 had a cast of 1,500 and an orchestra of
150, the London one a cast of 2,000 and and orchestra of
200. In New York in 1924 the parts of the Nun and the
Virgin were alternated between two noted society beauties –
Lady Diana Duff Cooper representing the British aristocracy
and Rosamond Pinchot its American equivalent. (The latter,
like the Nun, went to the bad, apparently as a result of her
sudden stardom. The Virgin in this case failed to intervene,
and she ended up taking her own life.)

In 1937 Reinhardt outdid this with an even more stunning excursion into show-business piety – this time Judaic rather than Christian, a Broadway show called *The Eternal Road*, which covered the entire history of the Jews, through the forty centuries of the Old Testament and on through the twenty centuries of the Diaspora. It's true that it had only a modest cast – 350 – but between them they wore 1,700 costumes, and the sets, which were four storeys high and covered almost an acre, required the rebuilding of the theatre. The result was a sellout – and beggared all who had been cajoled to invest in it.

Before the First World War Reinhardt was said to be the third most popular personality in Germany after the Kaiser and Count Zeppelin, and in Germany and his native Austria his name remains a familiar one. The tide of theatrical fashion, though, long ago turned against him and everything he represented, in favour of the kind of theatre associated with Brecht and Piscator. Even at the height of his success he was often dismissed as a mere showman, and his son Gottfried accepts, in his memoir of his father, that 'a slight whiff of charlatanism' has always hovered about him. Some commentators on the German theatre, however, now believe that there are signs of a reassessment.

And so, it seems to me, there should be. The spiritual force of his great religious extravaganzas may have become a little dimmed by time, but his real achievements were on no less a scale. In 1905 he took over the direction of the Deutsches Theater in Berlin, rebuilt it, and bought out its previous owner. Without any state or city subsidy he turned it into an institution that, in its scope, ambition, and output, came to occupy the same kind of position that the National Theatre now does in London. He did the great classics, and he introduced the most interesting new writers of the day to German audiences – Chekhov, Ibsen, Strindberg, Pirandello, Shaw, Galsworthy, Hauptmann. By the time he gave up the running of the theatre in 1932 it had produced over 450 plays – and he had directed about 170 of them himself. It was the only private art theatre in the world, he claimed, that had managed to support itself, without subsidy and without political or party connection, out of its own resources.

His energy and ambition were boundless. In 1923 he took on, in addition to the Deutsches Theater, the lease of the beautiful Theater in der Josefstadt in Vienna, and did for his native city what he had already done for Berlin. By this time he had also helped found the Salzburg Festival, in the teeth of considerable local reluctance, and was responsible for all the drama that was produced there. By the end of his life he had directed some 340 productions and built or rebuilt no less than thirteen theatres.

*

He was born Max Goldmann, in 1873. The Goldmann family had for generations eked out a modest living as small business-men in the little town of Stampfen (aka Stomfa, aka Stupava, depending upon which of the local languages was in the ascendant) near Pressburg (aka Bratislava), then in Hungary, in a district which had served historically as a dumping ground for Jews driven out of Austria on the other side of the Danube. By the middle of the nineteenth century, though, the Jews of Austria had been emancipated – and the German-speaking Jews of Hungary subjected to pogroms and forced magyarisation. In 1869 Max's father moved to Vienna, where he set up a firm trading in cotton goods and married a woman from Moravia. At first the business seems to have prospered, but by the time Max, their first child, was born, the stock market had collapsed, the firm had gone bankrupt, and the Goldmanns had had to move into more modest quarters. As the family grew so its fortunes declined. Another bankruptcy followed. Max's father sold bed springs and bedding feathers for someone else; took over the business; went bankrupt again; became a corset-maker. In the course of Max's childhood the family moved seven times. At the end of his life, after he had lost everything and was struggling to survive in exile, Reinhardt said that he had gone through the torment of sudden impoverishment before, in his parents' home as a child. It was, he said, incomparably worse than poverty itself.

From this shifting and straitened world he escaped into the theatre. When he wrote later, as he often did, about his boyhood passion for the Burgtheater, the vast imperial court theatre of Vienna (claimed to be the second oldest in the world after the Comédie Française), you get the feeling that he saw it as providing him with not just an alternative world to inhabit for a few hours in the evening but a complete alternative biography. 'I always say that I was born in the gods. There I saw for the first time the light of the stage. There I was nourished (for forty crowns an evening) on the rich artistic fare of the Imperial-Royal institution, and there the famous actors of the day sang their classic speech-arias around my cradle.' In Vienna at the time, he says, theatre was based exclusively on the spoken word. 'The stage was completely primitive, there were the bare necessities of furniture; everything else was the actor and his word . . . The Burgtheater was full of voices, that formed an incomparably well-toning orchestra, like old and precious instruments.'

He goes on to give a brilliantly evocative account of the excitement that theatre can sometimes generate:

The sound came to us out of the remote distance, pressed together as we were, up in the highest point of the house . . . My neighbours . . . were almost exclusively young people . . . I knew no one among them and in any case little was said. It was much too exciting . . .

As soon as it got dark and the curtain rose we melted together into one mysterious unity . . . Suddenly 250 faces broke into a single smile, then a giggle ran through the rows of people – and suddenly a ringing laugh broke out like a storm. You were swept irresistibly away, and you rejoiced that all the others were as drunk on merriment as you were. Then gradually it would become quieter and ever more still. The actors heard every stirring, just as we heard theirs. They would wait until we had settled . . . Things would become serious. Hundreds bent to the left, where someone had entered. The couple on the stage didn't see him. We were in the secret. Hearts beating. Breathing in time together. Two companies: the company of actors and the company of the audience.

The actors at the Burg tended to be elderly, and Reinhardt describes how they forgot their lines and had to be prompted – and were so remote that you could scarcely see them. But even this he saw as a kind of virtue. It meant that 'you had to play along with them yourself up there. The distance from the stage was so great . . . that you had to fill everything out for yourself.' He saw them as the real rulers of Vienna. 'The way they dressed influenced the way the aristocracy dressed. When one of the actors drank chocolate on the stage people watched with bated breath.' At the age of seventeen he became an actor himself, and adopted a new name, 'Reinhardt', to go with the new persona he was creating; and he became rather famous at the age of twenty, perhaps as a result of watching all those ancients at the Burg, for his ability to glue on a false beard and become an old man.

He worked in small theatres around Vienna, and in 1894 played a summer season in Salzburg. It was here that he got his first big break – a contract to join Otto Brahm's company in Berlin that autumn. Berlin was a relatively new theatrical centre, and Brahm was establishing for the first time its pre-eminence over Vienna. He had taken over the direction of the Deutsches Theater, accommodated in an old operetta house and now having a *succès de scandale* with the innovative naturalism of productions that introduced middle-class audiences for the first time to the social realities of poverty and sexual hypocrisy (Hauptmann's *The Weavers*, for example, and Ibsen's *Ghosts*).

Reinhardt's feelings about the revolution in which he now began to play a part were mixed. 'I was always acting in torn clothes, dirty and smeared,' he wrote later. 'Night after night I had to eat sauerkraut on stage. I wanted for once to play something else as well, something more beautiful and more enjoyable. At that time we had a club with merry and talented members. We allowed ourselves a good deal of professional fun at the expense of all the gloom in the art we practised.' The mockery was channelled into a kind of satirical cabaret, *Schall und Rauch* (Sound and Smoke – i.e. appearance without substance), which fought a running battle against the censors and was a great popular success. The team took over a small theatre to house the shows, and went on to produce first one-act straight plays in it, then full-length ones. Although one of these, Wilde's *Salome*, was seen as marking a decisive break with naturalism, it was a naturalistic production that propelled Reinhardt to the next stage of his career. He read about the opening of Gorky's *The Lower Depths* at the Moscow Art Theatre, sent a friend to Russia to see it and fetch the text, then produced it with such enormous success that he was able to take over a second theatre as well.

Here, in the Neues Theater in 1905, he first did the *Midsummer Night's Dream* that he was to direct over and over again in the following years, and that became the signature of his style. The production of a play is an event in time that vanishes once the run is over as surely as youth or summer, and it is impossible to reconstruct it or to know why it should have caught the audience's imagination. As Gottfried Reinhardt recalls in his memoir of his father, the play itself was only too familiar in Germany, where it was regarded as a rather tedious fairy-tale fit only for school matinees.

'What had made this tired warhorse a winning racer?' he asks. 'How could this drug on the repertory market suddenly transform itself into a smash hit and make its producer Europe's number one theatre man?' Not the text, evidently, nor even Mendelssohn's music, which had already been used to accompany many German productions. Not the actors, excellent as they were, nor the set, even though it was based on the novelty of a revolving stage. 'It was the *sum total* of all these elements,' says Gottfried, in a striking passage of critical description, 'or, to put it another way, the new element that made out of all of them a conceptual whole; the single idea to which all participants bent plus the generating force behind them; the unfamiliar ingredient of a new type of *direction*. The woods *acted*. The actors were a botanical part of the woods. Trees, shrubbery, mist, moonlight intermingled with the lovers, the rehearsing artisans, the trolls, the elfs, the spirits. The music, the wind, the breathless running, the clowning, the fighting were all of one key and came from one and the same source. So did the calm, the sweep, the dream, the poetry. Nothing was background, nothing foreground.

Passion, humour, lyricism, bawdiness, nobility, fantasy did
not have their allotted moments side by side or consecutively.
They were ever-present, simultaneous, feeding on one
another in multiple symbiosis.'

To achieve this, Reinhardt exercised total control over
everything, including the actors' performances. In the autobiographical notes that he wrote later in his life he describes
how he worked, reading and working over a text until . . .

Finally you have a complete optical and acoustic vision.
You see every gesture, every step, every piece of furniture,
the light, you hear every intonation, every rise in
emotional temperature, the musicality of the idioms, the
pauses, the different tempi. You feel every inward stirring,
you know how it is to be concealed and when it is to be
revealed. You hear every sob, every intake of breath. The
way another character listens, every noise onstage
and backstage. The influence of light.

And then you write it down, the complete optical and
acoustic vision, like a score. You can scarcely keep up, so
powerfully are you driven, mysteriously in fact, without
discussion, without labour. Justification you find later. You
write it chiefly for yourself. You have no idea why you see
and hear it this way or that. Difficult to write down. No
notation for speech. You invent your own signs.

I've never met any modern director who works like this. But
then nor have I met one who wears the kind of clothes in
which Thimig dressed Reinhardt – handmade suits of
tastefully restrained grey English flannel (though Michael
Blakemore, who has directed so many of my plays, including
Afterlife, wears handmade shoes). The style has changed.
Styles of dressing and directing, as of everything else, come
and go. Alan Bennett, in *Writing Home*, remembers when he
was a boy in Leeds seeing members of the Yorkshire
Symphony Orchestra going home on the tram after the
concert, 'rather shabby and ordinary and often with tab ends
in their mouths, worlds away from the Delius, Walton and
Brahms which they had been playing. It was a first lesson to

me that art doesn't have much to do with appearances and that ordinary middle-aged men in raincoats can be instruments of the sublime.' So, on occasion, can extraordinary men in handmade suits.

As Reinhardt's notes on his methods continue, and he begins work in the rehearsal room, he sounds for a moment as if he is prepared to set his carefully prepared battle plans aside and to work collaboratively with the actors, as most modern directors do, in a joint effort to discover what the text has to offer. 'You talk to the actors about their parts,' he says. 'You listen, you get new ideas . . . Some actors have their own ideas. They insist on playing cheerful devils as fallen angels. Tragically, magnificently. You nod in an interested way, agreeing with them.' This collaboration, however, soon turns out to be not quite what it seems. 'The individual opinions rarely have any importance,' he says, 'but you take them seriously. You allow yourself to be convinced.'

Modern directors, of course, also feign deference in this way more often than they would be prepared to admit. Once rehearsals begin in earnest, though, Reinhardt's methods are again quite openly autocratic. 'You play all the parts,' he says. This is something that no modern director, in my experience, would dare to attempt. According to Thimig in her biography of her husband, however, it is precisely what Reinhardt's actors loved about him – that at rehearsals he was himself an actor, and one who could demonstrate every kind of part – old men (of course) but also 'children, eccentrics, women, girls, and lovers'. One actor who worked with him remembers him having the same line line repeated over and over again, then saying it over and over again himself; another as guiding the player, 'without saying much, on invisible threads. With a look, a nod of the head, and then with one or two brief words, he leads him where he wants.' Then, when it comes to bringing an ensemble scene to life, 'he jumps in himself, takes actors waiting for their entrance by the hand, rushes them forwards into the middle of the stage, throws them (in one rehearsal it did actually happen) down on their knees, raises their hands – in a word, is now the leader who rushes into the battle ahead of everyone.'

One of Reinhardt's innovations, after he had moved on to the Deutsches Theater, had perhaps a more profound influence than even the revolving stage that he had introduced in *A Midsummer Night's Dream*: he added to the main house a studio theatre, the Kammerspiele. The auditorium of this smaller house comprised 292 seats – little bigger than the stage, and separated from it only by a couple of steps. This smallness and closeness allowed actors to develop a more intimate style, better suited to the new plays that Reinhardt was doing. It also created a luxuriously furnished space, closed off from the outside world, in which actors and audience felt themselves to be a single entity. 'Since I first came into the theatre,' wrote Reinhardt in a letter to Thimig, 'I was pursued and finally guided by one clear thought: to bring actors and audience together – pressed up against each other as closely as possible. Why? Theatre consists in essence of both these partners.'

Most major producing theatres now have a Kammerspiele of one sort or another attached, and in them (particularly in the National Theatre's Cottesloe) some of my best evenings in the theatre have been spent (and some of the best productions of my own plays done). Reinhardt himself, though, later changed his mind. 'I found that it was all a mistake,' he wrote in his autobiographical notes. 'The small house, the nearness of the stage, the all-too-comfortable seats. The Kammerspiele held too few people, and the quality of the audience grows with its quantity.' And also declines with its metropolitan sophistication. 'The so-called "good" audience is in reality the worst. Dulled unnaive people. Unobservant, blasé . . . Only the gallery is good.'

He seemed to be hankering for the kind of theatre that had first captured his imagination as a child in Vienna. But he went further. He turned his back, as other directors did later, on the concept of theatre as illusion, as an animated peepshow. His intentions remained the same: to dissolve the traditional boundaries between stage and house, and to involve the audience, the essential second company in which he had himself so memorably played at the Burgtheater. But now he thought that it could best be done as it had been in classical Greece, or in the medieval marketplace – by creating dramas that served as religious, or quasi-religious, experiences for a mass audience in a vast open arena. He conceived the idea of the 'Theatre of the Five Thousand', whose numbers were to be drawn not from *die oberen Zehntausend*, as the upper crust are called in Germany (and who, if they have been counted correctly and had all bought tickets, could presumably have supported only two performances of a production) but from the ranks of 'upwardly-striving workers and craftsmen' hungry for art and culture.

He tried the idea out at a summer festival in Munich in 1910, with a production of *Oedipus Rex*, in a new adaptation by Hugo von Hofmannsthal, before an audience of three thousand. The experiment was judged a success (though quite how many of the audience were upwardly-striving workers is not clear). He took over a 3,000-seat circus hall in Berlin and moved the production in, then next year followed it up with the *Oresteia*. That December he found time to go to London and produce *The Miracle* at Olympia, with a cast of 2,000 – and an audience of 20,000.

And in the same month, back in Berlin, he created his production of *Everyman*, the play to which he was going to find himself tied for most of the rest of his life.

*

By this time he had begun to construct a lifestyle on a scale worthy of the productions he was doing. He was surrounded by a court of advisers, assistants, hangers-on, and indigent relatives whom he had put on the payroll; he had a series of women; he dressed with fastidious elegance and ate only in the best restaurants; when he travelled he did it in the style of a prince on the Grand Tour. What all this cost he had not the slightest idea – his money was managed for him by his chamberlain, his depressive brother Edmund, whom he had rescued from suicide (and whom Helene Thimig thought was the greatest love of his life). He was, it was often said, a baroque figure. It was the opportunity of acquiring a baroque palace at a knock-down price in the great inflation after the

First World War that brought him back to Salzburg, where he had begun his theatrical career a quarter of a century earlier with a single suitcase in a single room.

Le style est l'homme même, said the Comte de Buffon, and it is surely true that in any human being it is difficult to make a distinction between the man himself and his outward expression in deeds and a way of being. In Reinhardt's case, though, the inner source of all that energy, achievement and display seems particularly elusive. 'Rarely,' said Heinz Herald, one of his associates over many years, 'has a human being remained so anonymous to those close to him, or has been revealed so totally in his work, as Reinhardt.' Another of his associates, the Austrian playwright Hermann Bahr, wrote: 'Paradoxically one could say of Reinhardt that the real charm of his personality consisted of his having none.' He had, said his son Gottfried, 'a reticence touching on the pathological . . . His paralysing reaction to direct contact with people, his inability to communicate with them freely, is indicative of the dark pockets in his soul.'

He often seemed to inhabit his vast carapace as thinly as a night-watchman in an empty warehouse. He was a legendary host (particularly at Leopoldskron), and, according to Helene Thimig, 'he loved big gatherings – but only to look at. He was mad to have people around him – but he was desperate at being alone with individual people.' He was charismatic, persuasive and articulate when he was dealing with actors, writers and people whose support he needed. But outside his professional life it was different. Thimig said 'he found it extremely unpleasant to talk *tête-à-tête*, particularly in a separate space cut off from the company. He never knew what to say.' Reinhardt said of himself that he found it difficult to breathe except in 'the true unreality of the theatre'.

It is impossible to know whether he consciously recognised any parallel between himself and Everyman, the eponymous protagonist of the play to which he now found himself yoked. I can find no record of his saying anything to this effect. So far as I know he had not intended to revisit the piece after its outing in Berlin, where it had had a poor reception from the critics (though a warm one from the public). For the opening of the first Salzburg Festival, in 1920, he had commissioned a young Austrian writer, Max Mell, to provide him with a modern mystery play about his future heroine the Virgin Mary, in Salzburg dialect. But it was not ready in time, and he fell back on the nearest equivalent to hand, the *Everyman* that he had done in Berlin nine years earlier. Would a play in Salzburgerisch rather than High German have caught on as *Everyman* now did? Many other plays were performed in the festival seasons that followed (some of them, including a suitably gigantic *Faust*, directed by Reinhardt himself). But it was *Everyman* that became its emblem. Reinhardt revived it every summer (apart from a couple of years in the twenties) until the Nazis came to power in 1938, and drove both him and the play into exile. It resumed its career and its emblematic status at Salzburg after the Nazis (and Reinhardt) had gone, and has now outlived him by over sixty years.

The play is by Hugo von Hofmannsthal, whose long collaboration with Reinhardt had begun with his version of *Oedipus*. Hofmannsthal derived it from an English morality play of the fifteenth century, *The Summoning of Everyman*, and it has a simple plot. God, outraged by the indifference and ingratitude of mankind, sends Death to summon Everyman to judgment. Everyman, suitably terrified, repents of his past failings, abandons his worldly possessions, proclaims his faith, and is welcomed into heaven, apparently redeemed.

How God, or Death, selects the individual who is to serve as an exemplar of humankind at large is not clear. The victim they hit upon between them, well suited as he is to be a popular target for retribution, is no more an average citizen than Reinhardt was. Like Reinhardt he is wealthy and rejoices in it. He lives in a grand house, and receives his unexpected summons during the course of a sumptuous banquet he is giving for his mistress and troops of friends. (He even seems to have some of Reinhardt's social inhibitions – his mistress has to urge him to join his guests.) At this point in the play, however, and at the point in Reinhardt's career when he first produced it, their paths diverge. As soon as they discover the identity of Everyman's visitor, and the nature of the journey he has been summoned to make, his mistress, friends, and servants all desert him, and he can derive neither help nor comfort from his wealth. Reinhardt had another eighteen years to enjoy his worldly substance and the company of his associates.

The English original now seems archaic and inaccessible. One of its modern editors says that it 'was written in the interests of the established faith; to uphold the papal authority; to emphasise the claims of the priesthood; to insist on the efficacy of the sacraments.' Another editor detects the hand of a priest in its construction, and the dramatic focus is plainly on Everyman's redemption. Hofmannsthal, a real dramatist (probably best-known outside Germany or his native Austria as the author of most of Richard Strauss's libretti, beginning with the magnificent *Rosenkavalier* – the first production of which, at Dresden in 1911, Reinhardt directed), has made it dramatically viable. One of the many things he has modified is the play's theology. The original is presumably among other things a contribution to the long-running debate about the relative importance of faith and works, and Good Works is the only one of the various personified virtues and faculties around Everyman who stands by him, and who single-handedly makes his redemption possible. Hofmannsthal has introduced the figure of Faith, and given her an equal role in Everyman's salvation.

Even in Hofmannsthal's version this aspect of the play is difficult for the non-believer to take much interest in – or to make much sense of. A faith hastily rediscovered under sentence of death and threat of eternal hellfire is surely as dubious as a confession obtained by torture. Good Works (or, as Hofmannsthal calls her, simply Works) is an even more curious figure. When we first meet her she is in a bad way as a result of Everyman's lifelong neglect – 'cold in the ground', in the original, 'pitifully weak' in Hofmannsthal – and unable to stir. How she regains her strength retrospectively, when she enters the story too late for Everyman to undertake any addition to his achievements in life, or any modification of them, it's difficult to understand. The moral would seem to be that there's no need to bother with behaving well, because you can always rewrite the record afterwards.

The strength of the piece now is its dramatisation of the unpredictability and inexorability of the end that waits for all of us, believers and non-believers alike. Any doubts I had about whether Hofmannsthal's handling of this could still be effective were abruptly shattered by seeing a DVD of Christian Stückl's production of the play at the 2004 Festival, with Peter Simonischek as a big, powerful, likeable, immensely human Everyman, caught in the rich fullness of his life by Jenz Harzer as a naked, grey-fleshed, burning-eyed Death. Even on the small screen it is an unforgettable experience.

In spite of the play's enduring power, and the success it had in Salzburg, the audience it found was not the one that Reinhardt had been aiming at. Ordinary local citizens didn't much like it, and in any case they couldn't afford the ticket prices. The customers (as always) turned out to be the rich and the tourists. Franz Rehrl, the Provincial Governor, was a strong supporter of the Festival – but for purely hard-headed reasons. 'Culture,' he said, 'equals business.' Not even the business, though, reconciled the intensely conservative citizens of Salzburg to the influx of the outsiders who brought it to them. One of these outsiders, of course, was Reinhardt himself. 'Philistines in Salzburg,' wrote Hofmannsthal to Richard Strauss in 1923, 'will never accept Reinhardt as president [of the Festival]. They hate him as a Jew, as a Lord of the Manor, as an artist and as a solitary human being whom they cannot fathom.' The tinge of anti-Semitism in local resentment was strong, and the most outspoken opponents of the Festival were the local forerunners of the Nazis. Already contemptuous of Catholicism as practised by Catholics, they were even more virulent about the 'hypocritical profit-Catholicism of Jews', among whom they included not only Reinhardt but Hofmannsthal, the Catholic grandson of a Jewish convert. Reinhardt was also a permanent target for the Viennese satirist Karl Kraus, still widely admired in *bien-pensant* circles today, who described him, with a wonderful combination of racial and social disdain, as 'an upstart from the Slovak working class'.

Leopoldskron, too, turned out not to be the quiet artistic and intellectual cloister that Reinhardt had envisaged. It became inevitable, said Thimig later, to invite politicians and money as well. 'Particularly unpleasant,' she says, 'I found the representatives of the so-called "entertainment aristocracy".' Money (as always) came to dominate the Festival, like Mammon springing out of Everyman's trunk. At first everyone involved in the play worked for nothing. But as the seasons went by the well-known actors who came to Salzburg began to demand the kind of fees they could command elsewhere. The Festival accumulated a considerable deficit, and not even high ticket prices could keep it afloat. It seems to have been rescued by a millionaire, Camillo Castiglioni, who had amassed a fortune building planes during the First World War and speculating in the great inflation that followed it (and another Jew, like so many of the philanthropists who keep the arts going).

So poor Everyman had to be preserved by the very wealth that had failed to sustain him in the play, and redeemed at the expense of patrons who did not believe in Christian redemption. It sounds more and more like the situation in the British (and the German) theatre today, which struggles piously to present plays about poverty and degradation to an audience not very closely acquainted with either – and which has to be subsidised by the charitable efforts of people on even more remote terms with them.

Well, perhaps they learn a few things that they didn't know, and are persuaded to go out and give all they have to the poor. Perhaps the audience of *Everyman* were moved to make some early improvements to the Good Works section of their CVs. It certainly seems to have spoken to the Prince Archbishop of Salzburg. Gusti Adler, in her biography of Reinhardt, reports that at the first performance quiet tears rolled down his cheeks, and that when he pressed Reinhardt's hand afterwards he said that the production was better than a sermon. But then, according to Reinhardt, he was a saint anyway.

It's difficult to know about the rest of the audience. Reinhardt himself certainly didn't change his lifestyle. Is that a criticism of the play? Of the production? Of Reinhardt? He may of course have felt that if the Deutsches Theater and

Everyman counted for anything, his record of Works was strong enough to counterbalance quite a lot of champagne and cigars. And Hofmannsthal was certainly right about the terrifying unpredictability of death. In 1929 his elder son shot himself, and Hofmannsthal himself died of a heart attack as he dressed for the funeral. Three days later the same unannounced visitor came for Reinhardt's beloved brother Edmund.

*

My play, like two earlier ones of mine, *Copenhagen* and *Democracy*, is based on the historical record, but perhaps rather more freely than they were.

Reinhardt himself, elusive and unforthcoming as his associates often found him, was in his letters and other writings immensely articulate, eloquent, sophisticated and prolific. Most of the ideas that he expresses in the play are drawn from what he wrote, but I have not even begun to do justice to the depth of his intelligence or the breadth of his culture. The external events of his life – his difficulties with local philistines and anti-Semites, the attacks on his house (and on the Prince Archbishop's), his expropriation and exile – are drawn from the record. And from the terrace of Leopoldskron you can indeed see Obersalzberg, above Berchtesgaden on the other side of the German frontier, where Hitler and other Nazi leaders had their villas.

Reinhardt's recollections of his childhood in Vienna and of his first arrival in Salzburg come mostly from his autobiographical notes. His working methods are described not only here but in the recollections of many professional colleagues, and also in three full-length memoirs – by his second wife Helene Thimig, by his personal assistant Gusti Adler, and by his younger son Gottfried. These are also the source for most of the details of his personal life – his relations with his brother Edmund, his efforts to support the rest of his extended family, the difficulties with his first wife, his princely travel arrangements, and his accommodation in Berlin and Vienna; for his distaste for handling or thinking about money, and his financial difficulties in exile, including his emergency cash arrangements (though he did have one success during his bleak American exile – *Rosalinda*, an adaptation of *Die Fledermaus* – which was produced in New York in 1942, and which just about kept him afloat); for his legendary parties; for his deferential consultation with Rothschild and other patrons; for his unfulfilled projects to commission a play from Shaw about the life of Christ and to film *Paradise Lost*.

Gottfried's memoirs (which he wrote in English) are particularly revealing, if somewhat overblown in style. His love for his father, reverence for his talent, and encylopaedic knowledge of his affairs (in every sense) do not impede him from casting a coolly observant eye upon his manifold weaknesses. Reinhardt, he says, was 'a precocious, hypersensitive, fantasy-possessed, play-mad, cruel-tender child to whom tenderness from others was as necessary as food and drink . . . an enthusiast and a skeptic, courageous and quickly intimidated, a gambler and an evader of decision, at one time trusting providence, at another taking refuge in procrastination, immune to fatal catastrophe, but an easy prey to the most banal mishap . . . '

The character of Rudolf Kommer, Reinhardt's man of business and master of ceremonies, is also very fully documented by Gottfried, including his division of the human race into the imposters and the feeble-minded. Gottfried says he 'played confidant, counsellor, caretaker, father confessor, procurer, arbiter, entertainer, to the international upper crust'. He was a kind of eunuch, continuously but harmlessly in love with a harem of other people's wives and girlfriends, whom he entertained and consoled, and who all called him Kätchen in affectionate gratitude. At the end of their long collaboration Reinhardt and Kommer became estranged from each other, though it's difficult to establish exactly how and why. Kommer wrote a long letter to Reinhardt 'enumerating, in Kommer's opinion, every error my father had ever committed and complaining about my father's ingratitude for his services.' Reinhardt responded with a farewell letter 56 pages long in which he gave a brilliant and generous account of Kommer's career and character, largely

in the third person. The guests at one of Reinhardt's great
parties, says Gottfried, would find themselves . . .

> staring in surprise at a person who happened to be in their
> midst as if by accident and who chatted nonchalantly and
> without ever stopping. He chatted with the virtuoso
> brilliance of a pianist, eliciting complicated cadences from
> the keys without seeming to touch them. He would turn
> from one to the other, called most by their first names and
> acted with such ease that one would think this centrifugal
> mass of people, alien and feeling alienated, were the oldest
> acquaintances and had simply run into one another again,
> and that he was continuing a conversation long since
> begun . . .
>
> There was no spoilsport who did not start to grin at the
> sight of him. He was the heart of the whole company and
> pumped blood even into its stiffest and most congealed
> members. He entertained and found entertainment in
> everybody. He formed friendship upon friendship and
> quarrelled with some to the point of physical violence,
> without, however, extinguishing his cigarette or his wit. He
> spiced the fat life of the rich with sharp truths, gave away
> boxes of candy, flowers and books, lunched, dined, supped
> (sometimes in repetition with first and second understudies),
> he debated, talked politics, criticised without surcease and,
> when he failed to incur enough contradictions, he started
> contradicting himself. He arranged divorces for excitable
> men, married off women, played with their children,
> concluded agreements between producers, poets, directors,
> musicians . . .
>
> At night, in the bar, he could make Jews yodel, Nazis
> *jüdeln* [talk with a Jewish inflection] . . . Without the
> slightest condescension, he could make every servant his
> friend and disarm every enemy with the perfect gallantry
> of a born aristocrat . . .

The originals of the other characters are somewhat less well
documented. Gusti Adler was the niece of Victor Adler, the
founder of the Austrian Social Democratic Party, and an old

school friend of Thimig's. She had started out in life studying art, and then become a cultural journalist. She worked round the clock for Reinhardt, says Thimig, and did everything for him, including buying rare books and antiques, and rare animals and exotic birds for the garden; the only thing she couldn't fix was the Salzburg weather. From her own book she emerges as devoted and totally uncritical.

Thimig, on the evidence of *her* memoir, was a little more detached. She came from a famous Viennese acting family, and had a successful stage career of her own. She fully shared Reinhardt's passion for restoring and furnishing Leopoldskron, but never, she says, a double bedroom, except in the bug-ridden hotel on the Mexican border where they were establishing their immigration into the United States as a preliminary to his getting a divorce in Reno from his first wife. Even on their train journeys between New York and Los Angeles they had a drawing-room suite with separate bedrooms. She is frank about the jealousy that she felt for some of the women who were drawn to Reinhardt – particularly Lady Diana Cooper, his Nun and Virgin, and Eleonora von Mendelssohn, the wealthy, beautiful (and drug-addicted) socialite who was closer to Reinhardt than she was herself in the last painful weeks of his life. She is (fairly) frank, too, about the triangle that developed when she herself fell for the actor she was working with in a romantic comedy.

The Prince Archbishop of Salzburg, Dr Ignatius Rieder, seems to have been admired and loved by everyone (except by the Nazis, and perhaps by the droves of people who were leaving the church at that time to join them). He was profoundly conservative in demeanour and outlook, and maintained contacts with the imperial family even after the dissolution of the Dual Monarchy in 1918. Thimig describes him as having a peasant's face capped by snow-white hair, and always wearing a peasant's heavy boots. She found him particularly noble and good; Reinhardt described him as a saint, and as 'the angelic archbishop'. The Archbishop reciprocated. 'A good Jew like Reinhardt,' he said, 'is dearer to me than a bad Christian' – a sentiment that would perhaps sound platitudinous in a churchman now, but that was not to be taken quite so much for granted in Salzburg at the time. He was one of the relatively few people in Salzburg who were enthusiastic about the Festival, and he gave Reinhardt permission to perform *Everyman* in front of the cathedral. (Reinhardt put his request in a letter; the reading of the play in support of the application is my expansion of this.) The two men developed a warm personal relationship. Thimig says that the Archbishop discreetly blessed Leopoldskron for them, in spite of its being a Jewish home, and she describes how he would sometimes tenderly stroke Reinhardt's arm and call him 'my son'.

Franz, Reinhardt's valet, has a slightly more oblique relationship to reality. The real Franz had, like mine, previously been valet to Luziwuzi, the transvestite Archduke Ludwig Viktor, who had caused much embarrassment to his brother the Emperor. (Franz's job description in his earlier post was not only valet but *Vorleser* – 'reader aloud' – though what he read I have been unable to discover.) But at some point, I think in the 1930s, Death came for Franz and he was replaced by Paul. Reinhardt retained Paul's services throughout the bleak years of American exile, even though he was often unable to pay him, which Paul seems to have been rather less sanguine about than my character. I have elided Paul with Franz.

Friedrich Müller is a degree more fictitious. He is based on a man called Friedrich Rainer, who shared with my character many of the political and racist views that were common at the time in Salzburg, as elsewhere in Austria, and who, like Müller, joined the Nazi Party and went into local politics. I changed his name partly because 'Rainer' sounds confusingly like 'Reinhardt', but also because Rainer grew up not in Salzburg but in Sankt Veit, and because it was not Rainer who conveyed to Reinhardt Hitler's bizarre offer of rebirth as an honorary Aryan.

This is an event doubted by some but confirmed by both Thimig and Adler, who agree that the messenger was Death himself. Or, at any rate, Werner Krauss, the actor who played the part for many years in *Everyman*, and who was also an outspoken Nazi supporter. Reinhardt was particularly fond of him. He had made his name in 1920, in *The Cabinet of Dr*

Caligari, but during the thirties he specialised in playing Jews in Nazi propaganda films. In 1933 Reinhardt cast him as Mephistopheles in his Salzburg *Faust* after he had agreed to sack the original casting, Max Pallenberg, because he was Jewish.

Müller's history, however, coincides closely with Rainer's after the Anschluss in 1938, when Hitler appointed Rainer Gauleiter of Salzburg. Up to then Rainer had called for the unconditional destruction of everything Catholic and Jewish in Salzburg. He now decided to preserve all the decadent baroque Catholic trappings of Leopoldskron – and to move into the house himself. During the war he continued his rise through the ranks of the Nazi administration, and ended up in charge of Friuli, the Italian province on the Yugoslav border. After the war he appeared as a witness at Nuremberg before being handed over to the Yugoslavs and hanged at Ljubljana in 1947 (though rumours persisted, as with other executed war criminals, that he had somehow survived).

*

My translations of the extracts from Hofmannsthal's text are fairly free, but I hope reflect something of the dramatic quality of the original. I have been pretty cavalier in my selection, taking only what suits my purposes, occasionally slightly changing the order of events, and skipping completely the sections dealing with Everyman's redemption. Hofmannsthal's text is written mostly in iambic tetrameters, but with occasionally longer or shorter lines, and rhymed mostly as couplets, though he often varies this, so far as I can see randomly. Since I was using only short extracts which needed to be clearly distinguished from their prose background I thought that I should stick strictly to regular tetrameters and regular couplets.

I feel uneasy about taking such liberties with a writer as good as Hofmannsthal. I can only say in justification that Hofmannsthal himself has made very free with his sources. The English text on which he has drawn, which may itself be taken from a Dutch original, is written in verse so irregular that its prosody is almost unfollowable. He has also heavily recast it, cutting among other characters Strength, Discretion, Five-wits, Beauty, Knowledge and Confession, and adding some dozen new ones. He has reshaped the action and made it genuinely dramatic, and changed the whole theological basis of the play by introducing the character of Faith. His German editor Heinz Rölleke identifies material imported from completely different sources, some of them highly anachronistic – a rhymed prayer of Dürer's, songs from the Minnesingers, and scenes from Calderon and Maeterlinck. He has also, says Rölleke, drawn on Burton's *The Anatomy of Melancholy* for Everyman's character and on the nineteenth-century German sociologist Georg Simmel for Everyman's and Mammon's philosophy of money (both of which I have quoted at length).

I have taken further liberties with names and titles. Actors often called Reinhardt 'Max', but this was a collegial informality, and Thimig says that she always referred to him as 'Reinhardt'. Even this was a wifely intimacy, though, and to most people he was 'Professor Reinhardt', an honorary designation bestowed upon him by the Duke of Saxonia-Coburg-Gotha; Austrians are notoriously meticulous about titles ('Doktor Doktor', for example, if you have two doctorates) – and open-handed about creating fictitious ones for citizens unfortunate enough not to possess real titles. Aristocratic ranks were abolished in 1918, but the old titles that went with them often continued to be used, and waiters in Viennese coffee houses are said to call any unfamiliar customer 'Herr Baron' or 'Herr Direktor'. One of the reasons that Thimig was so anxious to get married to Reinhardt, says his son acidly, was to be addressed as 'Frau Professor'. In America he apparently became 'Doctor', but in English these usages applied to a theatre director sound – to my ears, at any rate – so odd and egregious that I have left him as plain Herr Reinhardt.

He usually referred to Thimig, she says, as 'die Leni' – a characteristically Germanic usage that suggests both familiarity and respect, and that has no equivalent in English. To other people at that time, before her marriage to Reinhardt, she and Adler would have been 'gnädiges Fräulein' – gracious Miss – but a simple 'Fräulein' is the nearest approximation that sounds reasonable in English. Most of the references I have found to Dr Rieder, both at the time and since, call him *Fürsterzbischof*, Prince Archbishop, and when Reinhardt wrote to him he began his letter 'Eurer fürstlichen Gnaden' – Your Princely Grace. This is really another 'Herr Baron'. The last real Prince Archbishop of Salzburg was Hieronymus von Colloredo, whose tenure ended in 1812, by which time the office had been stripped of its temporal powers, so that all Colloredo's successors have been plain ordinary archbishops. Until the 1940s, though, they were still addressed as princes.

*

Real death is rarely the tidy and dignified event suggested by the mythic representation of it that forms the basis of Hofmannsthal's play. It wasn't for Hofmannsthal himself, who died still struggling to put his top hat on for his son's funeral. It wasn't for Rudolf Kommer, when he collapsed and died in 1943 in the lobby of his hotel room in New York, where the body had to be left until the coroner could be located – so that all the crowds of acquaintances who came to pay their respects had to step over him to do so.

Nor was it for Reinhardt when it came, slowly, over the course of three weeks and a series of strokes, in another New York hotel room seven months later, apparently after he had been bitten by a dog. Money ruled over his deathbed, as it had over so much of his life; Gottfried hushed up his condition for fear that it would frighten off the investors in the production he was trying to set up (an adaptation of Offenbach's *La Belle Hélène*, intended to follow up the success of *Rosalinda*).

Gusti Adler and Helene Thimig, however, both lived happily ever after – or at any rate for many more years after Reinhardt's death. Adler, who had followed him into exile in 1939, and worked for him unpaid in the evenings while she earned a living from her day job in the archive at Warner Brothers, continued at the studio until she was in her eighties, and lived on into her nineties. Thimig struggled back to Austria in 1946 to play her old role as Faith in *Everyman* at

Salzburg, then went on to resume her distinguished stage career in Vienna. For twenty-five years she lived happily with the Austrian actor Anton Edthofer, and died in 1974 at the age of 85.

Reinhardt's renunciation of Leopoldskron, I discovered as my researches continued, was not quite as simple as it seemed in the letter he wrote to his wife in 1942 that was quoted in the brochure. He continued to be profoundly anguished by his loss, and he never gave up the hope of recovering the house. In July the following year, three months before his death, he wrote another letter to his wife, 28 pages long, laying out what seems to be a deposition to an Austrian exile organisation preparing for the post-war restitution of property stolen by the Nazis, in which he attempts to catalogue the contents of the house, to list the improvements and additions that he and his wife have made, together with all the services he has rendered to the Austrian nation, and all the honours and recognition he has received for his work. It is rather like Everyman's account of his estate – but offered after he has lost it, in the hope that Death might relent, and return it to him. Death did not oblige, any more than it did for Everyman.

It was, however, after endless legal difficulties and battles, returned to his heirs – his wife and sons, who sold it to the American academic organisation that runs it today. And there it still stands, in all its lofty baroque elegance. The great impresario has gone, and so have the princes and financiers who were his guests, together with the actors and musicians who entertained them, and the thieves and murderers who followed them. Now the guests drifting elegantly about the marble hall and the terrace are a new privileged class – the conference-goers of the world. You can rent its facilities yourself when the Seminar is not in session.

And in its afterlife it has achieved a certain celebrity through its artistic associations – even become a place of pilgrimage that attracts coach parties from all over Europe. Not because of Max Reinhardt, but because it served as a location in the film version of *The Sound of Music*.

Sources

BIOGRAPHY

Leonhard M. Fiedler: *Max Reinhardt* (1975).

PERSONAL MEMOIRS

Helene Thimig-Reinhardt: *Wie Max Reinhardt Lebte* (1973).

Gusti Adler: . . . *aber vergessen Sie nicht die chinesischen Nachtigallen* (1980, but expanded from *Max Reinhardt – sein Leben*, 1964). The title of the 1980 edition refers to Reinhardt's reminder to Adler, as she left Leopoldskron to meet Lilian Gish off the boat from New York at Cuxhaven. She was to stop off on the way at Hagenbeck, the animal dealers near Hamburg, to buy flamingos, pelicans, herons and exotic ducks. 'But don't forget the Chinese nightingales!' he called after her.

Gottfried Reinhardt: *The Genius, a Memoir of Max Reinhardt* (1979). In English.

REINHARDT'S OWN WRITINGS

Max Reinhardt: *Manuskripte, Briefe, Dokumente* (1998). The catalogue of a collection made by Dr Jürgen Stein, but with many quoted extracts.

Max Reinhardt: *Ich bin nichts als ein Theatermann* (1974 in the DDR, 1989 in the BRD). A collection of his letters about theatrical matters, together with brief memoirs by some of his associates.

THE STORY OF THE HOUSE AND THE FESTIVAL

Johannes Hofinger: *Die Akte Leopoldskron* (2005).

Stephen Gallup: *A History of the Salzburg Festival* (1987). In English.

ESSAYS AND DOCUMENTS

Ambivalenzen: Max Reinhardt und Österreich (2004). A collection of press cuttings, other documents and photographs.

Roland Koberg, Bernd Stegemann, Henrike Thomsen, eds: *Max Reinhardt und das Deutsche Theater* (2005). Essays, including a particularly interesting one by Christopher Balme, 'Die Marke Reinhardt', on Reinhardt's theatre considered as a business enterprise.